CLASS AND CAMPUS LIFE

CLASS AND CAMPUS LIFE

*Managing and Experiencing Inequality
at an Elite College*

ELIZABETH M. LEE

ILR PRESS
AN IMPRINT OF
CORNELL UNIVERSITY PRESS
ITHACA AND LONDON

First published 2016 by Cornell University Press
First printing, Cornell Paperbacks, 2016
Printed in the United States of America

Library of Congress Cataloging-in-Publication Data

Lee, Elizabeth M., 1974– author.
   Class and campus life : managing and experiencing inequality at an elite college / Elizabeth M. Lee.
     pages cm
   Includes bibliographical references and index.
   ISBN 978-0-8014-5356-4 (cloth : alk. paper) — ISBN 978-1-5017-0311-9 (pbk. : alk. paper)
   1. Women college students—United States—Social conditions.
2. Students with social disabilities—Education (Higher)—United
States.   3. Elite (Social sciences)—Education (Higher)—United
States.   4. Class consciousness—United States.   5. Women's colleges—
United States.   6. Intercultural communication—United States.
7. College environment—United States.   8. Educational sociology—
United States—Cross-cultural studies.   I. Title.
   LC1756.L39 2016
   378.0082—dc23   2015036417

Cornell University Press strives to use environmentally responsible suppliers and materials to the fullest extent possible in the publishing of its books. Such materials include vegetable-based, low-VOC inks and acid-free papers that are recycled, totally chlorine-free, or partly composed of nonwood fibers. For further information, visit our website at www.cornellpress.cornell.edu.

Cloth printing   10 9 8 7 6 5 4 3 2 1
Paperback printing   10 9 8 7 6 5 4 3 2 1

In memory of Camilla Churchill

Contents

ACKNOWLEDGMENTS

In Dahlberg and Adair's edited book of narratives about class in education, which I read just before beginning work for this book, a scholar's experience of speaking "for" welfare recipients is recounted. Asked by a reporter "how much they really need to live on," she was chastened by one of the recipients to "answer that question when you have to live on the answer." This caution about representation has stuck with me. I worried a lot about the implications of presuming to speak "for" Linden College respondents whom I interviewed and "shadowed" during the research and writing of this book, particularly as that could imply that respondents needed someone else to take up such a task. Rather, the process of gathering the voices included here most likely has been of greater benefit to me than anyone else. I humbly admit this, with deep gratitude to the anonymous respondents whose experiences form the basis of this book. They not only carved out hours to speak with me over two to three years but, even more generously, they allowed me to ask very personal questions about a subject that can often be uncomfortable. I hope that the respondents recognize their voices, find that what they shared has been faithfully recounted, and that others who read this book benefit from their insights.

I also thank others from Linden College who spoke with me—administrators, faculty, and students—and generously supported this book with their time and attention. I specifically thank the Linden administrators who permitted me to spend two years hanging around campus and who proactively helped me connect with students and supported this book in other ways. I thank the several faculty members who not only spoke with me but also allowed me to sit in on their classes. Every person I met with was welcoming and interested in seeing work that supported low socioeconomic status students. The nature of sociological work is to engage critically. This is what I have done here by focusing less on what works well than what doesn't. It is important to be clear that the problems that Linden students, faculty, and administrators struggle with are shared across many campuses, both Linden's peer institutions and other, structurally different, selective colleges and universities (as I have discovered, in part, through conversations with students and alumnae from other campuses).

I could not have written this book without the support of friends at the University of Pennsylvania. I continue to feel very lucky to have landed in with such a great bunch of people. My thanks to Yetunde Afolabi, Jessica McCrory Calarco, Ksenia Gorbenko, Stefan Klusemann, Rory Kramer, Keri Monteleone, Liz Raleigh, and April Yee, and especially to Jacob Avery, Benjamin DiCicco Bloom, and Rachel Margolis. Kristin Turney and Elizabeth Vaquera were supportive role models and good friends. Janel Benson offered last-minute insights and encouragement. Charles Bosk, Grace Kao, Kathy Hall, and Camille Charles are researchers and writers I continue to look up to. Chuck in particular encouraged me from the beginning, and his influence is reflected throughout.

I received very generous financial support from the National Science Foundation Graduate Research Fellowship program and the University of Pennsylvania, Department of Sociology, Otto and Gertrude K. Pollak Summer Research Fellowship. I am sincerely grateful for their assistance. The University of Pennsylvania, Hamilton College, and Ohio University all provided support for attending conferences in which I have been able to share earlier stages of this research; I thank them and also the organizers of various panels at annual American Sociological Association and Eastern Sociological Society meetings for providing forums for valuable feedback.

Much of this book took shape during my time at Hamilton College, where I spent three years as a visiting professor. I could not have asked for a better place at which to begin my research and teaching career. My departmental colleagues, especially Steve Ellingson, Yvonne Zylan, and Dan Chambliss, were extremely generous guides and mentors, as well as friends. Chaise LaDousa and Bonnie Urciuoli, anthropologists who share my interests in education and inequality, also welcomed me immediately and supported me throughout, as did friends in other departments, too many to name but nonetheless appreciated. Particular thanks go to my Hamilton students, who were a pleasure to share a classroom with: I am grateful for their patience and their enthusiasm. Emma Bowman and Naomi Tsegaye were wonderful research assistants. Thanks also especially to Amit Taneja and Stephanie Guzman, co-leaders of the Class Matters group, and all of the student participants. I have been equally lucky in my new home at Ohio University's Department of Sociology and Anthropology, where I am surrounded by colleagues and students whom I enjoy. Ursula Castellano, Debra Henderson, Charlie Morgan, Steve Scanlan, and Deborah Thorne have been terrific mentors, and my students have made the transition not only easy for me but also fun.

Fran Benson at Cornell University Press has been a fantastic editor whose enthusiasm, confidence, and perceptiveness—not to mention reading suggestions—have helped me greatly. I also thank the three anonymous reviewers whose comments helped me to revise this manuscript and substantially improve it through their critiques and suggestions. Acquisitions assistant Emily Powers provided timely and specific logistical direction. Thanks also to Sara Ferguson and Katy Meigs for steering this manuscript into its final, more polished stages.

Adi Hovav helped me make key revisions in the early, painful stages of writing.

Of course, all remaining errors or gaps remain my own.

Finally, I thank my family, John and Annette Lee; Lee Metcalf; Camilla Lee; James Lee; Colbeigh Spero; and Thatcher, June, and Rumi

Spero, as well as my longtime friends Allison Mistry, Patty Jang, and, especially, Lauren Gutterman, who deserves extra thanks for having read this book in its early, middle, and late stages. It has been improved over and over again by her feedback and attention. My wife, Tan Nguyen, managed three moves, drove thousands of miles, and cooked me countless breakfasts during the writing of this book: without her I would be under-nourished in so many ways. Most book acknowledgments include a note about the solitary nature of writing, but family and friends have made this process much less so. Needless to say, customary thanks for patience and forbearance still apply.

CLASS AND CAMPUS LIFE

Introduction

Violet grew up in a small, distant suburb of Boston, the oldest child in a single-parent family. Things were not easy financially, and her mother, siblings, and she sometimes struggled to secure enough food and stable shelter. As in many families near the lower end of the economic spectrum, there were considerable challenges. Violet's mother was sometimes without work, and emergencies were made worse by a lack of supportive connections or spare cash.

Violet's high school drew from a regional mix of small towns and suburbs that covered a wide economic spectrum. She remembers the stigma of using her school's free lunch program as well as having friends and boyfriends who were from more economically stable families. Violet managed her college application process with help from these friends. She had always planned to enroll in college, but neither she nor her mother knew much about how to make this happen. She figured out how to use online resources to look for scholarships, kept track of application and financial aid deadlines, and was able to ride along with others on a few campus visits. Among other colleges, she applied to Linden (a pseudonym, as are all names and locating descriptions)—a selective women's liberal arts college located in the Northeast. She was accepted and offered sufficient financial support to make it work. Violet enrolled, and in the last days of a hot August, her mother dropped her off at Linden to begin her first year.

Here's where we might typically take leave of Violet. As a student at an elite college that offers plenty of financial aid, her chances of graduating are good. Her chances of getting a job after graduation that affords her a middle-class standard of living are also good. According to scholars, graduates of selective colleges are more likely to obtain high-paying jobs,[1] and over a lifetime they earn hundreds of thousands more in wages than those with only a high school diploma.[2] In many ways, Violet's story seems happily resolved now that she's made it to college—a success story.

But what happens from here? How do low socioeconomic status students make their way through largely affluent college communities? Despite decades of research on college inequality, we still don't know much about the experiences of low-income, working-class, and first-generation students who attend selective colleges such as Linden. We do know that their experiences are often more difficult and in some ways less satisfactory than those of their middle-class and upper-class peers. For example, although low-income students' completion rates are higher at elite colleges than at less-selective or nonselective colleges, they are still less likely to graduate than more affluent students at these same colleges.[3] We also know that low socioeconomic status students are less likely to participate in activities such as study abroad, sports, clubs, and Greek life.[4] Finally, there are indications that low socioeconomic status students attending elite colleges are on average less satisfied than their middle and upper socioeconomic status peers and may not form the kinds of social networks with peers that such colleges stress.[5] These findings tell us that merely gaining access to an elite college is not the end of the story. Rather, new challenges confront low socioeconomic status students during their college years.

Sociologists have begun to take a closer interest in the black box, so to speak, of students' experiences during college. Rather than looking at financial capital (how students pay for college) or human capital (students' academic preparation and capacities), scholars are now looking more closely at the ways that socioeconomic status matters for students' social and extracurricular lives. In particular, scholars have begun to focus on students' varying levels of cultural capital, which Paul DiMaggio concisely defines as "easy familiarity with prestigious forms of knowledge," and social capital, the resources we gain through network or personal ties.[6] Many examinations of class stratification in college life, however, leave out on-the-ground interactions across class: How do people manage inequality face-to-face within a shared space and ostensibly shared identity?

There is relatively little research on how people manage to negotiate class inequality in interactions generally. According to DiMaggio, although we may recognize class sociologically as one type of "doing difference,"[7] alongside race and gender, there has been "no comparably large ... literature [that] has focused on the production of class difference in social interaction."[8] Sociologists of education tend to write about class as constituting skills, knowledge, or attitudes that provide comparative advantage or disadvantage—for good reason, since class background shapes people's educational outcomes in important ways. Because of these discrepancies, sociologists often write about students from different class backgrounds as living largely separate lives.

Like other sociologists working in this area, I am especially interested in the experiences of first-generation, working-class, and low-income students. In this book, however, I foreground the way that elite colleges bring low socioeconomic status students into *a shared daily life* with more affluent peers in a space that is itself class marked. I show the ways that elite colleges provide a venue in which students become intimately connected to more and less affluent peers, whether sharing a dorm room or a classroom, a club or a dining hall, a friendship or a romance. Indeed, the college's goal is to provide these students with a shared and unified identity across this and other forms of difference. All of this provides an important and unusual opportunity to ask about how individuals interact across class positions in sustained ways.

Within this environment, cross-class interactions and class inequality must be managed among and between students and by the college as an organization. I specify inequality because I find that, while individuals and institutions are able to acknowledge difference, they are often unable to discuss the *implications* of difference—what it means that one person has more than another. I examine two inter-related sets of dynamics. First, I examine the ways the college as an institution attempts to talk about class inequality within its student body, creating a shared college identity that bridges differences, while at the same time framing class as an aspect of diversity. Second, I investigate the ways that low socioeconomic status students maintain relationships with the affluent peers who surround them and largely shape the social spaces of the college. I show that, at both levels, a coherent language of class inequality is lacking: students and college alike are poorly equipped to name or discuss class inequality in meaningful ways. In the absence of effective discursive tools—and indeed, often despite direct efforts to avoid acknowledging class inequality at all—class distinctions become infused with moral meanings that make differences even more personal and painful. I refer to these meanings as a *semiotics of class morality*: a set of definitions about group or individual worth that are associated with class positions but left largely unspoken. I thus unpack both the ways that lower socioeconomic status students' experiences at an elite college are "loaded" with deeply meaningful moral implications and the ways that both students and college are grappling with those implications.[9]

Although sociologists have long stressed that nonmonetary factors are important to education—particularly *habitus*, cultural capital, and symbolic boundaries around class differences—our understanding of the complex and nuanced social interactions across class-status positions remains underdeveloped. We have particularly few examinations of sustained cross-class interactions, as opposed to short-term or occasional interactions.[10] In asking about how class is managed interactionally rather than focusing on cultural capital or symbolic boundaries as other scholars have done, I am especially attentive to Julie Bettie's assertion that we are "discursively disabled" in talking about class. Bettie writes that class "slips out" of our discourse, allowing other characteristics, such as race, to take on multifaceted significance.[11] Thus, she notes, when we say "white," we often mean white, middle-class, and suburban; when we say "black," we often mean black, low income, and urban. Other terms, such as "inner-city," become similarly invested with extra meanings. I follow a similar line of thinking about the invisibility of class in our discourse. I suggest that regardless of race, ethnicity, geography, or gender, the additional meanings that adhere to class and class-referent language are about moral distinctions. I build also on the work of others who have elaborated on the links between class, money, and morality in more theoretical terms. I discuss these earlier approaches briefly before explaining my concept of the semiotics of class morality in greater depth.

Money, Class, and Morality

> Being poor is people surprised to discover you're not actually stupid.
> Being poor is people surprised to discover you're not actually lazy.
> Being poor is getting tired of people wanting you to be grateful.
> John Scalzi, "Being Poor"

These phrases, excerpted from a much longer list, get at some of the ways that (as bell hooks succinctly writes) "class matters."[12] Class matters not only in a material sense but also in the way it informs our interactions with others and our sense of self in context. Class connects to fundamental assessments—about how we spend our time, what we eat, how we raise and teach our children, whether we are understood as being hard workers, whether we are seen as upstanding citizens or mooching off the system, whether we can call ourselves "real" women or men, and whether we are competent to make decisions for ourselves or must be supervised by someone else. In all these ways, class raises moral questions about our worth and deservingness: how we got what we have and whether we have "earned" our place. We see these questions played out in literature, in popular media and political speech, in movies and TV. And, of course, we experience them in daily life.[13]

We understand class as relational, meaning it is not merely about where one falls in the spectrum of social and economic factors such as parents' education, income, and status. Rather, our class position is recognized *in relation to* others on either side of us in the socioeconomic spectrum. Moreover, our class standing is comparable not only to others around us but also to what we understand the successful American person to be, have, and look like. Mainstream culture provides discourses and images of what choices are socially legitimated and valued. This includes, for example, our lifestyle—having a smartphone or a newer-model car, home ownership, choosing beer or wine, or whether and where one goes on vacation. We might also think of world views or everyday beliefs—for instance, whether parents should schedule many after-school activities or allow children to grow up more "naturally" without a great deal of parental managing—class-related questions that arise in Annette Lareau's research.[14]

People who are able to live in ways that fit with the current ideal can feel confident that their choices are esteemed by society. They are legitimized through public discourses and by peers. As Andrew Sayer has argued, those who are not able to afford these choices, or who otherwise do not have the resources to secure them, may be looked down upon as failing to reach this ideal. Thus class differences are differences in ability to achieve socially approved ways of living and adhering to or failing to adhere to the "right" way to live. And, as Sayer stresses, these are not merely conceptual distinctions but distinctions with moral connotations.[15] By using the term "morality," Sayer means that people connote money, income, and socioeconomic status with deeply held (if often subconscious) beliefs about better and worse, good and bad, right and wrong. When we fail to attain a middle-class or upper-class way of living, we are marked as not merely materially deprived but morally lacking: our moral dispositions and competence as individuals may be called into question. For example, to say that someone is a "welfare queen" or "hillbilly" is not only to say that the person utilizes welfare or is a low-income person from a rural area but also impugns that person's moral rightness.[16] As was expressed by John Scalzi in the epigraph to this section, these charges are directed toward fundamental qualities of a person's worth such as intelligence, drive, and gratitude.

Constructing a Semiotics of Class Morality

Longstanding research establishes an American aversion to talking about class, while Sayer and others have established that class is freighted with moral meanings.[17] The implications of these phenomena for socioeconomically marginalized students on selective campuses, however, have not been examined: What do these silences and moral implications mean for low socioeconomic status students as class minorities in an elite space? What are the implications of these dynamics for cross-class interactions within such majority-minority spaces? Higher education, broadly, and elite colleges, specifically, are profoundly appropriate places for examining class-morality questions because the way we think and talk about higher education is itself so laden with moral discourse. Moreover, a significant aspect of contemporary sociological work on college and class variation is focused on low socioeconomic status students' holistic experiences and their relative abilities to navigate informal aspects of the college—in other words, not only whether they are adequately prepared for their course work but also how they are able to develop a sense of "belonging" on campus,[18] whether and how friendship ties and extracurricular activities help them persist to graduation or assist in postgraduation employment.

Applying Sayer's concern for morality to the context of elite colleges helps us to see that legitimated ways of being in the context of elite higher education have been historically set by elites themselves: white upper-class and upper-middle-class students, college personnel, graduates, parents, and trustees. Although many colleges' demographic profiles are broader now than in the past, the environs and the cultural practices of elite college campuses continue to reflect this history. Thus, what is presented by the college as best, ideal, or simply typical aligns with the experiences of white middle-class and upper-class students. For students who come from these backgrounds, college feels similar to home. For students from low socioeconomic status backgrounds, however, college may be a greater adjustment, as their previous experiences may seem to be less legitimate or valid. As Allison Hurst has written, the rhetoric of higher education presents working-class and low-income lives as less valued, something to become better than.[19]

The question of who and what is legitimated at Linden, as at other elite institutions of higher education, is not always communicated directly but rather through what I call a semiotics of class morality. A semiotics is a system of language, including texts, public presentations, visual representations, conversational exchanges, speeches, and other direct and indirect forms of communication. I use this term to convey the idea that interactional exchanges about the meaning of class take place below the surface—one need not name a hierarchy directly to communicate it effectively. I also use this term to convey the idea that there is a hidden language of moral associations around class that is communicated through personal and institutional discourses and that it is pervasive, occurring across many interactional venues. This semiotics of class morality is rooted in a larger hierarchical understanding of class and what class positions signify in American society—though we often prefer not to admit it. It is also inextricable from ideas about mobility, or how we get ahead in the world: according to the popular American narrative, through hard work and pulling ourselves up by our bootstraps. Although language and representation may seem to be merely about semantics, they pertain to fundamental questions of meaning and worth: better versus worse, more versus less esteemed, and more versus less legitimate. My research indicates that both students and the college are engaged in the creation and negotiation of this semiotics of class morality—a process continuously in play through discourse and interaction. The semiotics in turn shapes students' experiences across interactional venues.

Thinking about class and morality is especially important at an elite college in an era in which college admission and success is framed as being not only about academic merit (students' grades and standardized test scores) but also about their character, who they are as individuals. This includes their extracurricular activities including sports and clubs, volunteer work, travel history, and other nonschool accomplishments. Several people have noted the ways in which bringing these factors into the admissions process disadvantages low socioeconomic status students, who often do not have equivalent access, time, or funds for such activities. It is important, however, to note the ways in which this is a contemporary shift in how we think about what makes a person worthy of education or membership in a particular college community. While considering students as more than just grades and scores is important, we should also recognize the accompanying discourse that positions students' value as not merely academic achievers but also achievers outside the classroom in sports, clubs, volunteer work, travel, and ultimately in their abilities to translate these experiences into job applications. This does not stop with college admission but continues through college activities, as we can see in the push for students to become "campus leaders."[20] Thus we can also think about membership in the college community as being tied to personal achievement in addition to academic achievement. While this has the potential to valuably recognize students as whole beings with many facets, it also extends the pressure to "achieve" well beyond the classroom, making even one's personal life available for comparative measure. Consider, for example, an excerpt from a 2014 blog post by a liberal arts college graduate:

> We have no right to become the vulnerable women that our educations were meant to protect us from becoming. Even unintentionally. We cannot be weak. We cannot be average. . . . We cannot be poor or struggling. We cannot be abused. We cannot hold jobs that do not require a degree. We cannot be alone or scared. We cannot be in need. Our lives cannot resemble the less fortunate women we studied in school or for whom we've dedicated our lives to helping.[21]

This speaks volumes about the expectations that elite liberal arts graduates hold for themselves and believe are held for them—to be a worthy graduate of one's alma mater means being successful according to an "impossibly narrow" definition.[22] It is here that we get into potentially difficult discussions of what, exactly, students are becoming educated in: Is it scholarly knowledge, or is it lifestyle and class modality? Through this holistic matrix of evaluation, a logic of self-improvement from working-class or low-income backgrounds into the esteemed middle-class or upper-class future is applied, following a hierarchical ranking of social worlds.[23] This constitutes much of the way in which a semiotics of class morality is applied.

To say that there is a semiotics of morality does not necessarily mean that the college as an organization intentionally takes such a stance or that individual administrators or faculty intend to perpetrate these messages. Moreover, there may be conflicting representations or conflicts between the explicit and implied messages provided. Colleges work within larger fields of current practices that shape their own choices about how to talk about and represent class inequality on campus; they often must deal with conflicting priorities. Further, comparisons need not be explicit or explicitly framed in colloquial terms of morality such as good or bad, virtuous or indecent. Rather, a semiotics of class morality adheres to *locally relevant concepts* of achievement, merit, and deservingness. In short, moral rightness is defined as meeting what is understood as the desirable terms of community membership.

Sociological Approaches

Questions about the implications of class inequality in higher education have long interested sociologists. Scholars have attempted to understand the variations in students' experiences both in and outside the classroom through several lenses. Seminal works in sociology of higher education research focused on *patterns* of college attainment: the factors associated with how students got in and whether they graduated.[24] To simplify it greatly, scholars found that students whose fathers had attended college were much more likely to attend and graduate from college. Socioeconomic background was therefore understood to be highly influential in a person's subsequent attainment.

Although financial and human capital remain important to under-standing college outcomes, contemporary scholars stress other sources of inequality; even when these factors are mediated, we still see variation in students' experiences based on their symbolic capital. For example, even when students receive strong or full financial aid, thus mitigating financial inequalities at least somewhat, class-related challenges continue to stratify students' experiences.[25] Similarly, although precollege academic training may lead to some variation in students' college outcomes, low socioeco-nomic status students who move from academically disadvantaged high schools into elite colleges perform at high levels, as evidenced by data on the so-called "mismatch hypothesis."[26] Indeed, a 2012 study suggests that there are many more low socioeconomic status students who have the capacity to study in elite colleges, but, for various reasons, they are not applying, not getting accepted, or not enrolling when they are accepted.[27] Differences in students' finances and preparation for college, though important for in-dividual students, cannot explain the full extent of class stratification that arises once students are on campus.[28]

Cultural Capital

The approach to understanding socioeconomic variation in college out-comes shifted after Pierre Bourdieu's introduction of his concepts of *hab-itus*, cultural capital, and social capital as symbolic resources.[29] Cultural capital theory rests on an understanding that our dispositions—how we approach the world and our ideas about what seems natural to do, Bour-dieu's concept of *habitus*—are crucial for our experiences. Thus, col-lege success is not simply about affordability but also about the ability to navigate campus life. Cultural capital, one's familiarity with particular, usually elite, forms of knowledge, is important both for students' day-to-day comfort level and for their ability to excel in the classroom, as it includes both social and academic cues about status. Cultural capital also pertains to students' capacity to take advantage of college resources once enrolled through attitudes about seeking help, speaking with faculty and other college authority figures, and perception of what is both appropriate and valuable. In regard to social capital, low socioeconomic status students typically have fewer connections to white-collar elites in their personal and family networks than students from middle and upper socioeconomic status backgrounds.

Jenny M. Stuber's analyses of working-class and middle-class students' participation in extracurricular activities show that more-affluent students' cultural understandings about informal job-market benefits and connections on campus pull them in to campus opportunities.[30] These college opportunities—internships, study abroad programs, and other extracurricular activities—will in turn help them gain access to employment or graduate school in the future. Working-class students, by contrast, see less value in these experiences. They concentrate on practical, immediately applicable experiences. Moreover, they are less likely to be connected to peer networks that serve as conduits to in-college opportunities such as Greek life.[31] Scholars, including Elizabeth Aries and Maynard Seider, have investigated cultural capital by examining fundamental questions of students' senses of belonging and well being at elite colleges.[32] Low-income, first-generation respondents felt that they were not able to keep pace with middle and upper socioeconomic status peers, who had more elite cultural capital on arrival at college. This capital allows affluent students to transition into college seamlessly, as they already have experiences, such as travel, in common with fellow students. In some cases, low socioeconomic status students felt alienated and uncomfortable because they perceived that they did not possess the elite cultural capital valued in their college setting.[33] Cultural capital is therefore influential not only in terms of students' capacities to navigate college gatekeeping but also in terms of trying to fit in with peers.

Cultural capital sociological approaches are important because they crucially link students' backgrounds with their college experiences, thus helping us understand how students are variously equipped to navigate collegiate structures and how the dominant social tone on campus is set. There are two types of issues, however, that are not well addressed through this framing. The first has to do with peer relationships. Cultural capital analysis focuses on the possession of particular—typically elite—forms of knowledge that can be used for navigating systems. Examinations of the ways that cultural capital stratifies students' experiences are centered on how that cultural knowledge is utilized within particular venues governed by gatekeepers, rather than on relating to fellow students across class positions. These analyses lend themselves especially well to comparing low socioeconomic status students' cultural capital stores or facility at deployment with those of middle or upper socioeconomic status students. Working in this vein, Stuber, Elizabeth A. Armstrong and Laura Hamilton, and others have provided key analyses of the ways that institutional structures are successfully negotiated by students with elite cultural capital and the ways those same students create dominant social systems.[34] Although scholars have also examined the ways students understand and feel about these differences,[35] their primary attention is not on *interactions between students* who have dominant and nondominant forms of cultural capital or on the ways that students with relatively low levels of elite cultural capital approach these interactions as active negotiators. Indeed, Armstrong and Hamilton provide evidence that elite and nonelite students rarely occupy the same social spaces, because affluent students set the terms for membership in exclusionary ways.[36] While this may be true at large universities, it is less so at smaller campuses such as liberal arts colleges, which are important for thinking about the production of social and economic power for young adults.[37]

This leads us to a second question, namely how the college as an organization functions as a specific setting in which these interactions take place. Colleges, like workplaces, families, and every other venue have their own structures, values, and norms. Although contemporary sociological and anthropological research has explicated the ways in which elite colleges remain to a great degree exclusionary along class lines, many examinations of social-class dynamics in colleges focus either on students or on the college structure, with little emphasis on interaction. For example, Mitchell Stevens's ethnographic examination of liberal arts admissions processes clarifies the stratification outcomes for students, but it does not center on students' experiences.[38] Although Sara Ahmed, Bryan McKinley Jones Brayboy, Susan Iverson, and others have analyzed college discourses and procedures, they too aim their analyses at the institutional level.[39] Ann Mullen's examination of students' enrollment choices at Yale and Southern Connecticut State College showcases students' understandings of the admissions process and how their backgrounds lead them to choose where to enroll but does not discuss the actions of the colleges such as outreach strategies.[40] Armstrong and Hamilton's and Stuber's examinations are partial exceptions: both discuss the ways students operate within the constraints of their particular campus structures.[41] Neither book focuses on the practices of the colleges in question, however—rather, this area is one aspect of their larger analytical project. Thus questions remain about how colleges approach class inequality beyond providing financial aid, potentially either mitigating or exacerbating class distinctions among students.

Scholars have taken up similar questions in regard to earlier years of education, focusing on how high schools produce or reproduce class advantage among students.[42] Bettie, in particular, considers comparable dynamics between middle-class and working-class high school girls to understand how they perceive their social position and the structural factors that serve to advantage some over others. Shifting the analysis to college years means that students who have already stopped their formal educational trajectory will not be included in the analysis and those who do continue—both students seeking to reproduce an inherited elite class position and students from working-class and low-income backgrounds seeking socioeconomic mobility—are one step closer to adult outcomes. In this book I develop the implication that the college is important for providing internal mechanisms of class advantage or disadvantage. I do this by looking closely at the ways class position is contextualized, given meaning, within the Linden College institutional setting.

Symbolic Boundaries

To understand some of these issues more thoroughly, we can utilize a second theoretical approach, one that is directed at the ways that people determine the salience of differences among themselves as *symbolic boundaries*. Symbolic boundaries are based not only on ideas of like and unalike but more deeply on associations of what is right and wrong, honorable and dishonorable. They serve both to differentiate those who are unalike (the out-group) and to solidify the symbolic bonds or similarities of those considered alike (the in-group), further legitimizing one's own status position. For example, I may esteem people who are "like me" because they share my values or outlook on life, while simultaneously drawing an invidious distinction against those whom I perceive to be unlike me.[43] A number of scholars have therefore suggested that class is a powerful source of boundary drawing.[44] Scholars have observed, moreover, that people in different class positions tend to observe and mark these boundaries differently.

Michèle Lamont, a prominent scholar in this area, has argued that middle and upper socioeconomic status people tend to emphasize cultural distinctions of taste, such as sophistication, and markers of these qualities—for example, discrimination in wines or microbrewed beer. Working-class and low-income people tend to stress moral boundaries, such as hard work and honesty.[45] These different senses of what is important in oneself and others may lead to a devaluation of people who are "on the other side" or, conversely, may lead one to feel mocked or condescended to by others.[46]

Scholars looking at symbolic boundaries among college students have found similar dynamics in play. Stuber's research with working-class and middle-class college students, for example, examines how students perceive others across class boundaries. Her working-class respondents stressed their hard work and independence as strong positive qualities that would help them get ahead. They looked down on or even pitied middle-class and upper-class students, whom they perceived as having been born with silver spoons in their mouths and having too much parental support and lacking awareness of their many advantages.[47] Hurst has shown the complexity of this kind of boundary drawing.[48] She demonstrates that students from low socioeconomic status backgrounds largely took one of three positions in comparing their college and home lives: some tried to assimilate into the middle-class culture of the college, others worked to maintain their home-culture orientation, and still others tried to manage by keeping a foot in each world.

This theoretical approach complements cultural capital perspectives: while cultural capital asks what kinds of symbolic capital tools students need to succeed in the specific college venue and how they may vary by class background, symbolic boundaries analyses ask how students see class differences: What are the *implications* of difference? This theoretical perspective nonetheless leaves part of the puzzle remaining. Although symbolic boundaries arguments can help us understand how students make meanings around class difference, we also need to know what happens when these boundaries are blurred or crossed within students' relationships. Even though some scholars, notably Robert Granfield and Wolfgang Lehmann,[49] have examined the ways in which low socioeconomic status students have crossed symbolic boundaries relative to their histories or their families, we do not yet understand how students navigate those boundaries with respect to friends. What happens when students make cross-class friendships? How do students negotiate the deeply complex boundaries of class position within their intimate friendships and peer circles? How do individuals and organizations deal with class inequality when it is up close and personal rather than in the form of an abstracted other?

Focusing on the meanings of class and how these meanings are managed within personal interactions places such questions front and center. These topics are crucial to understand in the current American context as sociologists and others have documented the growing national levels of segregation by socioeconomic status or class, terms I use interchangeably.[50] (For more on this issue, see the methodological discussion in the appendix.) American children increasingly grow up around other children whose parents largely share similar levels of education, income, purchasing power, and occupations.[51] This dynamic has only increased over the past several decades. Because of the way our education system is funded and arranged, many Americans also go to school with others who are likely to share their socioeconomic profile.

This high level of socioeconomic segregation is largely maintained on elite college campuses. Demographically, these campuses comprise primarily middle and upper socioeconomic status students: according to Anthony Carnevale and Stephen Rose's calculations, 90 percent of students attending the top 146 colleges come from the top half of the socioeconomic spectrum.[52] For middle and upper socioeconomic status students attending highly selective colleges, therefore, the homogeny of their childhood neighborhoods and earlier schooling often extends through college. By contrast, class difference and cross-class encounters are pervasive for low socioeconomic status students entering higher education. First, low socioeconomic status students at elite campuses are the minority and therefore more likely to encounter class-different others, while adjusting to a middle-class setting that is more familiar to middle-class and upper-class students. Second, at residential colleges, and especially small liberal arts colleges, it is difficult to move outside of the so-called campus bubble to seek alternative social venues or relationships. Low socioeconomic status students must therefore develop interactional strategies for managing class differences because they cannot easily opt out.

For these students, then, college opens a venue for difficult questions about class inequality in one's immediate and personal life, moving from assessing cross-class others at a distance to assessing them up close. These surroundings and interactions bring students face-to-face with the difficult question: What does it mean to have class inequality within friendships and among peers? A similar question arises at the organizational level: What does it mean to have inequality among students who are supposed to share a community and common identity? These are the questions that make up the heart of this book.

Organization of the Book

In this book I examine class inequality at Linden College across multiple campus venues and in four different situations: in college discourse, in students' friendships, in a student club formed around the goal of class activism on campus, and in students' interactions with the college administrative structure. These chapters form the core of my analysis and trace the construction and impact of the semiotics of class morality across sets of interactions.

In chapter 1, I describe respondents' recollection of their lives before they arrived at Linden College, how they were able to go to college, and why they chose Linden. These narratives often revolve around students' motivations for seeking higher education and the people in their lives, especially parents, who supported their efforts. Some of the challenges that arise from moral undertones of class are presaged in these early stages of college preparation.

In chapter 2, I examine Linden's rhetorical construction of low socioeconomic status students as the college tries to establish a shared identity for students while framing certain differences between them as "diversity." I discuss the ways that this rhetorical placement matters for low socioeconomic status students. I show that the college, despite foregrounding its inclusiveness, creates a semiotics of class morality in which low socioeconomic status students are positioned as being less than fully legitimate members of the Linden community.

In chapter 3, I examine the ways low socioeconomic status students manage cross-class interactions within their friendships. I focus on how students either confront or avoid class inequality and discuss some of the ways that the college as an organization reinforces or undermines these dynamics—that is, why particular forms of interaction are more likely in this setting. I show that students rarely discussed class inequality directly. This dynamic is shaped by the moral semiotics of class and refracted through two locally meaningful concepts: community and merit.

In chapter 4, I look at Class Activists of Linden (CAL), a student club specifically oriented toward class advocacy for students. I ask how students can organize around class, given the interpersonal and institutional silences that prevail. It is clear that even the student club dedicated to advocacy for low socioeconomic status students had trouble figuring out how to talk about class inequality. While respondents often felt too vulnerable to share personal stories, abstracted political narratives that other groups on campus made use of opened up uncomfortable topics.

In chapter 5, I turn to experiences in the classroom and other formal interactions and ask what class looks and feels like in the classroom or in the dean's office. While the classroom was understood by many students and faculty members as a space in which real conversations could take place about class inequality—and a space in which students learned empowering analytical skills—these spaces were not immune to the same kinds of uncomfortable social dynamics that prevailed in other venues. When students sought to use formal resources provided by the college, silence around class inequality created not only difficulties for low socioeconomic status students but also often divergent views about the meanings of support for those students.

In chapter 6, I look at the other end of the education process, catching up with nineteen of the respondents several years after their graduations. I show the ways that respondents experienced relative levels of social mobility. While they had achieved several markers of middle-class status, other markers had not been attained, and respondents struggled to figure out how to think of their class status as adults.

I conclude the book by revisiting my primary findings and making some suggestions for ways that colleges like Linden might better support low-income, working-class, and first-generation students.

First, however, I will briefly contextualize my findings by describing Linden College as a campus and as an example of a specific type of college, including a brief discussion of how low-income and working-class students came to attend elite colleges. I will also provide a short discussion of my research methods. More detail about the latter can be found in the appendix.

Nonelite Students at Elite Campuses

Beginning with Harvard in 1636, elite colleges in the United States have predominantly served affluent white men, with greater availability for white women with the creation of women's colleges around two hundred years later. The first form of financial aid was a single private scholarship awarded annually to a "poor but pious" Harvard man (in 1643) who would take up a life of religious service after graduation. "Scholarship girls," as they were called at Linden, were relatively few and far between in the early years of American colleges. Excellent discussions of college admissions and financial aid policies over time already exist, and timelines of the history of federal financial aid are available online.[53] I will therefore only briefly outline some major points about admissions that help contextualize my subsequent discussions.

Working-class and low-income students were afforded considerably expanded opportunities to attend both public and private colleges with the advent of federal financial aid, which began after the Second World War to support veterans of the armed services. In addition to other benefits programs, returning servicemen were offered funds under the Servicemen's Readjustment Act of 1944 (GI Bill) to continue their education. These grants allowed thousands of (mostly) men to earn college degrees. Subsequently, the Higher Education Act of 1965 added federally supported loans for a wider swath of people at advantageous interest rates and with special benefits (such as not accruing interest while the student is enrolled at least half time).

These reauthorization provisions enabled students and their families who could never have paid for the tuition and other costs outright to finance higher education. As grants, work-study programs, and parent loans were added, greater numbers of students from wider ranges of economic backgrounds were able to attend college. Wealthy private colleges and universities continued to offer financial assistance and increasing the availability of support for middle-, working-, and lower-class students.

Financial aid had greater implications than simple financing, however. Colleges were no longer reserved only for those whose families could afford to pay the full costs. According to Rupert Wilkinson, private college aid has always had a connection to moral comparisons and meanings.[54] That first scholarship for a poor student at Harvard, who would use the benefits thereof to enter a life of religious service and thus material paucity, illustrates this. From early on, then, a sense of relationality between students was associated with funding: students receiving financial support from their college or university were often required to work for their keep—for example, by serving their fellow students. These earliest provisions allowed a small handful of young people to enroll at college, at the same time exemplifying their poor but morally worthwhile standing. Even schools like Linden that have made higher education available to low-income female students for most of its existence often did so in the manner of the times—in Linden's case, by creating dorms for scholarship girls. The dynamics of how financial support was provided were therefore not neutral but communicated a position or role for aided students vis-à-vis others. These institutional logics have changed—certainly low socioeconomic status students no longer live in a segregated space or work in a form of servitude, as was the case at some elite colleges. Nevertheless, the question of how financial aid positions students and discourse around low socioeconomic status students remains important.

Beginning in the 1970s and continuing into the 2010s, low-income students have become part of a new discursive project: diversity.[55] Selective and highly selective campuses that had long been predominantly white and upper class began to feel increasing pressure to "diversify" their student bodies. (Public institutions had already become considerably more diverse in terms of students' racial, ethnic, and socioeconomic backgrounds.) Awarding financial aid therefore became one aspect of speaking to the need for, and facilitating the increase of, student body diversity. This discursive relationship remains today: financial aid terms have become proxies for diversity, exemplified when colleges publish statistics on the number of federal Pell Grant recipients they have.

In the last decades, and especially since the recession of 2008, many elite colleges have been vocal about their support for low socioeconomic status students, in some cases supporting them through innovative financial arrangements. Despite these efforts, however, the numbers of low socioeconomic status students remain low at selective colleges. As intimated, low socioeconomic status students are a distinct and sometimes profound minority on campuses. Thus, the likelihood of a student making friends with another student who shares a low-income, working-class, or first-generation background is lower than for students who share a middle-class or upper-class background. Moreover, colleges typically offer little beyond financial aid in the way of programs to support low socioeconomic status students. These students therefore lack even a concrete venue to locate one another. This problem is exacerbated by college data-management practices, since colleges do not utilize financial or socioeconomic data for the same ends as they use, for example, data on students' racial or ethnic status.

When so few low socioeconomic status students attend elite colleges, why is it important to study how they fare? First, elite campuses are significant to the structures of power and class advantage in white-collar and creative fields—in other words, to the mechanisms of class advantage in adult and cross-generational life. Elite colleges play important roles in creating networks among elites and solidifying the socioeconomic positions of middle-class and upper-class graduates. Moreover, elite colleges may offer distinct benefits beyond a degree from a prestigious institution that can lead to upward socioeconomic mobility for students from low-income, working-class, and first-generation college backgrounds. Graduates of elite colleges (e.g., the top 146 colleges and universities out of the more than 4,000 currently enrolling students) are more likely than graduates of nonelite colleges to obtain white-collar jobs, to make more money over a lifetime, and to have access to postcollege opportunities, such as graduate school and alumnae networking services, that can continue to improve economic status.[56] Elite colleges and their students are therefore important to study because they are so intimately related to both socioeconomic power and stability.

However, elite colleges like Linden are also important research venues because their demographic and structural characteristics allow for significant examination of cross-class interactions. Like most other elite liberal arts campuses, Linden is entirely residential. Students not only attend classes on campus, but they also join clubs, play sports, party, study, spend time with friends, sleep, and (usually) work there as well. Students are required to live on campus for all four years of their stay, with the exception of time spent in study abroad and certain other academic programs. At Linden, the majority of students live in the same dormitory for their entire period of enrollment. Thus the social and extracurricular life of schools like Linden is deeply interwoven with the rest of college life, and students spend the majority of their time in this space—that is, students live out all aspects of their lives, not just their academic lives, on campus.

This provides multiple, interrelated venues for the experience of inequality to unfold. Moreover, it makes it difficult for students to participate only in limited parts of college life such as just attending classes and then going home. Rather, colleges like Linden are immersive experiences: community is an important institutional value, and students are pulled deeply into peer circles that bridge classes, sports, dorm life, work, romance, and virtually all other pursuits.

We might sum all this up by stating that elite college campuses remain profoundly classed spaces. They are spaces, moreover, in which class practices have particular, outsized relevance. I now describe the ways Linden College looks and feels in these terms.

Linden College as a Classed Setting

One of the key premises of this book is that we need to see students' interactions as located within a situated space—a classed space, both in terms of physical structures and social practices. I set the stage here for later discussions by describing the physical campus, how it looks and feels, and especially, the reasons why I call it a "classed" space. It's important to note that many of the structural (social and physical) qualities of Linden are similar to those of other liberal arts college campuses—or, for that matter, to larger campuses. Many of the campus traditions and annual events are also similar to practices at other elite college campuses.[57]

Linden is a compact campus that features a great deal of manicured green space and a host of well-maintained older buildings, with a few modern additions interspersed. The older buildings are brick, stone, or wood, while the more recently constructed buildings are either brick or concrete. A handful of the buildings have ivy crawling up their sides, and many have neatly trimmed shrubs or other greenery delineating the walkways that crisscross the campus.

The college is organized around a central cluster of historic administrative and academic buildings, and slightly farther out there is a student center. If we look out the front window of that student center, we see a beautiful lawn: very clean, very even, and blindingly green. To the left, there are more trees and another small brick building; directly across the way, a large tree stands beside Wilton Library; to the right there are more trees and Carter residence hall. In a style that is typical of Linden, Carter is a moderately sized building, constructed at the turn of the twentieth century out of red brick with a simple dark trim. Throughout both years of my research, as I walked from one part of campus to another, I found myself noting the number of buildings that had new coats of paint. There was evidence of virtually constant upkeep—fixing, building, repairing, repaving, replanting—to keep Linden looking perfect. Details such as these communicate a pervasive feeling about the class history and ongoing prestige of the college.

A fifteen-minute stroll down the central path leads to a cluster of student residence halls, while a ten-minute walk back in the opposite direction leads to another group of residential housing. Students refer to Linden in loose geographic sections: the "downhill" side (where the nerds and athletes are both said to live), center campus (where most classrooms and administrative buildings are), and the "uphill side" (reputed to be the party side of campus, sometimes compared to sorority houses). A peek inside the residence halls further demonstrates class distinctions. Much of the furniture in the residence halls suggests a comfortable upscale hotel rather than a stereotypical college dorm. Weekly Wednesday night study breaks feature coffee in matched china sets and cupcakes or other treats catered by the dining staff.

Virtually everything about the Linden campus, from the hundred-year-old oak trees and perfectly manicured lawns to the impeccably maintained historical buildings and contemporary design of the student center lounge, makes it impossible to call Linden class-neutral territory. The surrounding town of Connerston contributes to this classed appearance: the town's downtown has an artistic, upscale hippie feel to it because of its many coffee shops, art galleries, and relatively few chain or big-box stores. Whether weekday or weekend, the cafes and sidewalks are filled with people relaxing and chatting at all times of day, creating an air of easy relaxation and available spending money.

What Does Campus Feel Like?

Having described Linden's look, let us get a sense of the campus feel. Like many small colleges, Linden might be characterized as having a pervasive culture of what Michael Moffat refers to as "friend*l*iness."[58] Students and others on campus frequently smile in acknowledgment of others whose paths they cross, even if the person is not a personal acquaintance. Linden community members almost invariably hold doors open for one another, waiting a minute or so for the next person to reach the door. Several respondents recalled strong first impressions of how friendly the campus seemed during visits or tours.

Two contributing factors here are the small size of the Linden community and the lack of physical separation between living and working spaces for students—after a while, everyone begins to seem familiar. (Students who grew up in large cities, however, sometimes described how uncomfortable they felt at night in this small community when there were only the quaint lights of the walking paths and few people around.) This feeling of welcome and friendliness is communicated from students' earliest arrival on campus, when returning students play key roles in welcoming the new arrivals. For example, during orientation for new students, each residence hall had sophomore guides sitting or standing on porches and stoops and wearing hall T-shirts. Halls featured banners and hand-painted sheets with the names of incoming residents. Each arriving student would get help with her luggage and finding her new room as she was welcomed as a new member of the hall and the college.

Linden Students

I refer throughout the book to Linden as an elite college, as well as being selective. In using the term "elite," I refer to Linden's history, reputation, and selectivity of admission. I also refer to the current student composition: Linden students tend to be from middle and upper socioeconomic status families, have high SAT scores, and a long list of accomplishments. They come from all over the world but especially from the East and West Coasts. In many ways, Linden is similar to other elite colleges and universities, though its single-sex demographic sets it apart, and it is not as selective as Amherst and Williams or Harvard and Princeton. Around two-thirds of the student body receive need-based aid, ranging from one thousand dollars to over sixty thousand dollars per year in 2015. Linden ranks high among its peer colleges in the breadth of its students' class backgrounds: around 20 percent of Linden students receive Pell Grants, those federal grants awarded to the most financially needy students, and around 20 percent of Linden students are first-generation, meaning that their parent(s) did not complete college.[59] Finally, the college sponsors a small but long-running program for women over the age of twenty-six who are returning; these students are known as "Platt scholars," and many are first-generation and Pell recipients.

Students typically wear casual clothes, from worn-in jeans and tees to sweats. While I was there, many had adopted the latest hipster trend of tight jeans and hoodies, while others wore athletic or yoga gear and occasionally their pajamas. In my field notes, I characterized this as "not really a lot of on-purpose dressing." There were always a few students who looked like they were dressed to *go somewhere*, wearing dark-wash, well-fitted jeans and fashionable blouses or dresses. The following exchange I overheard one afternoon in the student center, however, illustrates students' typical expectations for dress. Seeing a friend wearing a skirt and casual blouse, the first student asked, "Why do you look so pretty today?" The object of her question responded that she "just wanted to" dress up a little. This line of questioning continued—Did she have a hot date? This exchange exemplified for me that, indeed, the Linden norm is not to dress up.

Once I began interviewing and spending time with students, I learned that the residence halls are understood by most students (and by the college) as the base for expected social life, the centerpiece of college community. Many students seemed to spend a great deal of time in their residence halls, whether hanging around with hall mates or on their own. Any given week-night or weekend features regularly scheduled TV nights, hall parties, and coffee hours; periodic cross-hall events such as a carnival or sports contests; annual events such as student potluck dinners, senior nights, theme parties (such as the polo party), parties for new students; and informal events such as watching the Super Bowl or going as a hall into town to see a movie.

While the Linden web site promises prospective students that "Lindies" do have active social lives (something I certainly witnessed as a participant observer), students were often very stressed about getting work done and meeting academic deadlines. This was in no small part because a good amount of their time was spent on extracurricular activities or, in some cases, working for pay. Conversations are frequently about classes, home-work, having too much work, and being behind on one's work. One of my respondents, Maya, described to me how "people at dinner were talking about people being on Prozac because they were so stressed—there is a culture of stress here. It's kind of sick—it's not right to be so stressed that you need to take pills for it."

A typical morning or afternoon on campus saw a constant trickle of students walking in ones and twos coming and going from the library, classrooms, and gym, without much lingering: although students are often out and about on campus, they are typically going somewhere and less often simply hanging around. One exception to this is when spring finally really begins and students gather outdoors for lunches in the final weeks of classes or spend the afternoon outdoors studying and playing Frisbee. The central areas of campus are not well navigated by car, so most students walk or bike their way around.

In many ways, Linden is a best-case scenario for low-income students compared with other elite colleges and universities. By providing high levels of grant support, Linden is able to utilize its endowment, alumnae donations, and other financial assets to reduce students' loan debts, though it is not able to eliminate loans entirely as a few colleges have done. The college is explicit in its goal of providing support for low-income and first-generation students, and each of the numerous faculty members and administrators I spoke with expressed their support for low socioeconomic status students. Indeed, a few years before my research began, there had been a faculty reading group on low socioeconomic student experiences as well as internal studies of how to support low-income and first-generation students better. Similarly, the director for diversity programming during the first year of my study was very committed to supporting low socioeconomic status students. (However, not all of this support was perceived by the students I spoke with.) Finally, there was a student-founded club, CAL, that specifically concerned itself with class issues on campus, something that was at the time extremely rare and remains only slightly less so. Thus, although—as with all qualitative findings—my arguments should not be generalized to all campuses or all students, it bears noting that the dynamics at Linden College may apply at similar campuses.

Methods

I selected Linden College as the site for research after meeting an administrator from Linden at a conference about low socioeconomic status student concerns. She mentioned CAL, the student club for low-income students, as a resource on her home campus, and I was intrigued—I'd never heard of such a campus organization, and it seemed like a great place to start for someone interested in understanding the experiences of socioeconomically marginalized students at elite colleges. Moreover, I knew that Linden was a relatively small campus and entirely residential. As an ethnographer, I thought that this would make students' social lives easier to see, both literally and figuratively, as they were played out on campus.

Linden administrators generously supported my project, welcoming me to campus. In 2008, I moved to Connerston to begin my research. Linden administrators introduced me to several student leaders from CAL. Linden administrators also sent an email to students whose families earned forty thousand dollars per year or less in adjusted gross income inviting them to volunteer as interview respondents. I selected the marker of forty thousand dollars per year as the marker of students at the lower end of the socioeconomic scale. Although the median income in the United States remains approximately, as it was during that time, fifty thousand dollars, the figure I selected is the approximate level at which a student would be awarded a Pell Grant, according to Linden administrators. This grant is the form of financial aid offered to the highest-need students, and it had a contextual relevance that was important. In order to expand the income criteria to include working-class students whose family earnings might be higher, I also invited students whose parents earned up to eighty thousand dollars per year, a figure I obtained by doubling the first. In both cases, I sought students whose parents had not obtained a four-year degree during the respondents' childhood and whose parents held blue- or pink-collar jobs (information obtained during the first interview). Thus with limited exceptions (discussed below), all respondents were first-generation college students, had parents who held blue- or pink-collar jobs, and came from households with adjusted gross incomes either below $40,000 or between $40,000 and $80,000.

I added two additional parameters to my selection of students to interview: US citizenship and traditional college age—that is, eighteen to twenty-four years old. I selected these measures because I wanted to minimize differences of experience attributable to age or nationality. An income level of forty thousand dollars in other countries might mean something wildly different than it does in the United States, and older students often did not live on campus and had very different social expectations from most of the Linden student body.

After interviewing a potential respondent, I asked the college to confirm whether her family income fell below $40,000, between $40,000 and $80,000, or above $80,000—in other words, did the student fit the economic parameters of the study selection. In addition to being roughly certain of a student's family income, I also asked about parents' educational backgrounds and occupations. (See the appendix for a lengthier discussion of my methods and a table of respondents.) Combining these data points allowed me to create a broader measure of what constitutes low socioeconomic status rather than strictly relying on a single proxy of income or parent education or parent occupation.

I characterized half of the sample as low income, first-generation students. Students in this group came from households with adjusted gross incomes below forty thousand dollars per year and had parents without four-year college degrees (with two exceptions), in most cases without any education after high school, and in a few cases without having completed high school. Typical parent jobs in this group included custodial or handyman work, home health aide, and other blue-collar and pink-collar work. Other respondents, whom I characterized as working-class, first-generation students came from households that were higher on the income scale. Parents in these households had not completed four-year degrees or, in many cases, two-year degrees but earned somewhat more through their work as skilled laborers, truck drivers, secretaries, and similar occupations. I refer to respondents who came from households with adjusted gross incomes above forty thousand dollars as working class.

Although a few parents obtained college degrees later in life, most respondents were first-generation college students. There were two exceptions, Alexandra and Lynne. Alexandra's father had completed a graduate degree before immigrating to the United States but then had been unable to gain white-collar employment. Her life and upbringing were therefore economically similar to other low-income students who were first-generation college students. Similarly, Lynne's father had completed a master's degree but experienced significant health problems that made work impossible. She therefore grew up in low-income circumstances. I refer to both as low income in my analyses.

Although I have included respondents' socioeconomic category in the data, I did not develop them in order to analyze differences—rather I wanted a holistic examination of status differences that was not limited to one or another proxy marker. I did not perceive systematic differences between the two groups and therefore present respondents collectively as being from "low socioeconomic status" households.

I do not analyze differences along racialized or ethnic lines, and therefore I do not identify students by these terms. This is primarily because the distribution of students' racialized statuses is so uneven in the sample, making comparisons difficult to draw. Information about students' race and ethnicity, however, can be found in the appendix.[60] Readers should not take this to mean that students' experiences are homogenous across race or ethnic positions. For example, I never heard stories about white or Asian American students being assumed to come from the "ghetto," "inner city," or "projects," while black and multiracial students did report being subject to these kinds of assumptions. In short, students of color managed issues of racism and being "othered" that white students did not, experiences that were sometimes told explicitly to me but not always. In my interviews with respondents, race and ethnicity were more often presented intersectionally through respondents' discussion of home communities, self-understandings, and other kinds of meaning making. I acknowledge that there are dynamics I am not able to include here because of the demographic makeup of the respondent sample and because my own racialized position as a white woman presumably shaped how respondents interacted with me. That being said, the arguments and phenomena discussed here are firmly based on interviews and field work with Hispanic / Latina, African American / Black / Caribbean, Asian American, multiracial, biracial, and white students alike. (To my knowledge, I did not interview any respondents who identified primarily as Native American.) The experiences I discuss were shared, if not by every low socioeconomic status student, then certainly by students located across these various racialized positions.

In addition to the e-mail message sent by Linden administrators, several faculty members and ultimately CAL sent out the same request for participation. (CAL's was accompanied by an informal introductory note from the club's president that year.[61]) I interviewed all students who responded but focused on those who met the set parameters. In total, I interviewed twenty-six low-income and working-class students. I also interviewed others who volunteered for the study, including more affluent students, older students, and international students. I interviewed all twenty-six students in the primary group of respondents more than once—in one case only three times, but typically five times, and as many as eight times. In total I had over 120 interviews with the primary group of respondents.

I also spoke with a small number of faculty (10) and administrators (13) who held key positions in shaping students' lives—for example, deans of academic divisions and of student services and directors of residence halls—or who were recommended to me as people who knew about or were sympathetic to low socioeconomic status students' concerns. Finally, I interviewed or spoke with five recent alumnae who were referred by respondents or who were former CAL members.

I supplemented the interviews with participant-observation field work. For this aspect, I took a three-pronged approach. First, I joined (with the permission of the student members) the Class Activists of Linden. (At the time of this writing, CAL has disbanded, and its future is uncertain.) A student-initiated and student-run club, CAL provided advocacy and support for low-income, working-class, and first-generation students. It also had the goal of educating other members of the community about class issues. The club met once a week in a classroom on campus to check in and plan events. I subsequently spent a semester attending the weekly meetings of the Hall Chairs Board, which helps coordinate and govern the residence halls. I selected this group because the residence halls are a significant part of Linden students' social lives, friendships, and campus identities. Residence halls are also places where students talked about class being revealed or hidden. Finally, they are places where students' enthusiasm for Linden seemed to take the most concrete shape, and it seemed to make sense to spend time around student leaders in this area.

Second, I attended Linden College events designed to introduce students to Linden or shape a Linden student identity—such as orientation programs and college tradition events—or that were relevant to financial issues, such as forums or workshops about class, college budget issues, or financial aid. I was interested in the latter group because of their clear connection to low socioeconomic status students. I was interested in the former because I wanted to understand how Linden students learned about Linden as a place, developed a Linden student identity, and learned about their peers. For similar reasons, I spent a semester attending a humanities course so I could understand in a more firsthand way what the classroom felt like. I selected humanities because I wanted a venue in which students talked frequently and might use personal anecdotes, something that seemed less likely in the hard sciences. I also spent time in the library, student center, and simply hanging around campus getting the feel of daily public life for students.

As the third ethnographic prong, I spent time with individual students. I asked respondents to take me either on a tour of campus or to an event that was part of their campus life or asked if I could "shadow" them—a term that describes well what field work entails. Respondents took me, among other places, around the campus athletic facilities, to residence hall coffee hours and governance meetings, and to a Seder dinner. I met students for meals, went along to classes and study halls and library sessions as well as to parties and other social events. My ethnographic understanding of Linden also included time spent simply being on campus—whether walking around between interviews or hanging out in the library or student center—and in the surrounding town of Connerston. Overall, I spent around 550 hours of observation time over the course of two years. Events I attended, especially parties, were sometimes awkward but they helped me better grasp the nonclassroom side of the college. I discuss my approaches and rationale in greater depth in the appendix.

To round out all of these practices, I periodically followed online and in-print presentations about Linden, both official and unofficial. These included an anonymous online student bulletin board, the college's official Facebook page, the Facebook pages of various student groups, archival records of the college administration, archives of several clubs and student magazines, and the college's official web site and YouTube site. It is important to emphasize that in all cases, names provided are pseudonyms chosen either by the interviewee or by me. In many cases, I have changed or omitted personally identifying bits of information—for example, a student's home state or the jobs her parents hold. Similarly, I have approximated many college statistics, quotes, and other texts to prevent them being identifiable, and I have blurred or changed descriptions of college places and events.

Big Questions

This book should be understood within a larger context of inquiry and public discussion. Socioeconomic status as a predominant constraint to college access and success is gaining scholarly, public, and administrative traction. Coverage in *U.S. News & World Report*, the *New York Times*, National Public Radio, the *Chronicle of Higher Education*, and other media has drawn national attention to the small number of low socioeconomic status students attending elite campuses, despite colleges' efforts to recruit them.[62] Many elite campuses proudly publicize the number of Pell Grant recipients and first-generation college students they enroll. Despite this, economically advantaged students continue to be the vast majority at Linden, as at selective colleges and universities overall. If we wish to see the numbers of socioeconomically marginalized students attending elite colleges rise, we must better understand how these students fare once they arrive, what kinds of social worlds await them on campus, and how their colleges can best support them. Ultimately, the big questions asked here are not only about what happens for these particular students but, more broadly, about how class inequality becomes interpreted through a semiotics of class morality within an elite institutional context, the effects of which have until now been left unexamined. In order to answer these questions, I follow the trajectories of Violet and other low-income, working-class, and first-generation students as they enter the Linden College campus gates and proceed through their careers as students at an elite college.

1

COLLEGE DREAMS, COLLEGE PLANS

When I asked Genesis how old she was when she first started thinking about college, she scrunched up her face as she thought back. She had been thinking about and planning for college through high school, but before that as well: "I think middle school, like eighth grade I started thinking about college. I remember working really hard in high school, and my main motivation working so hard was to get into a good college." College loomed large for Genesis in high school as a motivating factor and central concern, linked to other goals for adulthood such as career choice.

Genesis's account of college preparation sounds like that of many young American college students: years of planning, months of worrying over applications, anxiety while waiting for acceptance or rejection, joy at admission to a hoped-for school. However, Genesis, Violet, and other students from socioeconomically marginalized backgrounds who attend selective and highly selective colleges are by definition exceptional. The rates of low-income, first-generation, and working-class students attending four-year colleges immediately after high school are far lower than those of middle and upper socioeconomic status students. It is not an exaggeration to say that their representation at the top 146 most selective colleges and universities is tiny: according to one estimate, only 3 percent of students at these campuses come from the bottom income quartile, and only 10 percent from the bottom half.[1] I therefore begin this book by examining how these particular respondents began their lives at Linden by zeroing in on their decision to go to college, how they chose Linden, and their recollections of arriving on campus.

In examining this precollege process, I also highlight some of the ways in which moral questions related to class inequality were already coming into play as respondents and their families thought about college and the meanings of class mobility. In particular, I pay attention to respondents' motivations for attending college and for selecting Linden. Respondents indicated generally that they were seeking greater economic stability than they grew up with, and this positioned college as a path "out," as Genesis put it later in our conversation, but also a path away from the lives their parents and home-community friends typically led. I discuss parents both as sources of support and as what I call "conflicted role models." In this light, college aspirations often become tinged with moral associations, making the route toward enrollment and the thinking about what type of college to select more complicated. I close by discussing respondents' first impressions of Linden formed during visits or arrival on campus, the first face-to-face interactions between students and the new community they are about to join.

Parents: Sources of Support and Conflicted Role Models

In most cases, as we saw in Genesis's recollections, respondents had been thinking seriously about college since junior high or earlier. When asked how long they had known they wanted to go to college, some told me that they had always known; one respondent held out her hands about two feet off the ground to show the height of a young child and said, "Since I was this tall." Evelyn, for example, told me, she had "always" planned to go to college:

> Always. And my parents, I have to say, they were so good about saying, "We didn't go to college, and we want you to go to college and use your brain." Which is weird. They were so good with positive affirmation about my brain. . . . Doing whatever I wanted to set my mind to do as far as going

to college and becoming something. Especially my mom. Not so much my dad, but especially my mom. She was always, "Go to college. Go to college." So I just have always thought, "Well, I guess I'm going to go to college." And I wanted to as well.

The language that Evelyn attributes to her parents is evocative: going to college and "us[ing] your brain" means "becoming something." Evelyn portrays her parents as supportive of these goals, as we see through their long-term encouragement about using her abilities. Indeed, Evelyn seems to position her mother's push toward college as foundational and her own desire as almost secondary when she states, "I guess I'm going to college. And I wanted to as well." Many respondents shared this narrative of parental support and emphasis on higher education as an important goal.

We can also see a second kind of parental influence in Evelyn's description, positioning college as a way to avoid following their own pathways. Going to college not only means "becoming something" but also highlights an implied contrast to her parents' achievements. Evelyn's parents are equally clear about this as they are about their encouragement: they tell Evelyn, "We didn't go to college, and we want you to . . . use your brain." In Evelyn's and other students' narratives, this comparison positioned parents or other family as a kind of reverse role models in ways that could be uncomfortable for respondents. Parents play a key role in this chapter and in the broader sociological literature about educational outcomes. Sociologists have long been interested in the ways that parents' aspirations and expectations influence children's grades, progression through school, and indeed students' own goals for educational attainment.[2] Sociologists such as Annette Lareau, however, caution that we must also pay attention to the resources that parents have available at their disposal to support those aspirations.[3] While Lareau's interest is especially in cultural capital, other scholars have directed our attention to the role of information or "college knowledge": parents who themselves attended college not only understand the process of applying for admission more clearly than parents who have not but are also more likely to be immersed in communities that provide additional sources of information for their children, which increases the available sources of information exponentially. We might think of cultural capital and information as crucial for a shift from college dreams to college plans. Although most respondents reported the positive support of their parents, many also described this more complex undertone. I focus on this aspect because it tells us more about the complicated moral issues associated with college and has been less widely documented in the literature on parents' aspirations for their children's educations.[4]

Victoria's story is emblematic of this duality. When I asked Victoria about how she first began thinking about college, she was definite about how college had become a priority for her.

LIZ: Did you always know when you were in high school that you wanted to go to college? Was it always clear to you?

VICTORIA: Yes. I think I started looking at colleges when I was in seventh grade.

LIZ: Wow. How come? Was there some place specific that prompted that, and did your folks tell you that you needed to go to college or . . .

VICTORIA: No.

LIZ: Cousins or anything?

VICTORIA: No, no one told me. I think it was just—this sounds really bad. I think it was that I didn't want to end up living—this sounds terrible—because I love my mother and I admire my mother so, so much. And I'm so proud of her and everything that she's done for my sister and I. I think that I didn't want to end up repeating the cycle. I think in my day-to-day life I'm very, very conscious all the time, maybe overly so—I'm always very afraid of making a choice that's gonna repeat the cycle that my mother did. . . . It kind of, it scares me to think that if I don't go to school, if I don't educate myself, if I don't really learn how to support myself that I'll end up in some kind of bad relationship. And a situation where I'm stuck and I can't get out.

Victoria's emotional conflict comes through in her description of the role college plays in her thinking—namely, something that will hopefully ensure that she does not "repeat" her mother's life, not only in terms of work but in even more personal ways, like "end[ing] up in a bad relationship." Again, this positioning is a difficult one, seeming to show Victoria wanting something more or better than her family, which "sounds terrible" to Victoria as she compares her own life's path favorably to her mother's. She worries that she may be implicitly positioning herself as better than her mother, an impression she rushes to correct by mentioning how much she loves and respects her. We begin to see here the ways in which college plans, even when shared and honored by parents, can evoke fraught moral worries.

Violet, whom we met in the introduction, described how her mother had always encouraged her to go to college in similar terms, also highlighting the way that college was a way of avoiding the economic instability in which she had grown up: "My mom said you have to go to college. She didn't know what that meant or what [that might] look like, but this is what you do if you want to not clean houses. I didn't know anything about college at all." Thus, the *idea* of college was significant for making sure Violet did not end up repeating her mother's work history, even though neither of them knew exactly how to make the actual process happen.

For many respondents, then, college represented a "way out," a phrase that Genesis used—a way out of both specific childhood circumstances and a prospective undesired future: "I guess maybe I always knew I always wanted to get out, and I didn't like my childhood and teenager years so much. I wanted to . . . get out. Everything I did, doing it to get out, I knew college was like one way out, if I wanted a good job, a better life."

We see here strong links to what Richard Sennett and Jonathan Cobb referred to as the "hidden injuries" of class.[5] In thinking about college, respondents were often confronting difficult questions about what kind of life they and their parents envisioned for themselves and whether that life would be different, "better" than that of their upbringing. College was thus a source of desired mobility into a more stable economic position but also a path away from family and community. As we see in Victoria's response, this presented emotional conflicts for many respondents.

Immigration History as College Context

Respondents whose families had immigrated to the United States did not share this duality. These respondents did not report the same kinds of internal conflict about surpassing parents' educational or occupational attainments; rather, their families had come to the United States for this purpose, though this did not prevent later struggles with these same issues. First- and second-generation immigrants are more likely to attend college than those young adults whose families have been in the United States over multiple generations. This link between parents' immigration histories and students' college framing could be seen in my interviews with several respondents. Genesis, Alyssa, Georgina, Alexandra, Fiona, and Isabel were all children of parents who had immigrated to the United States. Alyssa told me that college was a priority in her family because her parents' "whole purpose . . . for coming to this country is so we could have the opportunity, that opportunity and so, they wouldn't want us to fall back . . . they only want to see us to go forward. So that was a big deal for them." Alyssa's sister was six years older, and Alyssa said that in her memories of childhood, "all I know is that she [her sister] was [applying to college], that college is a must in my family. It's either you go to school or you have to split the bills in the house. So it was: you do what you got to do, and so that's how that works." Alyssa's parents were also clear about what they saw as the benefits of a college degree: "It was definitely like, 'You're going to college. It's either you go to college or don't think you're going to come sit down [at home]. . . . You're going to be . . . either you're going to grow up really fast and have to split the cost of the bills or you can go to school and sit behind your own desk and do what you like.'" A college degree would bring the kind of extended transition into adulthood and independence as a worker that Alyssa's parents wished for their children—"sit[ting] behind your own desk and do[ing] what you like" rather than "grow[ing] up really fast."

Similarly, Georgina's parents, who had emigrated from China before she was born, recalled that her parents "didn't know [about Linden]. They said, 'You're going to college.' Okay, my family, my parents are first-generation immigrants. [In] Asian American families, in general it's a big [thing]." Like most students whose parents came to the United States, college was "a big thing" in Georgina's family, inextricable from family reasons for immigrating. Georgina's noting that her parents weren't aware of Linden as a college highlights an issue that a number of respondents described, that of needing to convince their parents and families about the importance of going to a college like Linden. For many families, simply going to college would have been sufficient, and staying close to home or going to a school with a lower sticker price might have been preferable. The ability to distinguish between types of colleges is yet another kind of "college knowledge."[6]

Exceptions: Unconvincing Role Models

The vast majority of respondents described family members as being strongly and explicitly supportive of their plans to attend college generally, even if not Linden College specifically. For most respondents, this consistent support was an important factor in their college stories. In some cases, however, respondents described their parents' efforts at convincing them to go to college as unconvincing. Harmony, for example, knew that her parents believed college to be important, but she did not see them as credible role models. She recalled: "My parents would stress education, but my father went to school and he dropped out, and my mom went to school after she had all of her kids, so it wasn't like [trails off]. And both went in the area . . . so I didn't really have an idea of all the schools that were out there." For Harmony, neither the full range of college possibilities nor higher education as something to be accomplished in her young adult life were represented in her parents' experiences.

Becca found that her parents also were not fully credible college advocates. She told me, "My parents would always be extremely kind of big proponents of college, but they also had jobs that you don't need a college degree [for]." Their support for college as a priority shifted over time. During her teenage years, when maintaining a college track in school seemed to represent a safe alternative to risky adolescent behaviors, Becca's parents stressed college: "They pushed college until I was older because it's a lot easier to explain to a sixteen to seventeen year old, who, if they didn't go to college would develop drinking problems or hang out on college campuses, get wasted then go to work— it was a lot easier to say no, you really need to go to college." However, after she enrolled at Linden and then took more than a year away from campus to work, the stress on going to college changed. Re-enrolled and a college senior at the time of our interview, Becca reflected that "as I got older, I realized, [my parents' advice] changed to 'as long as you're doing *something* [it's okay].' If I decided to be an apprentice and become—you know, as long as I was doing something productive, then they were really supportive."

In cases like those of Becca and Harmony, other college connectors became more important. In Becca's case, it was her older sister, who began graduate school at the time Becca began college. In Harmony's case, her high school mentor not only pushed her toward a four-year college but also to look beyond her own home city. These examples direct our attention to sources of information about college beyond one's own family.

Other Sources of Support

Family support and students' own aspirations for higher education were necessary but not necessarily sufficient in and of themselves. Particularly given parents' lack of knowledge about college, respondents often spoke about other sources of information and encouragement. Beyond these, respondents often described institutionalized pathways that had led them to college generally or to Linden specifically. By institutionalized pathways, I mean structured sets of opportunities through which, by accessing the first link, the student became connected to a chain of future possibilities. This most often took place in high school, especially for students who attended competitive public schools, magnet or charter schools, or through external scholarship programs. For many respondents, these sources of support worked in tandem with parents providing emotional encouragement or teachers or other mentors providing practical advice about how to make it happen and where to go.

Isabel's experience provides a strong example of this. She was part of a charter school system in which students joined the high school in seventh grade. During that first year, the preteens were not only encouraged to think about college as part of their future plans but also taken on college tours:

> Oh yeah, college was never really an option, like I had to go. And I never thought about it, but still, that was not an option. I started thinking about college. There was another program in my high school, and they started it my first year, because my high school was seventh through twelfth, so they started seventh grade and they ended my year, at my class, like a little guinea pig, in my class, and they started taking us to college in seventh grade.

Similarly, Harmony's high school, a magnet school in a large West Coast city, included a strong emphasis on college advising for all students that helped Harmony become more focused in her educational goals: "I kind of always thought about [college], but I didn't really think about as far as where I could go—[I was] also part of a high school preparatory program. . . . It's called TOP scholars, and they really showed me the importance of college—that you don't just have to go to a city school, you have more options, which at the time I didn't really take into consideration." For Harmony, the institutionalized college advising she encountered in her high school helped her move from "kind of [thinking] about it" to clear choices about college. She also honed her understanding about the different options for college, ultimately choosing a distant small private college rather than a large public campus in her immediate geographic area.

Similarly, Genesis spoke of a teacher who became a mentor and of being "exposed" to college by recent graduates who worked in her classrooms: "I did have one teacher I was really close with. She was awesome, like a second mom I guess. I guess she talked to me about college . . . all the teachers who went to college. We had teachers, fresh out of college type thing, [so] we were exposed to it." These high school mentors provided knowledge that parents could not, adding information that supplemented parents' emotional support, thus making going to college more likely and going to Linden, specifically, a viable option.

Friendships Providing College Knowledge

Of course, family and schools are not the only sources of information. A number of respondents reported that they were able to glean knowledge, both formal and informal, about college-going possibilities from friends, especially those who were more affluent. Violet's story was an especially strong example of this. Although her mother encouraged her to go to college, no one in her family knew what kinds of specific steps would be required. Violet's education about college and how to make it happen came through her friends and their families.

> I guess that was the year I got involved with my boyfriend of four years. He was from a different town that was more upper middle class, and it's always so sneaky—I had no real lens to see it until after we broke up and I came here, started thinking about class with tools to think about it. [It was] one of those things. I didn't know how different we were. I thought it was more like our families just had different styles. All my friends were from

his town more or less. They all grew up together and were way more privileged [than I was].

This privilege Violet observed in her friends manifested itself in important ways related to academics. Spending time with them "pushed" her to
begin to see school differently:

> [They] knew all these cool things, really hip, all this cultural capital . . . and
> that definitely pushed me to some degree to care about and think about ac-
> ademic stuff. It also made me feel I wasn't very good at it. Definitely being
> involved with his family for so long, a little over two years—I was really
> close to them. They were really strict, the always-had-to-do-his-homework,
> really managed life. Being exposed to that made me see this other way of
> living.

For Violet, her boyfriend's family and their circle of similarly privileged
friends played an important part of her getting to college. Although Violet's mother wanted her to go to college, neither she nor Violet had a detailed sense of what was involved in the college application process. Her
boyfriend's family, by contrast, with a "always-had-to-do-his-homework,
really managed" approach as well as their "hip cultural capital" helped her
not only to see a family life different from her own but also to gain information about college planning and to approach school work differently.
Friends and extended peer circles, therefore, were also important sources
of college support.

Extended Ties

In a few cases, respondents described more far-flung sources of support. As
with Becca, whose older sister was a primary role model, Meredith, Maya,
and Fiona described extended family, community members, and even parents' employers as sources of information and encouragement. In Meredith's case, an older cousin was the strongest—and at times only—source
of encouragement. Meredith's mother, for example, and extended family
had neither attended college nor were supportive of her intention to enroll
in a four-year program. But a cousin, a college professor at a prestigious
liberal arts college, supported her both emotionally and tangibly by taking

her on visits to colleges out of state. When I asked her when she began thinking of college, Meredith told me, "I started thinking about college really early, earlier than anyone I know. I think in eighth grade [I] went to one of my first college visits." For Meredith, having a cousin who encouraged her softened the discomfort of being at odds with the rest of her family, who looked askance at her vision for herself. Perhaps adopting the language of the rest of her family, Meredith described her cousin as "really snotty because she's always been just like me, just really loved school, and no one else in my family did. We've both kind of . . . been shunned from the family." Here we see the complicated interchange of loyalty, emotion, and mobility: while Meredith uses the word "snotty" to describe herself and her cousin (not seriously, but evidently expressing her family's perception), she also aligns herself with that quality. In other words, she positions herself as both a family insider, by using their critical term, and as an outsider sharing the "snotty" disposition of her college-educated cousin. For Meredith, family thus provided both a negative example of adults with whom she did not identify and whose life circumstances she wished to avoid and also with a clear role model whom she could emulate. This evident ambiguity coheres to the same moral complexity discussed previously: How will Meredith fit in with her family and with a future college world, the two of which don't seem to be able to occupy the same space?

In Maya's case, while her parents supported her college plans, meaningful encouragement also came from her wider hometown community. This consistent support from her early childhood onward was inspiring to Maya:

> I think ever since you're like little, you have to go to school. I think it's also, everybody says too, it's a luck thing. It's the only way you're going to succeed. Even though the community is like, "Oh, you left," but they're still like, "Oh, you need to go." Everybody just knows there's certain opportunities outside the community, but it's limited to who can go. If you look like you have potential, everyone is totally behind you—you should go, get good grades. Ever since you're little you're just, like it's drilled into you.

Having "everyone . . . totally behind you" was important for Maya, creating an impetus toward attending college as she developed her academic "potential." It's clear that she appreciated this support. Maya's recollection echoes others' in the duality it presents between being able to access valued opportunities and recognizing the possible costs of those opportunities that are "outside the community" and "limited." Thus, for Maya, achieving the goal of college enrollment puts her in an outsider position; she will need to leave the community—even though the community recognizes the "need" for her to do so. Again, this internal conflict between attainment and loss is important in shaping how respondents think about college in their lives. We see once more the implications of moral questions about who belongs to the community and how that belonging is maintained, implications that may become difficult as respondents move into their new lives on campus. Like Meredith, Maya understands herself as an insider who is also somehow pushed out, however supportively, of her home community.

In some cases, these outside resources continued to be important across the years of college enrollment. Fiona, for example, left Linden after her first year. Her transition into college was difficult both socially and academically, and she felt unsupported at the college. Throughout our interviews, she shared a number of recollections of microaggressions aimed at her because of her Latina heritage. Connerston was also a far cry from the big city in which she had grown up and from her large family who mostly still lived in that area. After leaving Linden, she spent a semester at a local community college and made plans to enroll at the flagship state university close to home. She told me:

> I went home, felt like shit, like let's leave the school—you know when you're fed up with things and make rash decisions. I said I'll go back home, finish the semester, and enroll in a local community college. I'll take courses there and transfer into [the state university]. Okay. It didn't work out that way. At first my mom was open to the idea, but then she started telling her bosses about that. They're like, "No, don't leave Linden, that's terrible." So she started telling me, but it was already too late. I withdrew [from] college. So then, I went back home, and she was so disappointed, and having your mom disapprove is terrible.

Influenced by the advice of her mother's employers—college-educated white-collar professionals—and her mother's disapproval of her plans to enroll at the local university based on that advice, Fiona decided to re-enroll at Linden and was about to graduate when I met her.

These low socioeconomic status respondents were largely able to put together multiple sources of support, collecting both emotional encouragement and "college knowledge" that helped them gain admission. One final narrative, from Rose, showcases how parents, schools, and other sources worked together to shape respondents' ultimate educational outcomes:

> I'm an only child, and I went to public school from the fourth grade on, so I think it was just more like my parents [stressed college], and I was always like the smartest kid in the class so it was just kind of like, you're smart so then you go to college. I don't remember actually sitting down with my parents and being like this is what you want to do—or them telling me you have to go to college. It was more of this kind of thing—[my] parents were really supportive, you know, wanted to do the best by me. And so, you know, I took a little art class for ten year olds or whatever at the community college, different stuff like that for middle school. They tried to get me in the preppy, $13,000 per year schools, did the whole interview process, which is weirdly similar to college, so all those things built up.

Rose recounts how her parents provided encouragement that was not forthcoming in her local public school and as one part of that encouragement placed her in other institutional settings that provided cultural capital resources and practical skills, such as managing interviews, that ultimately helped her plan for and obtain college admission.

Choosing Linden

Having gotten to the point of selecting college as an early adult pathway, how did respondents come to select Linden? Among students from working-class, low-income, and first-generation college backgrounds, enrollment in large public colleges and universities is much more common than attending private colleges—even among those students who are highly qualified for admission to the most prestigious institutions. Students with excellent high school academic records and outstanding standardized test scores often do not apply for admission to elite schools and, even if they apply and are admitted, sometimes choose not to attend.[7] Concern about the high "sticker price" is one reason; concerns about fitting in may be another—as one student in Ann Mullen's examination of the ways students came to be at Yale and Southern Connecticut State College described: "Actually, at first, Yale wasn't like my first priority or my first choice. I almost didn't apply to Yale and I applied on like one of the last days, and just randomly like typed an essay or whatever because at first I thought everyone here was gonna be very snobby and not realistic and not down to earth."[8] Social and moral worries about fitting in and what kinds of people attend elite colleges raise concerns for some low socioeconomic status students as they consider their options. It is worth remembering, however, that for low socioeconomic status students like Genesis, Harmony, and others, enrollment in a private college is linked to a higher likelihood of graduation, income, and occupational status as well as less immediately tangible effects like marriage, family formation, and health over the life course.[9] The stakes are therefore high.

There have been calls from the media and others on selective and highly selective campuses to do more to attract these kinds of students.[10] This is because elite colleges and universities arguably have special roles to play in the social and economic mobility of students with low socioeconomic status. Despite worries about cost and experiences on campus, low-income students are *more* likely to graduate from elite colleges than from less-selective campuses.[11] Elite private colleges typically offer higher levels of financial aid than public institutions, often with lower loan debt built in. And these campuses have extensive budgets for on-campus supports and services. Finally, elite colleges boast strong networks of alumnae who help undergraduates and graduates network into employment and other opportunities, helping to ensure success after college as well.[12]

As an elite institution, then, Linden offers the kinds of financial, academic, and extracurricular benefits that arguably help students translate academic advantages into postgraduate advantages. Despite these advantages, Linden does not enjoy the kind of name recognition that the most elite universities do. It is also not as well known as the top few liberal arts campuses, and, according to some Linden administrators, its status as a women's college means that some potential applicants may self-select out. So how did respondents like Violet and others select Linden?

Key Roles for Knowledgeable Insiders

Many respondents described the important roles of adults who suggested that they look into Linden College specifically. Teachers, guidance counselors, and other mentors were important in directing students' attention to this campus. Alice, who followed a college preparatory track in her charter high school, planned to go to college after high school. Although she hoped to attend a very prestigious college and was familiar with the Ivy League schools, she knew she did not want to attend a large university. A teacher introduced her to the concept of liberal arts colleges generally and Linden specifically:

> My math teacher, she went to [another women's college], and she was telling me about [her experience] because I told her that I wanted a school other than the big Ivy Leagues—something smaller. She told me about other schools, and then she told me about [another campus]. [That school] was my first choice. I thought, " 'Well, [it] is pretty hard to get in to, so what [schools are like that one]?" and then she told me Linden College. . . . I thought I'll try there just in case.

Alice didn't get accepted to her first-choice school and, she reported, said to herself, "Fine, I'll go to Linden." Like Alice, Alexandra knew she wanted to go to college and that she wanted to enroll in a competitive program. Also, like Alice, she had very limited knowledge of what kinds of colleges could fulfill her goals: "I always heard Boston—Harvard, all those big schools. I never heard of Linden. I researched. I didn't want to go to a big university [so I] talked to my favorite teacher, a Spanish teacher for three years. She gave me advice." As high schoolers looking for selective colleges, respondents knew about Ivy League schools. They knew about local community and state colleges, as well. Most respondents had little knowledge themselves, or in their families, about liberal arts colleges and schools that might sit between the Ivy League and local campuses in terms of selectivity and prestige.

Lynne always planned on going to college; like most of her high school peers, she figured she would attend the local very large state university. Good at school, she'd planned on the honors college campus. Her plans changed after a guidance counselor suggested Linden: "I just assumed like I was going to [a state college], the honors college. Then I had this guidance counselor who for some reason was really pushing all-women's schools on me, like Linden and [another women's college]. . . . I think because I was like the feminist of the school. Yeah, I was totally type casted, the one student openly into that kind of activism, and I started a feminist group in high school also." Because of Lynne's academic work and her activism, this teacher "pushed" her to think about Linden, about which Lynne recalls being totally uninterested:

> Yeah, basically, she was like you should go to Linden or [the other college]. So I came to visit a bunch of schools. Linden was the last I visited, and I really didn't want to. I really didn't like the idea of an all-women's college. My mom and I were actually driving back from [a visit to another college]. We were driving through this area, and my mom was like, "Why don't we just check it out?" And I was really reluctant, and she said, "Okay, either Linden or [a different liberal arts college]." I picked Linden, because I knew Connerston was a cool town. So we came here, and I took a tour, and for some reason it was one of those things where I took the tour and it just felt right. I could see myself being at a place like this.

Here Lynne's narrative echoes that of hundreds of other students across the socioeconomic spectrum: "It just felt right." Like their more affluent peers, many socioeconomically marginalized students were struck with emotional, almost whimsical attractions to Linden, often describing their feelings about the campus as having fallen in love.

In many cases, these key connectors had personal links to the college, either as alumnae or because they knew someone who had attended. This inside knowledge and personalized recommendation helped overcome students' hesitancy about Linden as a campus with which they were not already familiar. For example, Harmony's trusted high school mentor pushed her to think about Linden, a place she says she would never have selected otherwise:

> Funny story. I never thought I would be here—all girls, without men, that was like the last thing on my mind. I was talking to my college adviser and people from my program who graduated earlier than me. They came to Linden, and my college adviser is a really big fan of women institutions, so she told me just to consider it, just consider it. . . . I was at the table, and one of my teachers approached me, smiling. I'm like, "What's up Miss Patton?" She's like, "I'm an alum for Linden," and I love Miss Patton, so I got insight from her. And one of the admissions officers came to interview people in our program, Toni. I fell in love with her. She made me love Linden like ten times more, and so I just applied.

Similarly, Allison turned to a history teacher whom she trusted as a source of career advice, whose friend in turn had attended Linden College and recommended it for Allison:

> I started talking to my guidance counselor—"What do you think?" And I didn't look into it too much. People told me to go to Harvard, see if you can get in. I said, "Okay, sure, why not, it's Harvard." I applied to Harvard and six other schools. My history teacher—for a long time I thought I'd be a high school history teacher—said, "I had a friend who went to Linden. I think it would work really well for you. Check it out." I was really working on nothing; I was just doing blind searches. I'll look it up. My guidance counselor said, "That's a great program, great school." I applied.

Allison's narrative exemplifies many of the themes already observed. She asked a more knowledgeable college adviser, her guidance counselor. She got advice that recognized her academic talents and potential but that seems to have centered on what was most well known in her northeastern hometown. Outside of this, Allison recalls that she "didn't look into too much" and was "doing blind searches." Her history teacher, a trusted adviser, made a more personal recommendation about Linden, and Allison followed this advice successfully.

In some cases, key connectors' roles were even more significant because students had already provisionally looked into Linden or other liberal arts colleges and decided against them or had substantial concerns about the costs of these kinds of schools. In these instances, the encouragement or advice from connectors repaired misunderstandings and overcame students' hesitations about applying. This was most clearly the case for Victoria. Having already attended a local community college for two years after high school, she was ready to transfer to a four-year college to complete her bachelor's degree. As she recalled:

> I was getting ready to transfer to [the local state university campus], and one of my professors came up to me and asked me what my plans were. And I told him, and he just kind of shook his head and was like, no. And then he told me about a meeting of Linden representatives. . . . And so they came, and they did a meeting and talked a lot about how much financial aid they have to offer. And I would have never thought of it before, because I had looked at Linden's website and knew that I could not come here. And so

when they came and they spoke, I decided to apply. So I applied to all three, and it ended up being Linden.

Without her professor's intervention, which prompted Victoria to go back and give Linden another look, thus allowing her to learn about financial aid possibilities that she hadn't known about before, she would simply have transferred locally. While she would have likely completed her degree, many scholars argue that the credential of an elite institution continues to matter for postcollege opportunities.[13]

Although rare, there were also examples of students who were undermined by their high school teachers or counselors. Danielle, for example, had looked at both large and small campuses and chosen Linden because of its commitment to women's education. She could not get the support of her high school, however.

> I don't think my guidance counselor had ever even heard of Linden, and then coming here I'd heard some people talk about how their guidance counselor recommended Linden to them. It was so strange because I knew that this was my first choice and this—I felt this is where I'm going to college. At my high school, my teachers and guidance counselor discouraged me because of the catch that no one had much money when I grew up. And I just didn't listen to them.

In Danielle's case, her own determination that Linden would be the best place for her helped her to persevere in the face of others' doubts that she could afford it—or perhaps even be admitted. Students from her area didn't go to schools like Linden.

Family members also needed convincing: respondents sometimes found themselves needing to win over otherwise supportive family members to the idea that this *particular* college was special. For Alyssa, this was an issue that only resolved itself over several years. Although emphatically supportive of college in general, Alyssa's parents were concerned about both Linden's cost and the distance (four hours from their home). Alyssa's older sister had attended a college close to home and lived with their parents throughout, and Alyssa's parents had hoped for the same when she enrolled. I asked if they were excited about her plans to attend Linden. Alyssa recounted: "Not really, because they didn't really know. To them, college is college no matter whether you move to community college or to a public school or to a private college. I think now they're like—I've gotten to Linden and my mom and dad have been exposed to, well, [all that] is here, and I think they kind of like, 'Okay, yeah. This is serious.' . . . [At first] they couldn't tell the differences in it." Alyssa had a difficult time overcoming her parents' concerns—ultimately, Linden's all-female enrollment and residential requirements were important in persuading her parents because they minimized Alyssa's likelihood of romantic distractions. Although she overcame their initial resistance, Alyssa's parents were still not completely convinced that this campus provided more than others. As she moved through her four years, they occasionally urged her to rethink her decision and move home:

> At the beginning . . . they were like, "So expensive!" I'm like, "*Come on!*" and they're, "Why can't you just go to [state college]?" Actually, at one point school got really expensive for me. And so I had people telling me, "Maybe you should transfer and go to [the state university]." And I'm like, "No, I don't want to. I like Linden. I love being here. It's a really good opportunity. We meet great people. You have great connections—once you're Linden, it's simply forever." People just were not understanding why I wanted to stay at Linden, when like it was getting so expensive. My mom and dad [too]. Like, "No, I'm not going to leave school, because it's a really good environment. And then Linden, like—*Hello, it's Linden!*" And so they kind of weren't really getting it.

Alyssa's conflict with her parents shifted slightly over time: although their worries about her being out of the house and farther away than they would have liked were resolved, they still didn't see Linden as any different from a local campus. When Alyssa had difficult times or challenges at Linden, they urged her to come home, where they could more closely support her. And they—like others in her home community—didn't understand why Linden was worth the economic struggles that Alyssa was taking on. Alyssa, however, understood clearly Linden's value in her life; she was able to attain firsthand research experience in a professor's physics lab and develop strong connections with other faculty members. Her exasperation— "*Hello, it's Linden!*"—comes through clearly, as well as the fundamental value she sees here: it needs no elaboration.

    In the end, Alyssa thought that over time, after her parents had visited Linden's campus and gotten to know it over her first several years there, their feelings changed: "And so they had [had] a really hard time of understanding that Linden is a really good school. . . . And so that's an insight to them, 'Oh, okay. She's on the right path. There's a difference between colleges.'"

Amber, who transferred from a local community college to Linden, also had to work to convince her mother that Linden was a smarter move than enrolling in the state college system. Like Alyssa's and other students' parents, Amber's parents were generally supportive of her college goals and supportive of her intention to get a bachelor's rather than an associate degree. However, also like Alyssa's parents, Amber's mother thought that Linden's costs of attendance made it prohibitive:

> My mom, after I went to [visit a community college], and I started looking at smaller liberal arts colleges, and I started bringing home information about these schools that were $40,000 a year. She was a lot more resistant. I did what I wanted without listening to her because her idea was, "You'd never be able to afford these schools, or if you do [you'll be] $200,000 in debt, [so] just go to a state school—nothing wrong with our state schools." But I just wanted a different experience. Both my mom and I are really stubborn. I found resources, made up a good argument, and supplied [that information]. Once she realized how much aid I got, she was a lot more excited about it.

Here we see echoes of Alyssa's discussion with her family: Why take on debt or extra expenses when one could just as well go to a state college closer to home. We also see hints of a different kind of conflict that makes going away to college especially difficult for many socioeconomically marginalized students in the refrain "nothing wrong with our state schools." In other words, do you think you're too good for the state schools? The struggle between Amber and her mother around this matter gets to a deep question about a student's socioeconomic mobility and how family relationships will change as the student experiences this mobility.[14]

Financial Aid

Amber's narrative also highlights a crucial aspect of students' choices that I have not yet discussed. As a private liberal arts college with a well-funded endowment, Linden is able to provide students with a substantial amount of grant aid—financial support that does not need to be repaid after graduation. This ability to support students financially sometimes tipped the scales for students considering different options, and it would be incomplete to talk about how students came to Linden without mentioning the importance of financial aid.

Genesis was one such student for whom aid made a difference. Genesis lived some six hours from campus in a midsized city. She did not visit campus before enrolling, though she told me she had looked at videos of the campus on the college's website. She narrated how she chose between Linden—a place she had never been to that was much more rural, homogenously white, and wealthy than where she had grown up—and other campuses: "I applied to [a lot of colleges]. I did the common application, the top twenty. I was sure that they had good academic [options]. Other factors, like I said, a huge factor in my decision, I had been to small schools all my life, [so I was] hoping for a good university. BU [Boston University] was my first choice. I was in love with it." Neither Boston nor Genesis's second choice university came through, however. Genesis continued:

> Then Linden came in, a couple of days after I decided—like Oh, Linden. I had a conversation with my teacher who actually graduated from here: "You should go to Linden, I can see you there." So let me do some more research. I know it's good, I checked it, did some research, spoke to someone who went there; they seemed happy with their experience there. I took the virtual tour online; it was pretty good. I knew it was going to be different from the city, but I'll just adjust to it, that's my motto. I can't turn down a financial aid packet—this is it. So I called Linden. I even missed a deadline to notify them. I called them. They had waived my deposit, so I didn't have to worry about it. . . . Okay, good, Linden it is.

Although Genesis selected Linden knowing it was "good" and that people seemed happy there, the extent to which she was still unsure comes through in her final comments on her process: "People asked me what school I was going to—a popular question because I graduated in the top 1 percent of my high school. A lot of people asked me what school. I said Linden. They'd go, 'Wow!' It's like I didn't make a bad choice after all." Only when she heard others' responses did Genesis realize she had really made a good selection. This suggests that the financial aid really was a significant factor for Genesis, who had not even visited the campus. At the end of her college search process, Genesis chose a school very different from what she had envisioned for herself, more rural than urban, and certainly small. She observed that she could not turn down the financial aid offer when Linden met the important baseline requirements of being a respected campus academically. The last portion of her quote is especially telling, however, in that it displays the way that Genesis was still figuring out the value of Linden even after she had been accepted. She was still learning from others' reactions what the reputation of the college was. This tells us even more about the value of the financial aid award, as well as Genesis's determination to select an academically strong campus even if it's one she knew little about.

Georgina also recalled not knowing much about Linden as a place—like Genesis, she had not visited the campus before applying—other than its being "a good school." But after being admitted and offered a strong financial aid package that exceeded that of her other choices, she decided to accept the offer: "I just got into Linden . . . and Linden gave me pretty good financial aid in [comparison to] all the other schools, and like it's a good school, right? I don't know much about it, and so like, it's got the most financial aid. When I went to visit [after being admitted], we considered it a good area." Georgina prioritized the aid as the impetus to choose Linden over other schools: Linden met her baseline criteria for being a good school, and she thought it was in a good area, but the aid set it apart from other places and made it stand out.

Linden's strong financial aid awards were also sometimes used by low socioeconomic status students to avoid being perceived by others as wealthy or snobbish. Lynne, for example, told me that when she speaks with hometown friends, she often tells them immediately that she attends Linden because of the financial aid award she receives from them—this allows her to sidestep what she sees as a prevalent stereotype of Linden students as having enough family wealth to cover most or all of the costs. Lynne stressed that her parents did not pay for any of her education at Linden.

> For a lot of my friends at home, college culture or whatever was never part of their lives. They don't know; they don't already have an understanding of what it means to go to Linden. They know I'm going to college, but they don't know if it's a high-caliber school; they don't know or care. But people who do know what Linden is and do have an understanding, especially in the area, whether it's people in town or friends who go to [the nearby

state college] . . . I sometimes feel I need to, if I can sort of sense that people are judging me a little bit, I say, the only reason I'm going there is because [they] give me a ton of money. I want them to know that I'm not a traditional Lindie who's especially—I don't like people who assume because I'm going to such an expensive school that my parents pay for the whole thing.

In some cases, then, Linden's wealth and ability to provide strong financial aid awards—ironically, an important aspect of its very elite status as a campus—enabled students to dodge moral disapproval that might arise from being seen as able to afford a private college education. Moreover, it gave students a narrative to frame their choice that did not position them as privileged or advantaged, which allowed them to remain in the same narrative circumstances as hometown friends.

First Impressions of Linden

First impressions of Linden figure large in students' narratives. Respondents and other Lindies I spoke with often described idyllic expectations and strong emotional connections to the college. This is so much the case that one admissions counselor I spoke with at Linden joked, with a big grain of truth, that in years when it rains on the day accepted students visit campus, the proportion of students who attend the following fall drops dramatically, whereas the sunny visiting day allows students to feel a deeper emotional level of excitement about the college. I was interested in how my respondents first experienced Linden. Sociologically, we might expect many students from lower-income, working-class, or first-generation families to experience what some scholars have dubbed "culture shock,"[15] while students from middle-class and upper-class backgrounds might experience a more seamless transition. And, indeed, it is exactly this sense of disjuncture or seamless transition that can be crucial for students in their first months in a new space: Does it feel like home? Is it a place where one can hit the ground running? Or is it a struggle to find a sense of fit?

Many respondents recalled their first impressions, either on a visit or on first arrival for their enrollment, with the same kind of emotional and even idealistic enthusiasm for the campus highlighted by the college itself. Amber, for example, described how she compared Linden with other places she'd been to on her college search in aesthetic terms; she linked her impressions of this "cool place" with her sense of "empowerment" of her potential enrollment:

> I was kind of speechless. I remember standing next to [the college green], [thinking] like this is a cool place, a really beautiful campus. I'd seen a lot of ugly campuses. Realizing I was at this great college with so many successful women who came out [was] really empowering. I remember [during orientation] all sitting there, when we were hearing the speech, I was thinking how awesome it is to be surrounded by so many women motivated to do all these different things.

Brianna, by contrast, had been to only one other campus, but she was just as impressed by Linden:

> I was just shocked by how nice it was, really, on the whole. I'd never really spent any time in a college campus before, just the closest one to my house, which was probably a state school. . . . Cold War architecture most of them, but Linden is gorgeous. I think probably mainly my first impression was just being, "Is this a school?" They'd just built the student center, and I was . . . walking around and totally in awe, and the dorms were so big to me, and I was like, "This is so nice." The food was nicer than the food I eat at home. It was just . . . just this totally mind-blowing experience.

I asked Brianna if she thought Linden would be her top choice for colleges after that visit. She told me that she "had a pretty good feeling about it, yeah. It was like, "Yeah, you know what, I could live there. That would be good." Here we get a sense of culture shock, but not in a negative way. Rather, we see the campus through Brianna's eyes as beautiful and awe inspiring. This sense of awe was also linked to the rhetoric of the college—for example, as we see in Amber's comments, to the achievements of alumnae and current students, which are widely publicized to prospective students. By implication, new students see the possibility that they will similarly achieve, that they will become part of this idyllic world. This kind of understanding is an important aspect of the construction of a shared Linden identity that takes place as students move through these first weeks, especially.

This understanding of what it means to be a Lindie was both exciting and challenging for many respondents to assimilate. We can see an example of this in Violet's recollection of arriving on campus. In addition to mentioning "how beautiful this campus is," she remembered feeling alone: "I didn't really—couldn't relate to any of the people in my res hall, definitely lonely." Despite this, she made a close friend right away:

> I met [her] right away, in preorientation. We became fast friends and spent all our time together. . . . But she was definitely upper middle class [with] highly educated parents. She was really influential [to me]. Also we were really at odds, class-wise. I didn't really know what to expect from Linden. All the people I'm friends with came in knowing what to do in college, knew how to do the system, the homework, and like—yeah. So I kind of like picked up these things from other people, but it seemed like the longest month of my life, and I didn't get a huge part of why it was so stressful—it was just this total clash of class cultures.

Violet's relationship with her first friend presages much of what respondents discussed in their experiences being part of the Linden community: affluent friends were important sources of support and, in some cases, new cultural knowledge. They were emotionally important and provided valuable close ties. Yet they also brought low socioeconomic status respondents into contact with cross-class differences that were difficult to manage: difficult comparisons, uncomfortable interactions, conflicts that became more important because of the emotional connection.

Not all students recalled feeling so inspired on their first visit to campus. Respondents moving from cities, in particular, described having a more difficult adjustment. For example, Genesis told me that on family road trips out of the city, she'd "wonder to myself, like people in those houses, this is the middle of nowhere. If they needed something, it must be a long walk." Linden, with its small-town surroundings and tree-lined campus, felt somewhat similar to Genesis:

> We got on campus, and I thought this is really pretty: the grass is fresh, no snow yet of course, just like green, trees. People were friendly; the cars stopped [when you] cross the street. [Where I come from,] no one wants to stop. People [here] are so friendly and respectful. Like alright, it's not a bad atmosphere; it's definitely different. But at night I get skeptical. I always wonder if someone is hiding. It's a bad mentality. Of course no one is hiding behind trees. It's just so dark you don't know what's going on inside those trees. It took getting used to, but I know compared to the city it's safe to walk back from the library at night.

Genesis paints a whole picture of her new small community, in which the buildings and trees and slower pace are linked to people being friendly and willing to stop when you cross the street. Although friendly, it also felt eerie and too quiet, and when we first spoke two years after her arrival, she was still getting used to this atmosphere.

For Meredith, the reality of Linden clashed a bit with the way she imagined college, and this campus specifically. Having been one of only a few liberal people in her small high school, she had looked forward to moving to a new area and going to classes with more people who shared her political ideals. On reflection, however, she said: "Well, it definitely wasn't as liberal as I thought. I thought everyone was going to be like all about [politics] and stuff like that and really extreme. It wasn't, which is good in some respects."

Macy, a recent alumna I interviewed, had likewise looked forward to conversations with people who shared her interests in social justice and inequality. During an orientation workshop, however, she found that this wasn't the way she'd imagined it. As she recalled, the workshop was designed to facilitate conversations about class, race, and gender. Macy was "really excited" about that because it was "the first time I was around a bunch of people who wanted to have real conversations about the kinds of things I was interested in." She remembers, though, noticing that there were few mentions at all about class, and she felt hesitant to share much of her background. During one of those exercises where people step into and out of the circle, she was the "only person in the circle for first-generation, out of twenty or thirty people. It was terrifying, isolating, to be the only one. For almost everything, there were at least a couple of people." This feeling of being exposed rather than fitting in was echoed by other respondents. Here, also, we begin to see clues about how Linden could become a difficult space in which to interact.

Examining respondents' expectations, desires, and plans for college allows us to see what kinds of mobility they sought and the kinds of moral questions implicated by that mobility. These are particularly clear in respondents' reflections on their parents as both positive sources of support and yet also as examples of an adulthood respondents hoped to avoid, what I refer to as conflicted role models. Reflections like Victoria's show the way that, at least for some, the search for a more economically stable life—something "better"—seemed to imply a negative judgment of parents' lives or choices.

As suggested at the start of this chapter, many respondents seem to be superficially like their economically advantaged peers. In looking more deeply, however, we begin to see differences. In particular, the meanings respondents attached to college attendance were significant. Rather than understanding college as a birthright or a taken-for-granted activity, college attendance for the respondents fulfilled other kinds of symbolic expectations, such as being a way "out" of difficult family circumstances, a way of leading a "better" life or "making it." These goals underlie the later questions that arise for students about what college means in terms of class and how to relate to family. The initial impressions and experiences of Linden as recounted by the students I interviewed also presage subsequent interactional dynamics among students and between students and the college as an institution.

2

"SCHOLARSHIP GIRLS"

Creating Community and Diversity on Campus

On an early September evening two nights before the start of the fall semester at Linden, a few hundred new students stream into a stately old auditorium. There's an excitement in the air along with the crisp feel of fall, and everyone seems to be chatting and laughing with new friends. The students gradually make their way to their seats, and the evening's event, an orientation session required for all incoming Linden students, begins. The evening's topic is diversity—what it means, why the college values it, how to learn about it and from it. After an hour of remarks, the speaker begins asking groups of students to stand up: those from New England, those from California, those from the South, those from the Midwest. Students who are the first in their family to attend college, who were born abroad, whose mothers or grandmothers went to Linden. She asks the students receiving financial aid to stand up and students who will be studying the sciences, the arts, or the humanities. There are whoops from the crowd as each group is called out; New England and California get especially boisterous cheers. The speaker then closes the evening by emphasizing that all of these students are important, each one belongs here. She says, "You are all Lindies now!"

This event represents a particular organizational response to the puzzle of welcoming low-income, first-generation, and working-class students at Linden. As Mitchell Stevens has pointed out, elite colleges must balance two seemingly contradictory priorities: becoming more accessible to students who would previously have been excluded from admittance due to racialized, ethnic, or class position, and at the same time preserving the schools' essentially elite character in order to remain appealing to alumni donors, wealthier new students, and other stakeholders.[1] On the one hand, Linden as such an elite school needs to make students who are actually in a minority feel like "Lindies" who fit in and belong. On the other hand, Linden also calls attention to the diversity of students and their backgrounds as an institutional priority. Discursive framing is important to this process. As Susan Iverson writes, university discourse "contributes to producing a given campus reality, transmitting a code for conduct, and shaping students' perceptions of themselves and others in a particular context."[2] Whether written, verbal, or graphic, a college's "presentation of self" (to borrow a term coined by Goffman that sociologists usually apply to individuals) establishes important meanings for students and other community members.[3]

Linden uses discourse to create two sets of relationships, one around the idea that we are all the same and another around the idea that some of us are different.[4] These presentations facilitate Linden's efforts at creating *both* community and diversity by presenting a framework outlining students' roles as community members and the parameters of that community.[5] There is even a required session during orientation week entitled "Being a Linden Community Member." By extension, these presentations tell students not only who they are but also who they are to one another. This discursive structure provides the context in which students operate, just as much as the physical space of the residence halls or the social space of students' friendship circles.

In this chapter, I examine the college's rhetorical work as a primary effort in managing inequality in the student body. I ask what messages are communicated, and how. I show that despite an emphasis on community that is framed as fully inclusive, Linden's rhetorical efforts create a system of meaning—a semiotics—in which students' class positions are linked to insider and outsider roles, which makes them more or less legitimate as community members. Students who do not match the class presentation of the college, which is presented as cohesive, are presented as providing diversity, a rhetorical frame that creates a special category of student and student roles. My thinking in this chapter is heavily influenced by the work of Sara Ahmed and Ian Hacking, both of whom are attentive to the impact of categorization on shaping social experience.[6] Here, I suggest that categories such as *diverse*, *first-generation*, or *financially needy* are underpinned by moral connotations and structures, positioning students in relation to one another and the college as a whole.

"You are all Lindies now!": Framing and Characterizing Community

Linden students take in a stream of messages about who they are as a group and what being a Linden student entails over the course of their enrollment. These messages come in the form of exhortations, encouragements, warnings, portrayals of Linden students, and more subtly as implications derived from what is not included in the above. We can think of these messages as normative in the sense that they establish a standard for student behavior, especially for new students. These are some of the first ways that new students learn what is expected of them as members of their new community—the meaning of Lindieness—and indeed the importance of that community to its members. This is perhaps especially explicit during the first few weeks, when many students are new and the tone is being set for the school year. As I tried to learn about Linden identity, I therefore sought out Linden events for new and returning students: orientation sessions, the all-college assembly that kicks off the fall semester, and other smaller gatherings that took place during the two years of my field work.

The importance of community at Linden is emphasized from the very first hours of students' arrival on campus. At the first event of the orientation week, new students—those entering their first year and transfer students—and their families gather in a large auditorium. As they file in, students are provided copies of the college's song, in Latin. Over the evening, they will learn how to sing this song "like a Lindie"—when to stomp in time, when to sing extra loud, when to yell and whoop for their graduating class (an event still four years away for most in the auditorium), and who their new peers are as a collective group. After the president's welcome and a short speech by the first year and transfer deans, the dean of enrollment stands to add her welcome. Dean Fallon tells students that she can feel their energy and excitement, the potential and talent of the new students, and that they are the few selected from the largest ever pool of applicants in Linden's history. She asks for a round of applause for all the new students.

Leaning in, Dean Fallon then says, "I will tell you something," and continues in a conspiratorial tone: "Admissions staff do not make mistakes. Each of you was carefully chosen. You may wonder about that in the coming weeks. You may become anxious. You may feel that others have different, perhaps better, preparation than you. Remember, you belong here, you *earned* your admission. As of today, you are officially a Lindie." The dean related to me in a subsequent conversation that she hopes this short talk will give two messages. The first is that students belong—they are not there by accident or mistake; they will fit in and do well. The second is that they are not alone—whether they are from Bangladesh or two towns over, whether their grandmother went to Linden or their parents never took a college course, there is someone else to whom they can relate. These messages help to create a shared identity of being a Lindie by assuring students that they all belong there, one just as much as the other. Students should have no doubts about their own spot or, implicitly, anyone else's. In this sense, the dean's comments are intended to homogenize, to highlight a new, shared identity over other, dissimilar backgrounds. She closes by telling the families gathered in the room, "You have carried a great weight in [your child's] development to this point. Now, you must [do one more thing for them: you must] go home," symbolically and literally leaving the new students to enter the Linden community.

The same message of community membership is repeatedly communicated through other presentations. For example, the student chair of the Discipline Advisory Board tells new students in her presentation several days later: "I already trust you. Faculty already trust you because you are a Linden student." Another student speaker on the same panel tells her new peers, "Once a Lindie, you are always a Lindie." As in the case of Dean Fallon, these remarks let students know that whatever their backgrounds, they are now all Lindies, downplaying differences in the face of a shared membership and identity. As we will see, this new identity is a deeply personal one, as Linden students tend to talk about one another as "sisters" or "family."

This message of community is central—both as something that is at the core of being a Linden student and also to Linden's message of inclusivity. Community framing develops shared identity around membership and prioritizes this symbolic similarity that implicitly or explicitly communicates other key similarities: the college selects shared qualities to highlight as befitting a Lindie, leaving others aside or in some cases denigrating them.

This process takes place through the normative character building implicit in these discourses. Alongside the normative community building, students also receive messages about what *kind* of community this is, the expectations to which they and their new peers must now adjust. Some of these messages are very direct. Deans, faculty members, and even other students share impressions of and predictions for new students, folding newcomers into the existing culture of Linden. They use phrases like "you will . . . ," "you are . . . ," and "you all . . ." to tell students how the college perceives them and what it expects from them. For instance, speaking to the incoming class at a Tuesday afternoon mandatory orientation meeting about academic life, the dean of faculty exhorted these newest Lindies that they would "be challenged at Linden, to know what you stand for and to defend it vigorously. You are a group of highly motivated and success-oriented students. Your resumes are already bursting with your high school accomplishments; you will become overcommitted here, as well." This short talk tells students directly about the rigorous and challenging community into which they have been admitted and implicitly that they will be able to keep up with, perhaps even relish, these challenges—that this is what they were seeking. It also tells them about themselves and their peers, specifying an audience: not only highly motivated and success oriented but also those with "resumes already bursting with . . . accomplishments." The language of challenge and defense, of being driven and overcommitted (and with a near future of even more overcommitment) tells new students what to anticipate from their lives on campus.

Normative messages are also communicated more implicitly. One example of this that struck me particularly was that incoming Linden students were admonished over and over during orientation week to get as much sleep as possible. This message was repeated by deans, faculty advisers, and student service professionals. For example, as the final suggestion in his "Top Ten Best Habits of Successful Students" the provost admonished the listening new students:

> Get enough sleep. I tell people you need seven hours, and they laugh at me. Professors also don't get enough sleep at the beginning of the semester. But you really need to sleep. You need to make yourself go to bed. If it's a question of staying up another couple of hours to study or do a problem set or write a paper or read or go to sleep, maybe it's better to go to sleep and turn in something less good. I know it's hard, but you gotta do what you can.

The reaction to this advice that he described—"they laugh at me"—is in some ways the real message here: you're in a place where getting enough sleep is a joke, including to professors. The wink-wink, nudge-nudge tone used by the dean also communicates that the dean knows that these listeners will also find this advice somewhat laughable. New students were similarly urged to "try to stop multitasking at least once every day. Put down the cell phone, iPod, etc., and just lose yourself in a book, concentrate on one thing" by a faculty speaker, who then confided that she has trouble doing this as well. The implication is that Linden students are so driven to work hard or to be "overcommitted" in other ways that they don't sleep, relax, or even focus on a single task at a time. Through this imagery, new students learn what being a Linden student looks and feels like.

These messages also tell students what success looks like in this community—what they should be striving for. Generally, as we see in these snippets, success involves managing numerous academic and extracurricular activities and not getting much sleep. It involves having an "already bursting" resume of accomplishments. Success is even more specifically represented in the form of selected Linden alumnae. By sharing these women's profiles as embodied ideals, Linden communicates who is worthy of emulation and what kinds of paths are worth following as Lindies. The happy lives celebrated in these narratives are generally shaped around careers, and although the fields vary, they are heavily weighted toward professional, white-collar and other high-status positions such as international aid worker, elected politician, author, business executive, or green innovator. In one such instance, President Hartigan, discussing the value of a liberal arts education, described a conversation she herself had recently had with an alumna who works as a senior executive in a national consulting firm. As President Hartigan retells it, the alumna noted that she looks not for a specific course or for grades when making a decision about hiring but for a broad education, because that person will be working with clients and needs to have a wide conversational range and should be someone who has passion and drive. A Linden parent, who was speaking as a panelist during a fall workshop, similarly spoke about the ways in which work and personal life will be hard to separate: "We live in a world that is now 24–7 work life. You bring your computer home; you bring your work home; your cell phone's always on; your Blackberry is right there next to you; you can be reached at any time. It's very hard to find any kind of boundaries between work and personal life." Here again we see the ways that a particular kind of career and lifestyle—professional, busy, requiring a laptop, Blackberry, *and* cell phone at your side—is presented as the presumed common future for Linden students.

Collectively, these discourses allow Linden College to communicate to new students their inclusion in a defined Linden community. Linden uses discourse to manage expectations and identity, to tell students who they are as a body and thus normatively who they are as individuals. As new and returning students, Lindies understand that by virtue of their membership, they and their peers have or will develop these lauded qualities. In this sense, community messages are both welcoming and homogenizing (or, again, normative): we're the same here, Lindies now and forever. This kind of rhetoric also marks the boundaries, helping students to learn symbolically who is in and who is out. However, these same markers of membership and implicit nonmembership also undercut the inclusionary thrust of community discourse. We can therefore understand these presentations as creating moral comparisons between students who meet these implied expectations of what it means to be a typical Linden student and those who do not.

Cracks in the Whole: Recognizing What We Are Educated Not to Be

Although intended to be welcoming, community discourses do not always seem to encompass socioeconomically disadvantaged students. They are built around ideals that are more often associated with middle-class and upper-class world views and educational backgrounds in multiple ways.

For example, locating the resources and opportunities to study abroad or get an internship requires a large amount of cultural and social capital, which is a periodic complaint among low and even middle socioeconomic status students at Linden. As Annette Lareau shows in her theory of concerted cultivation, middle-class and upper-middle-class parents train their children through conversational practices and participation in activities how to benefit from opportunities for advancement provided by academic gatekeepers. Low-income and working-class families are less able to provide these lessons. Despite this, presentations on Linden student life most often include students who have taken advantage of study abroad, internships, and less-formal opportunities. Similarly, descriptions of having "wide conversational range" and a "broad education" speak to an adult, fully realized version of Lareau's concept of concerted cultivation, in which value is accorded to conversational ability rather than task-specific skills. The intertwining of work and personal life referenced during the orientation panel is also a hallmark of middle-class and upper-class careers rather than low-income and working-class jobs.[7] Conversely, many occupational identities are not included in these presentations, most notably blue-collar work. Descriptions of success are explicitly about white-collar careers or implicitly about white-collar skills. As one student put it, we learn "what we are educated not to be."[8]

Perhaps it is not surprising that references to work will be references to white-collar careers and lifestyles. Indeed, many of the respondents held similar goals for themselves. In the context of creating a class-marked discursive structure, however, references to white-collar work serve to show which lifestyles and careers are prioritized or esteemed, while others are rarely mentioned. For those students whose families include blue- and pink-collar workers, Linden's organizational presentation of self is a disjuncture and places the student in a different, seemingly more esteemed category than members of their families and communities.

Along the same lines, administrator presentations of what is normal or expected from students at Linden both behaviorally (as seen in being "well-rounded") and in terms of material objects (as seen in the call to put down one's "cell phones, iPod, etc.") imply a background among Linden students that is middle or upper class. Corresponding expectations about students' backgrounds and available resources also contribute to the conflict between inclusive and exclusive community making. For example, a student who had just recently joined the Class Activists of Linden during my second year of field work explained at length at a club meeting her irritation with both faculty and administrators as she adjusted to campus life—interactions that solidified her interest in joining CAL, as I described in my field notes:

> The new student described going in to meet with her major adviser. She's a new transfer and planning to declare an English major, so she went in to talk about this, and one of her concerns was, "What can I do with this degree? Will I be able to get a job?" Her adviser's response was "Well, Linden is not a vocational school." [Reaction of outrage in the group.] She felt like "You don't understand. That is why I am here: I came to get a job to earn money! That's why a Linden degree is worth it!"

Listening students chimed in with advice, including suggesting that she go to the Career Center. She had already been to the Career Center, however, and had gotten a response similar to what she encountered with her adviser. She explained that she is considering law school as an option. My field notes report, "She can't do it right off because of loans and money but wants to figure out how to make it happen. She's never had an internship or a law job and wants to set something up." But the Career Center, through which she hoped to gain insights, was no more helpful than her major adviser:

> The career adviser asked, "What experience do you have that would qualify you for these jobs?" And she replied, "None." The adviser's comment was then, "What have you been doing with your summers? Why don't you have law experience?" [Again, reaction of outrage in the group.] The adviser's suggestion was, "Talk to your family and ask them for advice"—essentially, network to find a job. Again, the student felt like "You don't understand. That's why I came here, because I am not from a doctor-lawyer family. No one I know could help get me a job like that, and I've been working every summer to earn money."

The expectations of the career adviser were totally at odds with this student's life experience and the kinds of support she needs from the career office—indeed, the type of support she is requesting seems to be obviated by her assumed class standing and resources in the mind of the adviser.

In a similar example, an orientation session about women and money in college posed implicit comparisons to a presumably normal Linden student through the examples shared. In an optional orientation session for new students and possibly their parents, a faculty member dressed in chic head-to-toe black informed her audience about Linden's program on financial leadership and decision making. The office runs programs throughout the year, primarily speakers and workshops, ranging from retirement investment basics to budgeting strategies to understandings stocks and bonds. In this session, the professor who coordinates the program introduced it.

> She tells the audience of mostly students that once you are living on your own you need to know about these things, when you are thinking about your independent life at college and managing your money (the implication is, for the first time). The faculty member tells the student audience, "Even though you may not be thinking about these things now and it seems far away, you should start planning your financial life. Start to be an independent person."

Already in these first few sentences of the session, a schism emerges between the life experiences of the presumed Linden student who has never needed to manage her money or been independent and the realities of working-class, low-income, and first-generation students, for whom money management has likely long been part of life. The implicit comparisons became more vivid as the talk continued and the session moved into a discussion of budgeting, something the program has found that students often say they wish they had known about when they started college.

As a way of beginning this discussion, the faculty member asked for volunteers to say what a budget is. The way she phrased the question implied that it's almost a difficult question, as though she were silently adding the phrase "just make a guess." Students' answers included a limit on what you can spend; planning ahead with your spending; don't spend more than you have. The faculty member affirmed that all of these are part of making a budget. She then went step-by-step through making a budget in the most elemental terms: "Start by tracking your expenses." She explains that a budget is your income versus your spending, and if you have some left over you should save it. She provided an example of saving in the following terms: "You save your money for spring break. You decide to go to the south of France to take in some sun [meaningful pause] and learn some French." The audience giggles at the addition, which I take to be an inside joke about how it's just like a Lindie to be learning French while on vacation or knowingly sarcastic about how one could justify a vacation with "learning."

In the course of talking about budgeting, she brought up the term "cash diet," asking, "Does anyone know what this is?" "No, but it sounds horrible!" replied one student. Indeed, no one in the audience volunteered an answer. The speaker explained that this is when your spending limit is your cash on hand. You take out as much as you can afford to spend for the week or the month and only spend that amount. She informs the audience that not only students do this, many grown-ups do this as well. As a final anecdote in her discussion about spending, she talked about her hairdresser, who says that at the beginning of the semester lots of students come in with their friends and their parents' credit cards, and they get a cut and a dye and buy the shampoo and they spend three hundred dollars. (Not surprisingly, the salon is really happy about it.) Then as the semester goes on, the parents get the bill and say, well a three hundred dollar hair cut is maybe a little too much. Then students come in and one gets a dye job or a trim and the other one gets a shampoo.

It's hard to miss the glaring differences between a world in which the idea of only spending what you have available is completely foreign and in which a three hundred dollar hair cut and color is "maybe a little too much" but possible, at least at the start of the semester, and the financial positions of students coming from low-income and working-class families. The presentation of these examples as normal, as though the anticipated reaction is a knowing nod, communicates implicitly what the understood reality of the presumed typical Linden student is. Ultimately, this is part of the challenge: How can Linden be both a place that needs to explain what a budget is *and* a place that feels like it makes sense to low socioeconomic status students?

In each of these examples, a cohesive similarity is presumed among students—that Linden students will identify with the dilemma of too-expensive haircuts or the expectation of traveling to France or having family members who can connect her to white-collar internships. Expressed both as uniform and unproblematic, these presentations tell listeners that the speaker thinks these things are typical for Linden students. Middle-class and upper-class students who fit these descriptions are positioned as the norm, as the definition of a Linden student. Students who do not fit such descriptions are positioned outside of this norm, the odd ones out. Indeed, working-class and low-income images are absent, as are first-generation images for the most part. And given the congratulatory celebration of these normalized middle-class or upper-class images, absences and exclusions of other class locations or experiences are rendered not merely different but less-than, unable to achieve the markers of normal Linden identity.

When working-class and low-income narratives are presented, they are most often implicit and contextualized within a diversity rhetoric. At times, however, an explicit hierarchical comparison between class positions is made in which vaunted Linden expectations are presented as on one side of a divide with working-class or low-income cultural markers on the other. For example, at an all-college welcoming celebration, a faculty member from the history department gave a talk encouraging students to truly invest themselves in their academic work. She spoke about "furnishing your mind, because it is where you will live for the rest of your life." Continuing this metaphor, the professor noted: "Faculty will recommend furniture for you, pieces they especially like—a Queen Anne settee with chinoiserie pillows, for example. If you prefer Aunt Sadie's pull-out couch from Sears and knitted pillows, mediocrity is an option." The invidious comparison between Queen Anne settees and "Aunt Sadie's couch from Sears" is inescapable, linking the college to an elite class position. A similar example could be found in the book given out to graduating seniors during the first year of my research. Containing life skills tips about managing postcollege life, the book featured a cartoon on the first page showing a woman going for a client meeting over dinner. In a crude caricature of a rural working-class woman (she is wearing overalls, speaks with a twang and poor grammar, and mentions hog farming), the cartoon shows how having bad table manners—like putting your feet on the table—may appall future (upper- or middle-class) clients. The working-class daughter of pig farmers is clearly the bad example, whom Linden grads do not want to be, and her evident working classness is clearly marked as offensive in the affluent expected postcollege lives of Lindies. Such examples were rare in their explicitness but form part of a larger set of moral conflicts about what is legitimate and illegitimate at Linden.

We can see these conflicts in some ways as struggles about Linden's institutional identity, deeply linked to class and questions about what kinds of students attend the college and what kinds of graduates are produced. Such conflicts were exhibited not only through discursive presentations but also through questions of what was or was not understood as being worthy of academic credit, as I learned through my conversations with faculty, administrators, and students on campus. Respondents described a thread of comparisons made periodically by Linden administrators and faculty intended to illustrate Linden's status, contrasting "excellence" with "vocational" or "remedial" education. Students, especially those who are transfers, reported being reminded that Linden is not a professional or vocational college or, as explained to one student who transferred from a community college, "not high school anymore." Rather, it is a liberal arts college focused on academic excellence.

A conversation between the director of the Linden internship program and the students at CAL, who had invited him to their meeting to discuss the program, showcases this nicely. The director explained that funding would be provided only for "professional" experiences. Genesis, a student who was in the middle of applying for summer funding herself, asked whether an internship was ever not approved. Yes, sometimes, replied the director: "Only in the following circumstances: First, if you were totally on your own, not getting any supervision or guidance, like a campus rep who was working alone rather than in an office. Second, the work needs to be at least on some level professional in nature. If you were folding towels in a yoga studio that would not be okay. If you wrote your application essay saying, I want to run a yoga studio and I am going to be working with the owner of the studio on new outreach programs, then that would be approved." A second student, Sherry, asked, "What about learning to build homes—that's professional, right?" "Yes, we have had students do that. You need to demonstrate how the activity is a valuable learning experience," replied the director. The meaning of professional—and the college support that stems from that designation—is therefore a source of potential contestation, one in which it turns out that the CAL students held different ideas than the college.

After the meeting, I talked with Heather, CAL's club president that year, and the other CAL students about the presentation. Heather and the others agreed: "It's bullshit that the [Career] Center won't give you money for folding towels—hello, most internships are filing and typing; that's the same thing as folding towels!" From the college's perspective the policy is intended to insure that students are obtaining internships that will give them "real" and résumé-worthy experiences—indeed, the director of the Career Center may have intended his comments to be advice about how to frame one's application materials. But as the CAL students did in this instance, socioeconomically marginalized students sometimes grumbled that the college prioritized some kinds of work over others, determining what a "real" or appropriate job for a Linden grad might be—that is, not the areas their own parents or siblings work in. (Of course, this presents an additional hurdle in social capital terms: those internships deemed worthwhile are easier to arrange for students who have personal connections in those fields.)

The message implicit in these comparisons is again one of hierarchy and exclusion. We see the importance of institutional identity as determined by what activities get credit and other forms of validation. And, as we have seen, this also tells students what kind of place Linden is by indicating what kinds of jobs are considered worthy of validation. Rhetorically, this puts students in a position of justifying how work that is like their parents' is as worthy as some other kinds of work. This is an especially fraught comparison for low socioeconomic status students. On the one hand, upward mobility is precisely the goal for many—they and often their families have prioritized college as a means of increasing economic stability and sometimes social standing. On the other hand, the kinds of distinction highlighted here between white-collar and blue- or pink-collar work, in which one is deemed more worthy, feels like just one more in a long list of exclusions. Symbolically, these distinctions are not only about the worth of the jobs being done but also the worth of the people doing them. Socioeconomically marginalized students are thus placed on one side of a hierarchical line, while those who hold the jobs their parents, siblings, and friends hold are on the other. This is a challenge for students who seek to belong to both "sides."[9]

Where Do Low Socioeconomic Status Students Fit?

Within this classed world, where does discussion of low-income, working-class, and first-generation lives happen? Although these students are welcomed alongside other Lindies in the catch-all community rhetoric—and indeed explicitly welcomed in Linden's web and in-person presentations—the very outlining of that community seems at times to exclude them. However, low socioeconomic status students are also folded into a separate discursive structure of college diversity, one that creates a particular role within the larger community for them. Here again, we see conflicts between the surface message of community inclusion and the actual positioning of socioeconomically marginalized students. Let's turn, then, to diversity.

The Same but Different: Creating and Valuing Diversity

In contrast to community discourses, diversity discourse seeks to emphasize differences between students rather than minimize them. As with discourses about Linden identity, diversity narratives were presented both directly—for example, as statistics, rates, and figures—and indirectly, through stories and pictures. Diversity rhetoric is extremely common on American college campuses, particularly those that are on the lower end of diversity scales. Although nonselective and somewhat selective campuses are often diverse along multiple axes such as age, income, work status, race or ethnicity, and immigration status, selective and highly selective campuses like Linden remain predominantly white and middle to upper class, as well as homogenous in terms of age and other markers.

It's important to understand diversity as both historically contextual and as socially created. Although diversity is nominally about students (or other persons), we can more accurately think of diversity as a category creation and discourse within a specific context. Diversity can only be produced through defining sets of same and different prioritized characteristics that are meaningful within a particular location. We can therefore think of college diversity as being *embodied* by students but *created* through the construction of difference. Though it comprises a collection of people with various appearances and histories, diversity is created through presentations that normalize some statuses while rendering others as marked. In the case of creating class diversity, it is Linden's demographic homogeny and classed environs that position students at the lower end of the socioeconomic scale as "diverse": these students would be the norm at many colleges and universities that reflect the broader American population.

As an administrator or archivist can tell you, Linden has enrolled "scholarship girls" (as they used to be called) from the start of its existence. However, the issue of what is now referred to as "diversity" is different from what it was 150 years ago when these few "girls" lived in a designated dormitory and worked off their tuition by serving their fellow students' meals. While Linden has "always . . . enrolled and supported outstanding young women from a wide range of backgrounds"—in the words of President Hartigan—it must be more public about its pursuits in the contemporary world of higher education. Given Linden's cost of attendance, selectivity, and history, as well as its association in the broader culture with success and achievement, presenting socioeconomic diversity is a complicated rhetorical and representational process. And yet diversity is as important to Linden as to other elite campuses. Diversity within the student body has become an important measure and descriptor of a college. Calls from policymakers and news sources for increased concern with income and parents' education level as important facets of diversity have increased in recent years; these calls have further increased since the recession starting in 2008.[10]

The pressure to enroll more low socioeconomic status students comes not only from the media, however, but also from what sociologists call the "organizational field"—in this case, competing peer colleges. Linden is one of a small number of selective liberal arts colleges in the United States. It must constantly vie with peer colleges to maintain its high position on college rankings lists such as that of the *U.S. News & World Report*. Selected priorities, such as small student-to-faculty ratios and class sizes, sports teams, and average time to graduation have become institutionalized key points of comparison through these rankings.[11] Campus diversity is one metric included in different ways across sites—diversity is noted but not made part of the overall *U.S. News & World Report* rankings. Elite colleges are therefore ranked, even if only informally, among other things, according to their ability to enroll and graduate low socioeconomic status and other so-called diverse students.

For both women's colleges and liberal arts colleges, competition with highly ranked co-ed colleges and universities is particularly difficult. Liberal arts colleges must differentiate themselves within the small range of similar organizations that tend to sound alike in their promotional literature. Emphasizing a school's individual qualities—in Linden's case, for example, particular school traditions and the residential hall system—helps create a strong and distinctive identity. This is especially important for women's colleges because very few high school students will consider applying to a women's college, and a presumably a smaller number of those who do so actually enroll.[12] In this, Linden is further disadvantaged because the students it accepts are often also offered places at other colleges with either more famous names (e.g., Ivy League campuses) and male students.

Moreover, some of these competing colleges have upped the ante by providing grant-subsidized low- or no-loan packages for students. The first of these programs was begun at Princeton in 2001. Since then, a number of the most highly ranked colleges and universities, including Williams, Amherst, and Harvard, have created new ways of funding students that minimize or do away with loan obligations. Such innovative approaches set a high bar for student financial support and provide a difficult comparison for those colleges that cannot meet it. These trends also take place during a period of eroding federal and state financial support and rising tuition and other college costs for selective higher education.

On elite campuses like Linden's, diversity has become what Ahmed terms a "national property," a positive symbol for the college as an institution and by extension all of its students, given that minority students provide diversity for majority students. In this positioning, "'they' are diverse, which is what allows the claim that 'we' can 'have [diversity].'"[13] Because diversity is an institutionalized characteristic, a widely publicized component of national college rankings, attending a school that is diverse is seen as a positive statement. Students may think of themselves as members of a diverse organization and by extension as people who value diversity, regardless of their actual social networks. Diversity, including socioeconomic diversity, therefore becomes an organizational priority for the college and for its students—including those students who would not typically be considered diverse in organizational parlance—that is, white and middle or upper class.

Linden administrators refer to diversity as a "core value." At a forum convened to discuss possible budget cuts during the recession in 2009–10, the dean of enrollment reassured the audience of mostly students that financial aid would remain a priority of the college: "Financial aid is the only budget item that will continue to go up—the college will continue to meet full need. This is a core value of the college. You've heard that phrase, and providing financial aid ensures socioeconomic diversity and all kinds of diversity." Showcasing diversity as a "core value" of the college frames it as a public value shared by all students. Presenting diversity to the current student body therefore takes a celebratory tone that invites all Linden students to see it as a shared quality. Similarly, President Hartigan remarked during an all-college address: "As many elite universities and colleges struggle to support economically diverse student bodies, Linden is gaining new recognition for what it has always done: enrolled, supported, and graduated outstanding young women from a wide range of backgrounds." As the college president notes, maintaining diversity "gain[s] recognition" for the college. Her words are especially evocative in this speech as she reaffirms these particular students' value as "outstanding young women from a wide range of backgrounds." Diversity, consisting of students who can be tallied and measured as diverse, is therefore a positive quality benefiting all Linden community members.

Diversity is likewise used to create positive meanings for external consumption by parents, alumnae, donors, and other off-campus community members. Similar rhetorical approaches are directed at these groups to confirm the institutional value of diversity and the students who provide it. For example, in a "talking points" document provided to alumnae fund-raisers, the college's rank (quite high) on the *U.S. News & World Report*'s list of percentage of high-need students (measured as those receiving Pell Grants) is stressed each year, as are the figures for first-generation students. These are included with other accomplishments, such as number of Fulbright awards received, percentage of alumnae attending graduate school, and famous alumnae. For example, a Linden brochure features the heading "Educating Tomorrow's Leaders," under which is the following information: "With over 20 percent of students receiving federal Pell Grants, Linden is an established national leader in creating access for low-income and first-generation students." Through examples like these, we can see low-income, working-class, and first-generation students as individuals—valued members of a community—yet also as fulfilling specific organizational goals. Low socioeconomic status students are therefore holders of specific roles within Linden's organizational system.

Fulfilling Diversity Roles

In the service of creating diversity as a sort of public good, so-called diverse students are positioned as *providers of diversity*, rather than simply Linden students like anybody else. This process marks them as other even as they are also being welcomed as insiders. In the process of framing these students as providing a public good, the comparison between diverse and unmarked or "regular" students seemed to some respondents to imply that some added reason was needed for their inclusion.[14] The institutionalized position of providing diversity to the campus therefore creates tensions for students who are designated as diverse because they are seemingly placed outside the norm.[15]

Diversity narratives therefore raised questions about who belongs at Linden and under what auspices. What do students in different categories "bring" to justify their organizational membership? As Heather, a president of the Class Activists of Linden, asked rhetorically in a meeting on class at Linden, "What do upper-class students, who aren't financially 'needy,' need? Going by the state of the campus, they need *something*. But there are no mandatory requirements for them to do anything." Her comparison is low socioeconomic status students, who (by being positioned as outsiders) seem to require additional claims to membership. Why is it that affluent students are not called on to showcase their special membership through, for example, a required course on social justice or community service (Heather's suggestions)? Or, if maintaining good grades and campus participation are sufficient indicators of membership, why does that not hold for low socioeconomic status students? An illustration of what Heather refers to implicitly here can be found in a draft letter sent to CAL students for review (who subsequently shared it with me) regarding a diversity-training pilot program one fall semester in which working-class students are described as "bringing practical skills to campus." The authorship of the letter was unclear, and it could have been written by an external proposal writer. However, the letter was circulated by the Linden administration and written for Linden administrators and stakeholders. As one CAL student noted, this rationale seems akin to wording about the Platt scholars program, which is often framed as older students bringing "real-life experiences" to campus. Both seem to suggest that these students require some kind of justification for their inclusion as Linden students above and beyond their academic and extracurricular preparation.

This implication arose in other ways during students' campus lives, particularly around issues of representation—the ways the college positions low socioeconomic status students in relation to other students and to the college as a whole for both internal and external consumers. Like other colleges, Linden makes a variety of efforts to represent student body diversity in meaningful, emotionally engaging ways, ranging from pictures of students in their materials to student profiles on their website that highlight the student's background and experiences at Linden to presentations of alumnae accomplishments through panels, individual speakers, and publicity mentions in college materials. For example, in an article about first-generation students written just before I began my fieldwork, photos and background stories of two such students are presented, along with their recollections of Linden's support. Their stories detail the difficult road to college, for example noting that "[this student] has struggled against remarkable odds to get to Linden. When her family arrived in the States they lived for a while in a homeless shelter in New York. Still, she managed to excel in high school—even though she had to work to help support her family—and eventually ranked third in her senior class with a 4.0 grade point average." The second student profiled stated, "I feel privileged to be a Linden student because my time here is something I think my aunt [who raised me] would have loved to have had for herself." The article closes by citing "Linden's long-time commitment to providing an academically rigorous education to qualified students from diverse backgrounds."

As we see in these two excerpts, representations of low-income, working-class, and first-generation students were often framed as stories of upward mobility and gratitude to Linden for making that possible.[16] This framing was also evident in interactions between students and alumnae designed to promote increased alumnae donations; these interactions range from materials profiling current students intended to be viewed by alumnae to thank-you notes requested (but not required, it should be stressed) from students who have received alumnae-funded grants to in-person presentations organized by the college. These kinds of requests—for testimonials and thank-you notes—undermine the inclusive welcome extended to all Linden students, telling students collectively that they earned their way but then also asking certain students to say thank you or framing them as outside the typical student body. For example, Lynne shared her experiences attending an event sponsored by the Development Office to encourage students to write thank-you letters. As Lynne recalled:

> The meeting started with congratulating us for getting scholarships, and then . . . the director of the program read us examples: actual e-mails and letters they've gotten from alums who have written thank-yous for the

thank-you notes they've gotten from students. Like, they'll say, "I don't normally thank people for thank-you notes, but your story touched me so much. I am so glad I know my money is going to a good cause, and for that reason I will continue giving money to the school." Then it always says, "although our stories are different, and I grew up in a fortunate environment," basically coming down to these alums giving money were never people when they went to Linden who needed money. They came into Linden privileged and left privileged, and it's just a whole, I guess I feel like it's not even a question that we're going to be normatively, economically successful when we get out of Linden; it's just, they seem like they want these rags-to-riches stories.

Michelle had also been asked to participate in this kind of event, having received scholarship funds donated in part by Linden alumnae. She told me that she always meant to participate but ultimately chose not to:

It was weird. It was like, thank you for your money; here's a snapshot of who I am; this is what I accomplished. And I was just like, number one, I don't have very much to write in the accomplished thing . . . like I have a better hand on who I am, I'm pretty happy. Things like that, and those aren't interesting. . . . Obviously I'm grateful, and who are these people who are expecting me to send them a letter to tell them so. I was just like kind of offended by the idea.

Being asked to testify to her accomplishments was uncomfortable for Michelle, and it did not seem "authentic" (as she told me elsewhere in the same interview). She did not think that her accomplishments were of the kind that Linden seemed to want, being too broad and not the kinds of things one could put on a résumé like "having a better hand on who I am" and being "pretty happy." The letter writing asked Michelle to elaborate on something obvious: as she noted, "of course" she was grateful to be supported. To provide evidence of her accomplishments or measurable gratitude seemed "kind of offen[sive]," perhaps exploiting that gratitude.

Rose was involved in a similar project of testifying about her Linden experiences as a woman receiving college support. She said: "Linden does these legacy teas. So there's a woman down . . . in the alumnae building that usually does major gifts. So what she'll do is get four or five students together, and we'll do a panel, and usually a dean or someone will come along, and we'll all go to some town, have tea in someone's house, and we just go and talk about Linden or our experiences." When I asked Rose about how she felt about being selected to talk about Linden and whether she thought that her selection had to do with her particular background, she replied, "We're like, you know we kind of felt exploited almost, but the woman that does it is just so nice. She's a Lindie. Her son's biracial [like Rose]. I knew that she wouldn't—whether or not your intentions were this, this is how it comes off. But at the same time I really like talking about Linden." Rose's response exhibits some of the complicated rhetorical internal exchanges that socioeconomically marginalized students underwent in weighing the personal intentions of the administrator ("she's just so nice") and genuine pleasure in representing the college along with doubts about their own roles ("whether or not your intentions were [exploitative], this is how it comes off").

By making their stories known, students like Lynne, Michelle, and Rose provide important personal testimony to alumnae and others, either through thank-you cards for funds or more broadly for sharing with alumnae donors about "our experiences." Linden students who are marked as socioeconomically diverse are thus asked to make their individual stories into data that support key organizational narratives. This is a crucial function in representing upward class mobility and diversity to several constituencies. Interestingly, although college administrators sometimes noted that (as is the practice at many liberal arts colleges) *all* students' tuitions are subsidized by thousands of dollars, a reduction from the actual cost of a Linden education made possible by the college's funds, I never heard of instances in which the general student body was asked to write thank-you notes. (In 1999, Winston reported that private colleges discounted student tuition by \$7,700 on average.)[17] Indeed, while middle or upper socioeconomic status students also sometimes provided narratives of achievement or gratitude, or even thank-you notes for grants, these requests take place in a broader context in which their presence is continuously reflected in college presentations as not only the majority but also the norm, affirmations unavailable to low socioeconomic status students. Having such requests made of them therefore does not undermine their membership.

Campaigns featuring individual stories of accomplishment are important for fund-raising. As we see in Lynne's comments, alumnae and other donors are genuinely moved and motivated by such narratives. They are effective tools for raising funds, including funds for future student grants.

They can even be meaningful presentations for students themselves. For students requested to make such personal testimonies, however, they can be difficult to negotiate. On the one hand, respondents like Rose, Michelle, and Lynne were truly grateful for financial assistance in the form of grants. On the other hand, being *asked* to be grateful and to express that gratitude seemed to put them in a stance resembling recipients of charity from the college or from alumnae.[18] Indeed, I heard about one recent alumna who referred to these kinds of financial aid efforts as "Tiny Tim campaigns," referring to Dickens' heart-warming character who convinces Ebenezer Scrooge to become more generous through his irreproachable goodness in the face of hardship. Moreover, they felt uncomfortable sharing stories about what is a sensitive topic—namely, needing help from others to maintain their status as Linden students. And, as some respondents told me, they felt compelled to offer "rags-to-riches stories" of the benefits they've received by virtue of being at Linden—that is, to package their presentations in ways that reflect the priorities of the college rather than their own. Thus, while their personal narratives were requested, students often perceived that those narratives were reshaped or packaged to serve the needs of the college.

Respondents and others in special groups were sometimes suspicious about Linden's choices about which categories are highlighted and which are left aside and how these categories are used for representational purposes by the college. They expressed concern that Linden is "only" interested in students who fit categories of racialized or economic minorities in order to demonstrate diversity in the student body, rather than as individuals with inherent value and individual paths. Like college professionals, students are aware that "diversity" is important for a liberal arts college presenting itself as progressive, and they worry that they have been included to help the college meet that goal. For example, Amber, a student attending an event held by the Class Activists of Linden, complained that "I feel like they [the college] don't want relationships, they want statistics. . . . They gain financially by us being here." She explained further that colleges use data on low socioeconomic status students to apply for foundation funds and raise money from alumnae on the basis of having a diverse student body, claiming high Pell Grant numbers. Amber explained her concern about balancing pride in her working-class status and excitement in being open about that status with feelings about the uses of her personal story by the college. She experienced this conflict at an annual spring event, held just before a visiting day for prospective students, in which current Lindies write declarative messages around campus in chalk. She told me afterward: "With that chalking thing that they had a couple days ago, you know, I'm still kind of conflicted about it. Because I wrote stuff. I wrote something about how . . . I think I wrote, like, I'm Midwestern and proud, working-class and something, and then like, something about being under-represented at Linden." Amber's "conflicted" feeling was rooted in wanting to express her reality and at the same time not wanting to feel like a pawn or an advertisement for the college, allowing the college to show her off as a kind of asset through her status as "under-represented." Students suspected that the college's real valuation of their membership lay in what they could provide in filling a categorical need.

To the degree that low socioeconomic status students' needs went unmet—when they felt alienated, when they could not participate in the ways they wished, when they struggled to pay for books, when CAL could not get money for many of its projects, and when individual students had difficulty finding internships and vocational assistance—students perceived an unfulfilled bargain in which "diverse" students provided their presence and categorizable identities for the benefit of the college in exchange for membership and college support. Respondents felt that the college benefitted from their presence in ways beyond their participation as students and specific to their evidence of campus diversity but refused to provide additional support necessitated by virtue of those same so-called diverse characteristics. As a student noted in a documentary made by CAL, "You bring me here, but then you don't want to support me." At a CAL meeting early in my field work, club president Heather expressed frustration at CAL members' being asked to volunteer time and funding for an upcoming event. She vented that the college likes to talk about the presence of CAL and socioeconomically disadvantaged students but doesn't want to support the club. She said, "Now that there are people coming to our meetings, graduate students studying us, undergrads from other colleges calling to ask about how to start a similar club, a faculty panel being planned about class, and other college events—obviously there's admin support for this issue that we should be able to leverage." The implication of her comment was that the college supported CAL's presence as evidence of diversity—and the college's support for diversity—but it was not prepared to offer more tangible support.

Amber also mused about this relationship, continuing her thinking about the significance of speaking out about her working-class identity at an annual event in which students were encouraged to write in chalk short statements around campus that expressed something important about themselves or a belief. Not coincidentally, the event takes place around the same time as a visiting day for prospective students, described above. On the one hand, Amber felt good about declaring herself both a working-class Midwesterner and a Lindie, both for herself and for the college as a whole: "It was really kind of empowering to write my identity like that out on the chalk while people are walking by and seeing like, 'Oh, you know, she's, you know, low, working class, whatever,' not that I thought they were judging me or anything, but just to be that open about it." She also wondered aloud whether she was, in essence, allowing herself to be exploited in some way in service of the college's need for diversity: "But at the same time it's totally a way that Linden can, as an institution, capitalize on that and kind of use my minority status, being that I'm from an under-represented student background or whatever, as kind of like a commodity to sell the college. Like, why were they doing that? Because they're trying to get all these other students to enroll next year."

Amber linked her own thinking on this issue to questions other students had raised, questions about a working-class student's position in the broader college community. Like other respondents, Amber thought that institutional designations of class background came with extra expectations for her as a student: "I'm not here just because I'm a capable, good student. I'm also here because I'm supposed to give that other perspective to students who don't come from my background. And that's definitely not a bad thing, but . . . I don't know. I don't think it's an entirely, I don't want to say moral, but like, ethical kind of thing to do." Amber's ambivalence and doubt comes through clearly toward the end of this comment. On the one hand, it's not "a bad thing" to share her perspective as a working-class student with others who don't come from the same background. On the other hand, the idea of being expected to perform a role in that way of being "like a commodity" and having a value to the institution beyond being "a capable, good student" seems somehow not "ethical."

These reflections touch directly on the semiotics of class morality being created in which some students are symbolically positioned as bringing, or perhaps needing to bring, something extra to the college beyond their academic achievements. (Earlier in this interview, Amber remarked that her reflection on this was sparked by a classmate with concerns about race as part of diversity, which reminds us that the impact of diversity discourse is also important for students of color on campus. A strong literature critiques the deployment of such discourse.)[19]

As Amber's and others' narratives indicate, students were well aware of how valuable diversity is to the college. They sometimes worked to use this categorization to their advantage, a bargaining chip in getting group recognition or to meet other goals.[20] For example, at one campus forum, a student who was a Platt scholar argued for maintaining the program's funding. Standing up in order to make her comment heard clearly by everyone in the room, she said Platt scholars should be acknowledged as an aspect of diversity: "We offer an aspect of diversity that needs to be included in the list of what makes Linden great." Platts bring experience, she said. She shared an anecdote about being rejected from another college because of her age and said, "We are a face here not seen at other institutions, part of all the wonderful diversities at Linden."

Here, being one of several "wonderful diversities" is a source of validation and legitimation. It provides value and, in this specific case, insurance against losing funding. (The Platt program was in danger of being reduced in numbers.) In another college forum, however, in which similar issues were raised (i.e., the possibility of budget cuts), another student defended the same program by exclaiming, "We're not just a source of diversity—we bring a lot to this campus!" The meaning and value of diversity is clearly a conflicted subject among the students who provide it.

Administrators used the same kind of conflicted wording in these discussions. For example, in a presentation about the reasons why the Platt program might be reduced in size, the dean for the program explained that Platt scholars use a significant proportion of the total financial aid budget, being the "most socioeconomically diverse group of students on campus." She continued, "For better or worse, Platt scholars are part of that rising cost of financial aid." She closed by stating, "We love the diversity that Platts bring." Thus the financial need that provides this diversity is exactly what is causing the program to be reduced—and yet, in the same breath, she asserted that this diversity is something the college "loves" and wants to maintain.[21]

Socioeconomic Status in the Context of Campus Diversity Rhetoric

Although socioeconomic categories and terms were invoked to tell stories about diversity, the term "diversity" was not often understood to be "about" socioeconomic status per se: in discussions about the meaning of diversity on campus, class was frequently left aside. For example, note how diversity was presented at a campus meeting of the Linden Social Issues Forum (a periodic open meeting to discuss campus issues). During a meeting in spring 2010, President Hartigan presented changes to the campus structure that deal with diversity. Where there had formerly been a designated officer overseeing programming, compliance, and serving as an ombudsperson for complaints, there would now be a committee to focus on long-term planning and three positions (already existing) taking over the core responsibilities of the former diversity officer. The newly created committee met several times over the first year of its existence, and President Hartigan gave a preview of its findings—as she phrased it, "where we are by the numbers." She shared the change in percentage of minority faculty members from 1999 to 2009, a dramatic increase: "not yet diverse enough, but an upwards trend," as she put it. For students, the change was smaller, from under 20 percent to under 30 percent. She briefly ran through the race/ethnic groups to which she was referring—Asian / Pacific Islander, Black, Hispanic, and Native American (in order of percentage). She also mentioned staff numbers, which were also much smaller than the faculty numbers and almost unchanged in the past ten years. Finally, President Hartigan noted that she wanted to know more about the data. For example: "For students of color, what are their experiences like? Are they different than those of white students? What are the statistics for different types of participation on campus, such as study abroad, internships, and those types of opportunities?" In each of these statements and questions, the diversity statistics presented are solely about race or ethnicity. Socioeconomic background is not covered at all.[22] Effectively, then, although class is positioned as an aspect of student body diversity, "diversity" as a term refers almost exclusively to race and ethnicity, leaving class inequality in a sort of institutional-discourse limbo. There may be a presumed conflation of race and class, as though class diversity is already built into the race discussion because racialized minority students are also the providers of class diversity.

This connection of race or ethnicity to diversity could also be heard in other meetings on this topic. For example, one administrator noted during a discussion about a newly vacated job as "diversity officer" that "no one person can be the person for all people of color to go to. Maybe they can function as a sort of clearing house—they might not be able to solve the problem but can refer the person elsewhere." Comments from the audience reflected the same associations, such as a question about whether the diversity office could encompass *both* race and disability services not to mention other issues associated with diversity, of which class was one of several mentioned. Here again, race is the first. The second was disability, and only after that in a longer list of attributes is class mentioned. This instance was one of the few times class was mentioned during that meeting about campus diversity. As these excerpts suggest, class must be made to fit into unspoken choices about what the term "diversity" means, thus raising questions about who brings diversity and how race and income are conflated.

Here we see that college administrators tend to link diversity to race or ethnicity rather than socioeconomic background in discursive circumstances where the conversation is not specifically about socioeconomic status. That is to say, while socioeconomic status is spoken of in reference to diversity in order to frame it in a particular light, *diversity* is spoken of in reference to race or ethnicity.[23]

Choices about how to track diversity and what constitutes diversity are often guided by external factors rather than solely internal college choices (as implied by the discussion about the pressures that impel colleges to participate in such tracking). Thus, regardless of Linden's own interests, data have to be in the correct form to meet various requirements. For example, as the college president noted during the event described above, the college's tracking of data on race is tied to affirmative action wording of the 1960s and 1970s. This can be problematic as we now live in a more complex ethnic landscape with more multiracial people, more international students, and so forth. Thus, the definition of what makes diversity is changing. Categorization therefore also reflects shifts in the social and professional landscape when terminology comes into use or becomes outdated. In some cases, the tracking of data exposes tensions around such changes. Many campuses, for example, have begun tracking the categories of "multiracial" and "first-generation" students. These newly institutionalized terms alter the ways we now think about diversity and serve as contemporary important categories.

In this chapter we have seen how class inequality is largely left aside in college discourse except when it is framed as part of campus diversity. Although class inequality is rarely discussed directly, it is often communicated implicitly, though stories, jokes, images, anecdotes, and other communications about Linden as a community and Linden students as a group. We see the ways that these quotidian presentations are geared to middle-class or upper-class experiences and presented as unproblematic, to be expected. The portrayal of middle-class and upper-class life as the norm structures the semiotics of class morality: one set of experiences is presented as expected while the other is either left out, exoticized as diverse, or explicitly portrayed as less-than. Although Linden includes all students explicitly in narratives of community and belonging, these communications are undercut both by carving out special roles for "diverse" students and by the creation of a class-normative Linden student identity. These students are then discursively pressed into service to provide diversity, mobility, and sometimes gratitude in institutionally usable ways. Respondents and other students I spoke with sometimes felt frustrated that their stories or pictures were being used as examples of diversity for the college at the same time as they wondered about how this positioned students who received financial aid relative to other "less needy" students and to alumnae.

It's important to note that college can, indeed, serve as a source of upward mobility and empowerment and that low socioeconomic status students (like others) are often happy to attend Linden, grateful for the variety of benefits they receive. These stories are important, not only to the college (especially those tasked with raising money) but also to the students themselves and their families. They should not be discounted. Being asked for tokens of gratitude or being positioned as having a special role to play in relation to what might be called "traditional" students, however, contributes to a semiotics of class morality, altering low socioeconomic status students' experiences of membership.

These issues are genuine challenges for administrators and for faculty members, and not taken lightly. Indeed, these struggles are likely familiar to students and others at any elite campus, and Linden fares well in comparison to its peer colleges and universities in terms of numbers of students from low-income and first-generation backgrounds. Linden and other elite colleges must manage a delicate balance when it comes to representing a broad socioeconomic spectrum within its student body, creating both diversity and community. While Linden welcomes the students who make up this diversity, the college must also package that diversity for other constituencies as contributing something to the whole. In this case, Linden utilizes discourse to create meanings of both community, in which all members are equal, and diversity, which necessarily involves highlighting students' inequalities. Through their presence, low socioeconomic status students allow the college to fulfill a pressing contemporary organizational priority, supporting not only the college's image as an organization but also contributing to the organizational identities of their fellow students, who do not stand out because of their family background or relative disadvantage. They also demonstrate Linden's priorities through their own mobility and further laud Linden by demonstrating their gratitude to generous donors. To the extent that providing diversity overshadows students' other, individual merits as members of the Linden community, however, it is something of which low socioeconomic status students are wary. Ironically, it is precisely their individual identities, their personal stories and experiences, that are called on to fulfill a responsibility assigned to them by virtue of their status in one particular category. The inclusivity of the community narrative is therefore undercut in other spaces by the college's own rhetoric that presents middle-class or upper-class lives as normal on campus.

This is consequential for all students, not just those from low socioeconomic status backgrounds, because students' identities are entwined with that of the organization (as Ahmed points out[24]). Low socioeconomic status students have special roles to play within these schema, and these roles belie the idea that all students attending Linden do so on equal footing. Moreover, Linden must fit the celebration of diversity into a larger set of organizational narratives that speak to its core identity as a selective college. These dominant narratives are classed, representing what is ideal or (ostensibly) the norm at Linden. For low-income and other nonelite students, these narratives form a sounding board of comparisons between this and other locations and status positions. Furthermore, upward mobility does not fit seamlessly into the institutional presentation of diversity more broadly, which, when not explicitly tied to socioeconomic status, is generally used to refer to race or ethnicity.

Of course, the challenge of managing low socioeconomic status student enrollment in elite colleges is not only an organizational one; low socioeconomic status students themselves must manage these complexities on a daily basis. In the next chapter, I examine how socioeconomic inequalities are manifested among peers and within friendships.

3

"ARE YOU MY FRIEND,
OR ARE YOU CLASSIST?"

Confronting and Avoiding Inequality among Peers

At lunch, Daniela and her best friend Mari talked over what they will do after graduation, two years away. Both are ambitious and want to be involved in education or social activism, perhaps government or nonprofit work. They've clearly had this conversation before and trade light-hearted digs. You will get a job first says Daniela to Mari, because you have glasses and are smarter. No, you will get a job first, replies Mari, because you are lighter-skinned and have class privilege. Both young women smile a little mischievously and laugh at each other, making light of what are actual differences between them.

While Linden wrestles as an institution with managing both inequality and community, students struggle to manage socioeconomic inequality within their friendships and peer circles. Most low-income, first-generation, and working-class Linden students I met reported having middle-class and affluent friends on campus; only a few reported having only or primarily friends from similar backgrounds as themselves at Linden. Middle- and upper-income peers were part of their inner circles, romantic lives, and broader acquaintances. These friendships are unusual—people most make friends with people who are similar to themselves, what sociologists call "homophily." Spending money, food preferences, and choices about how to spend time all shape the ways we develop social ties. Furthermore, there is evidence that socioeconomic origin influences what people value in their friends, suggesting that cross-class friendships may be difficult to maintain.[1] As we know, most Americans grow up in socioeconomically homogenous neighborhoods and schools, which provide few opportunities to forge friendships with people who have very different backgrounds.[2]

When I planned my research at Linden, I assumed that most people would have friends from pretty similar backgrounds; the number of students I met who had friendships across socioeconomic differences surprised me. While these cross-class ties offer students important potential resources and are likely to support positive academic outcomes,[3] they also open up venues for difficult interactions: how do students manage friendships that likely include frequent comparisons of having and not having? In this chapter I look at how students managed inequality encountered within friendships, both close relationships and in broader social circles. I examine two possible ways—direct and indirect—for tackling this proverbial elephant in the room. Daniela and Mari's conversation at the opening of this chapter turned out to be the exception: respondents rarely spoke directly about class inequality. Their silence, parallel to that at the institutional level, is shaped by the same semiotics of class morality.

As we saw in chapter 2, students locate themselves as similar-to or other-than the self-presentation of the college and, by extension, the purportedly typical Linden student. These presentations are highly classed, if not explicitly classist—though they may be that, as well. Moral comparisons are created as students understand themselves to be affirmed or othered through the college's normative presentation of self. Students incorporate the same semiotics, or systems of meaning, into their own relationships, making class inequality very difficult to negotiate. This meaning making is especially clear as it comes through in the expression of two key values in Linden student life: community and merit. Thus the semiotics of class morality is understood through locally important cultural concepts and shapes students' strategies for managing class inequality.

Making Cross-Class Friendships

Cross-class friendships are atypical in American society. For perhaps self-evident reasons, forging relationships across socioeconomic boundaries is challenging. Indeed, the very markers of socioeconomic status—income, education, and occupation—are strong factors predicting the demographic similarities among people in our lives: we befriend, partner with, and marry those who are similar to us in socioeconomic measures. Flying in the face of these statistical patterns of like finding like, the respondents in this study were exceptions to the rule. Of the twenty-six respondents, only four (Fiona, Meredith, Alyssa, and Isabel) reported primarily or solely having friendships with peers who shared their socioeconomic backgrounds, and only two reported no friends with class-different backgrounds (Fiona and Alyssa)—the others each reported at least one close friend who was more affluent.

Alyssa came to Linden through a local scholarship program along with three other young women who shared both her working-class background and her ethnicity, and they quickly connected with older students from the same program. Fiona chose not to pursue close campus friendships at all, focusing on her studies, her long-distance boyfriend, and spending time with a hometown friend who went to a nearby college. However, even in these cases where respondents reported having mostly same-background friendships, the lines were not clear-cut. Meredith, for example, reported that her closest friendships on campus were with two other young women who were working class. In subsequent interviews, however, Meredith mentioned that while both friends had grown up in low-income circumstances, the family of one had become upper middle class by the time this friend reached high school. Making same-class friends was therefore not always cut-and-dried, especially as students had different constellations of privilege and hardship over different times in life.

I more often heard stories like those of Aleisha and Violet, whose girlfriends were from middle-class and upper-middle-class families, and Lynne and Becca, whose best friends were from upper-class families. Hearing about these friendships in interviews with respondents took me off-guard and immediately caught my attention. Once I began spending time on campus, however, two factors that make these cross-class friendships less surprising became clear. First, students from socioeconomically disadvantaged families are a minority at Linden. Despite Linden's having a larger percentage of first-generation students and students who receive Pell Grants than many similar colleges, students from working-class or low-income backgrounds remain proportionally few—less than 20 percent of the traditional-age students, if we estimate according to the institutionally tracked data. Thus, in a classroom of thirty students, perhaps six will come from socioeconomically marginalized backgrounds, while twenty-four will come from middle and upper socioeconomic status households.

Moreover, college friendships tend to be driven by proximity. Students establish friendships primarily with their roommates and hall mates—who are not grouped by socioeconomic background—and then secondarily through club membership, social preferences, and classes.[4] The scarcity of low socioeconomic status students is therefore especially important at residential schools such as Linden, where students are required to live all four years in campus residence halls, to which they are assigned by preferences for relative noise and being a morning or night person rather than demographic factors. Even if students were interested in locating other low socioeconomic status peers, there are few clear gathering places for students who share such a background. Although these students, like others, periodically go to the Financial Aid Office and hold jobs on campus, these are not social-support locations and are far from exclusively occupied by students from socioeconomically disadvantaged backgrounds since middle-class and even some upper-middle-class students receive financial aid in the form of loans, work study funds, or smaller grants. Ultimately, like most new students, respondents from low-income, working-class, and first-generation families made friends with people they met during orientation, in clubs formed around shared interests such as crafts or environmental activism, and in their residence halls, with fairly little regard for one another's backgrounds. As respondents often noted, *everyone* wants to make friends as quickly as possible during the first year: by the time you figure out just how different another's precollege life was from your own, you're already friends.

Second, students reported that it could be difficult to make accurate determinations about peers' socioeconomic backgrounds without some investigation. As noted in the introduction, fashion choices at Linden tend toward thrift store finds rather than luxury goods, with "hipster" and androgynous looks being predominant—second-hand clothing, fit-ted cotton tees and flannel shirts, jeans, sometimes worn with more ornate accessories, and a tolerance for a range of second-hand "vintage" 1980s styles—rather than more formal dress, making outfits alone unhelpful for determining class. Students often spent most of their time on campus or in walking distance of it; many socialized inexpensively by going to cam-pus parties and drinking cheap alcohol before going out or by going to campus events such as movies and arts performances. For middle-class and upper-middle-class students, this socioeconomic "passing" was often achieved by being "cheap" (in the words of Quinn, a working-class junior) or simply modest in spending habits. Just about everyone seemed to talk about being "broke." Casual or visual assessment of another's socioeco-nomic background was therefore difficult, especially when students first encountered one another. While some students stood out as "snobs" or as "flaunting" their wealth through clothing, cars, or stories about travel over Spring Break, those students could be avoided in favor of others who were more unassuming. Those who were less open about their wealth or not quite as high up the socioeconomic scale were harder to place.

What low socioeconomic status students *did* have was a general idea that most students, including their friends, were more affluent than them-selves, whether by a little or a great deal. While they often had a sense of which friends were more financially advantaged, they did not always know by how much. As I discovered, students mostly do not talk about class directly, even including seemingly banal and basic details like par-ents' jobs. Class-indicative language and subjects were found instead in more subtle ways. As Aleisha said, by observing people one may note that "they have like, A out of A, B, C, D, and E; it doesn't take much to figure out. . . . Okay, appearance isn't the distinguishing factor, and maybe there isn't just one. It's a little more complex . . . but it's not impossible." Thus the listener who wishes to make note of differences may gain at least some indications without direct discussion of parent income, education levels, or careers. When I accompanied Michelle to dinner in her residence hall, I overheard conversations about food preferences ("What are capers? Are they a berry? A fruit?"), students who used big vocabulary words, and discussions of summer vacation or internship plans. All of these provided clues to the backgrounds of the speakers.[5]

Respondents were also aware of the college's status and overall demographics. The college's statistic of socioeconomic diversity—roughly 60 percent of students receive need-based aid—was often cited during the years of my research. This figure did not communicate as wide a range of economic variation as the college may have intended, however, to low socioeconomic status listeners. As Aleisha pointed out, "there might be 30 percent that . . . may only need ten thousand dollars, which is nothing to scoff at, but it's not the same as having a group of very needy [students]" like herself. And, furthermore, she reasoned, if some 60 percent of the students are on financial aid, then "that means that the rest can pay for it themselves," meaning they are quite wealthy. Overall, as Quinn observed, "I think it's really just an environment that is so clearly high class, because it's education that's worth fifty thousand dollars a year."

One additional factor that made assessing class more complicated was that the scale of comparison was fairly extreme. A small proportion of students were open about having very high levels of affluence or privilege in ways that seemed to set the benchmark for comparison quite high. Respondents talked about peers who variously had a brother who dated a famous movie star; whose parents had bought her a yacht for her birthday; and who spent upward of five thousand dollars a month on phone bills, for example. By comparison, a quieter upper-middle-class status student may be more innocuous. It may also be the case that a similar dynamic functioned at the opposite end of the socioeconomic spectrum: there was periodic Linden media coverage of students who had grown up in extremely difficult circumstances. These stories, similarly, make the circumstances of students whose families were only slightly better off perhaps less noticeable.

Thus, while respondents often did not have a specific sense of the socioeconomic positions of their friends, they were generally aware of class inequality on campus and the classed status of their environment. Within this setting, socioeconomically marginalized students' friendships and romantic relationships encompassed a wide but often murky range of socioeconomic backgrounds, including more-affluent others ranging from best friends to dates or girlfriends to wider friendship circles. As I settled in to campus, my questions shifted from how and why students formed these friendships to how they maintained them in the face of deep interactional complications and powerful symbolic boundaries. I became less interested in how students assessed whether friends were affluent and more interested in how they managed inequality within their friendships. I found that students seemed to take two routes. The first was to be open and upfront about class differences, to talk directly not only about their own background but also, more important, to confront those who made classist comments and to point out privilege and inequality when they saw it. I think of this as a "rocking the boat" approach. I heard about these interactions only rarely, and students more often took what I think of as a "see no evil, hear no evil" tack. In these instances, respondents worked to render class difference unimportant, effectively invisible. Students were not Pollyannaish in their avoidance of the subject and were often (though not always) perfectly clear about the sometimes stark class differences between themselves and others. Rather, what they negotiated was the salience of those differences and the implications of inequality for their friendships. Thus low socioeconomic status students were often active participants in maintaining a silence around class inequality, sometimes adjusting to this approach because of negative feedback from peers after trying to be more direct.

Managing Cross-Class Friendships

Rocking the Boat

Inequality was sometimes acknowledged directly and purposively among peers and friendship groups, as in the example that opens this chapter. Students who chose to highlight inequality had various goals for this stance. Some perceived their emphasis on class inequality as political, even when not as a form of direct activism. Making sure not to simply let classist comments pass or to gloss over inequalities felt important even among friends. Macy, a recent alumna from a low-income family, encouraged students at a conference held by the Class Activists of Linden by saying, "If *we* have to be uncomfortable here, we might as well make it uncomfortable for other people sometimes!" Students often used humor to make their points. For example, when a speaker invited by CAL to talk about class and race in higher education appeared unlikely to attract much of an audience, several CAL students began to update their Facebook statuses to encourage friends to come to the event. Violet wrote on her Facebook page, "Are you my friend or are you classist?" While her intention was to offer two reasons why viewers should come to the event—namely, if one was *either* classist *or* her friend she should attend this event, rather than if the reader was not her friend, *then* the reader was classist—the confrontational tone of her implied judgment received the amused laughs of a Freudian slip that has a strong grain of truth to it. Similarly, during another meeting of CAL students, Violet joked that rich students "suck . . . just kidding." These instances acknowledge the potential for animosity stemming from inequality, and for discomfort.[6] They also suggest a complicated moral balancing act, as Violet's girlfriend and her two best friends were from considerably wealthier backgrounds than her own and would probably fit into the "rich students" category.

Other students accomplished a similarly jarring outcome simply by being matter of fact in discussing socioeconomic differences and being open about their lives. Michelle, for example, told me that she was very comfortable talking about money because it had always been a topic in her family growing up—What can we afford? How can we pay for what's needed right now? When she was open about money with friends, however, they often reacted with discomfort. Michelle told me:

> So, talking about money, I think people are a little surprised because I'm like, "I can't do that, I'm poor," and they're like, "What!" And they also sometimes think I'm joking, and I say it in a joking way, but I really do mean that. One of my friends was actually appalled. She was like, "Ah, look you're poor!" I was like, "No, really, I'm below the poverty line. The poverty line is twenty-two thousand. We're at eighteen, and probably not even that anymore since my mom is unemployed." I guess some people are really surprised when you're candid about money.

When I asked how people reacted to her in these moments, her answer was unambiguous: "They get uncomfortable. Some people—and they won't say, 'Oh, I'm uncomfortable,' but you know when people are uncomfortable—sometimes they change the subject or go really quiet. I change the subject. It's fine." Despite this discomfort, Michelle and a few other respondents remained fairly open about their backgrounds and worked hard to spur more open discussion or acknowledgment of difference.

Choosing whether to be open or confrontational about inequality was not easy, however, and it often threatened to bring respondents into conflict with friends. In one such instance, Becca described how her first year at Linden had included a lot of fights with peers: she had frequently gotten angry with students she saw as unaware of their class privilege and didn't hesitate to point this out. She described getting "into fights . . . verbal, like slightly aggressive." She recounted also that during that year "my friends were like, 'You are not going to have any friends if you don't stop.'" This recollection of "heated" interactions and admonishments about the possible costs suggest that a direct approach may be socially risky. Here Becca was not confronting her own friends but rather classmates outside her social circle. Her "heated" and direct approach was nonetheless perceived by friends as socially risky.

Moreover, respondents were not always sure about how to go about pushing people to deal with class inequality. For example, at a CAL meeting, students discussed possible slogans for a T-shirt. While some students wanted to put a provocative statement on the back, others were concerned about causing offense. During a discussion of how to recruit more members, several students brought up the idea (used once by previous years' students) of confrontational language on the front, such as *Get your mommy to pay for it!* This idea was quickly discarded: people didn't want to be too snarky, and they came up with some ideas that seemed a little less snide. Specifically, the students present worried about offending middle-class and upper-class peers, arguing that it is no one's fault what kind of family they were born into and that upper-income students might feel uncomfortable about class, too. As Genesis, one of the presidents of CAL during my second year of field work, explained in an interview, "I don't often compare myself to others. I don't blame them for the situation they're in. It's just how fortunate they are—that's not their fault." Similarly, Meredith thought that upper-income students "are always going to feel like the bad guy because they're privileged, and it's not their fault they were born into it." And Alice, another CAL member, told me later in an interview that CAL should be "more open to everyone . . . open for discussion so that people can come, everyone from all backgrounds can come." Thus, even in a club founded to engage in activism around class inequality, students were hesitant about rocking the boat too hard. Class inequality is hard to name, even for students who want to engage with the topic, because it threatens to bring uncomfortable comparisons to the surface. This brings us to the second approach and the reasons why that approach usually prevails.

See No Evil, Hear No Evil

Most low socioeconomic status respondents noted that although they had affluent friends, class and family income were not discussed. Violet told me, "Obviously it [class] was present in my relationships and friendships, but like I couldn't really talk about it or think about it clearly. I know people are going through these tension things with their friendships but don't know how to deal with it or talk about it." Similarly, Meredith told me, "It's not something people discuss here." And Becca stated, "I think class issues have never been something I have actively spoken about to friends."

This inclination to avoid talking about class inequality is shaped by two important cultural understandings that arise, at least in part, from the semiotic structuring of the college. The first is the very strong emphasis on community and the particular, local meanings of community discussed in chapter 2. The second is an association between merit, or legitimacy as a Linden student, and socioeconomic status. Interestingly, students at both ends of the economic spectrum seemed to feel vulnerable to these concerns, which provided many of them with a disincentive to discuss financial issues.

Community: "Like family away from home"   As discussed, community is a predominant discourse at Linden. Community is a guiding or encompassing aspect of Linden identity, part of what is expected. This emphasis on community—and, more specifically, the very personal and emotional meanings that undergird Linden's specific understanding of community—mapped onto the broader semiotics of class morality and shaped the ways that students managed inequality among themselves.

Community discourse is not unusual on college campuses, and most, if not all, liberal arts campuses emphasize this as part of the college experience. Linden's language around community, however, is greater than many conventional campus interpretations of community that simply promise friendship, school identity, and extracurricular activities. Rather, Linden's discussion of community is interwoven with associations of deep emotional ties, often in terms of family or sisterhood. Linden students therefore hold an expectation of membership in a tightly knit social group, many having selected Linden in part because of this promise. This was most clearly seen in interactions in and discussions of the residence halls. Linden emphasizes its residence hall system to prospective students, and the halls are an important reason students choose to attend Linden. Among current students, there are frequent discussions about which residence halls have the best "community." As one administrator remarked to a group of newly enrolled students, "Your hall is your family and your home."

Language that interprets community as family is used explicitly by new and returning students alike. For example, new students and sophomores both discussed and enacted these expectations in an orientation meeting. The new students were called up floor by floor to get cupcakes, helping them to see in an immediate sense the others who lived around them. The returning students, who were running the meeting, then asked the incoming students to talk about their ideas about what the hall should be like in the coming year. The new students jumped in quickly and readily, shouting out words to be added to the growing whiteboard list. By the end, the list included community, hall identity, sisterhood—the young woman who shared this last desire specified, "I have two sisters, and I really miss them, so I want the hall to be like sisters. Like, sister*ly*"—to be friendly with people when you come in, to recognize everyone and know who they are, community again, field trips, dance parties, and nail painting.

Community, listed at least twice during that evening's brainstorm, was clearly a priority, and its specific contextual meanings are spelled out here as "family," "sisterhood," and participation in activities to create these bonds. The meeting continued with a further icebreaker. All participants had been asked to bring three items that were important to them. People went around again and talked about their items. Several have brought stuffed animals; other items included a shot glass, framed photos, posters, iPods and phones, blankets, T-shirts, a Wii control, jewelry. The students explained their choices in personal, sometimes intimate terms that—as is the goal of the exercise—helped develop a sense of interconnection. Students talked about keepsakes from hometowns; jewelry made by hand at a much-loved summer camp job; pictures of themselves with best friends from home, siblings, and pets; a stuffed animal to symbolize a long-held love of animals and dreams of becoming a vet; and a quilt made by a grandmother. One young woman's item was a vial of nail polish: she introduced it by saying, "I am not really girly, but I just love nail polish. I have fifty bottles [of nail polish] in my room, so if you ever want to use some, stop by." Someone across the room called out, "Nail-painting party!" As an observer, I could almost see the gathering as a slumber party of old friends, especially given the surrounding blankets and stuffed animals. Here again, the development of community as a process of sharing and support, the strong interpersonal ties that are fundamental to this vision of community, are begun early. Social activities such as painting nails together and even more formal arrangements such as in-hall student advisers for academic issues encourage students to see the residence hall as "home."

Linden's definition of community—strong emotional support, like family—is undergirded by the structural arrangements of student life on campus. As described in the introduction, the campus is small and almost entirely residential; indeed, a large majority of students remain in the same residence hall for their entire time on campus. Thus the emotional tone of close ties is complemented by the long-term stability and physical closeness between students as they move within a tightly interwoven universe of residential, academic, social, work, and extracurricular spheres that largely include population overlaps.

These structural and discursive arrangements of community result in several constraints on students' capacities to manage inequality. First, Linden's close physical quarters make for a lack of anonymity. Like other small residential campuses, students often felt that they knew "everyone" and often had interconnected friendship groups. What students do and say can follow them across venues: comments in class will likely be repeated not only in gossip circles but will connect back to a student's residence hall and vice versa. This concern shapes campus practice, as one faculty member noted when describing her belief that students have difficulty engaging with many issues in classroom discussions because if "you say it in class, it follows you out of class." In this system, one's neighbors and hall mates are important community members, rather than merely nameless or faceless others. This is even more strongly emphasized when community is defined as not simply members of a shared space but involving supportive, emotional ties to peers and being "like family." Leveling criticism is therefore even more emotionally complicated.

Second, participating in community is an extremely important aspect of what it means to be a Linden student, a crucial and virtually obligatory component of a full Linden identity. As a dean told new students during a welcoming event: "Linden has an exceptional sense of community, or communities. We are all part of the Linden community, with a shared sense of tradition, mission, and identity. You will also be a part of many other individual communities, which will overlap." In this presentation, Linden is described as being made up of layered and overlapping communities. The centrality of this "shared sense of tradition, mission, and identity" could hardly be overlooked: community seems to overtake the very meaning of the college. Consequently, in order to truly be a Lindie, students may feel pressured to enjoy the community and are sometimes pressed to participate more fully if they are lackluster in their enjoyment or involvement. For example, a student attending a workshop discussion about class issues in the residence halls talked about how her peers gave her funny looks when she chose not to spend time in the living room or go to periodic get-togethers over coffee. On the Linden online student bulletin board, students periodically posted about feeling unhappy in their residence halls but being unable to admit it because everyone else seemed so happy. Even critiques of the college as an institution seemed to be made difficult by this sense of community membership and ties to friends. As an alumna related to me: "The institution is giving you the message about community and what you should mean to each other. For me, what was weird is that in high school me and my friends rebelled against the institution, whereas here, the expectation is that you will love the institution, be part of it. And there is a conflation: to love your peers, your peer group, is to love Linden, to love the institution." Thus to express concerns about the college as a classed location, or to express feelings of difference from the generalized organization, is to refuse love for one's peers and friends. Evelyn, the transfer student quoted earlier in the chapter, described a similar experience. During an interview in which she said how difficult it had been for her to adjust as a new student, I asked if she shared that feeling with others. She replied: "No, because everyone's like, 'Oh, we love Linden College so much. Oh, Linden College is the best place ever.' And I really severely disagree." This vision of community as an important aspect of college life is not dissimilar from that expected at other campuses,[7] but it may be more heavily stressed at Linden and other small residential colleges that require students to live on campus.

Finally, when inequality conflicts with community, it becomes reframed in ways that obviate acknowledgment. This could be seen in action one evening during a residence hall orientation. The returning students explained to new students what they could expect as members of Brownleigh Hall, including rules and regulations. One rule involves hall dues, a fee collected each semester to cover shared social events such as study breaks, parties, and field trips. The sophomore describing the dues said they are required from each student, but the hall chair corrected her to say that they are not *required*. The person making the announcement said, "That's right, they are not required—if you're busy and you don't want to participate in hall events and stuff, you don't have to pay, but that would just be sad." This version of the hall policy goes uncorrected and unchallenged, despite being inaccurate: financial hardship is an important reason why students may opt out or make other arrangements for paying the residence hall dues. Here difference—an inability to pay dues, or a need to prioritize money—is instantly reframed as a lack of interest in participating, which is "just . . . sad." It's notable that students in hall leadership positions are actually trained to inform new students that these fees are nonmandatory and that all students are welcome to participate in hall social life regardless of ability to pay. The framing used here, however, diminishes the possibility for low-income students to opt out for financial reasons, since these appear to be preemptively reinterpreted as opting out because they are bad citizens.

This discursive positioning echoes the college's presentation of itself in middle-class or upper-class terms and lack of presentation of working-class and low-income lives. Here, a conflict is created between appropriate community participation by some and lack of participation by others, but the socioeconomic roots of that lack are made invisible. Students not participating are simply presented as poor community members.

One implication from this example is that, while inequality may be swept under the rug as in this instance, it is precisely through the ways that residence halls practice community that inequality is made very real for many low socioeconomic status students. Indeed, students who don't pay dues are sometimes told directly that they will be excluded from hall life. Genesis, for instance, was not able to pay the hall dues. She recounted during a CAL meeting that she was told, "If you don't pay, [then] no cocktail party, no storage room, no hall T-shirts." Genesis described how she was "getting threatening e-mails that her name would be on the list and her stuff would be taken out of the storage room." ("The list" refers to a list of nonpayers posted in this particular hall.) Although Genesis didn't care that much about missing parties, she resented being excluded from the hall's social events and the threats of revoked hall privileges such as storage of belongings in the residence hall over the summer and breaks. Although students are often told that they can pay what they can as long as they explain, students in CAL spoke of resenting having to offer this information, which made them feel vulnerable. This was especially the case when others framed the request as, "But it's only ten dollars!" While Genesis and other low socioeconomic status students are told that they are part of Linden's community, they are simultaneously pushed to the side by peers as part of the practice of creating that community. Thus the heavy and pervasive emphasis on community as part of a successful Linden experience and as part of Linden identity has left little room for expression of inequality. Normative community expectations therefore render class inequality silent and low socioeconomic status students as morally wanting because they are unable to be full community participants.

Merit: Achieving Moral Legitimacy on Campus   A second aspect of the moral semiotics of class emerges in students' academic practices and the meanings derived from them. The presentation of what it means to be a Linden student, discussed in chapter 2, is rooted in themes that would be recognizable on any elite campus: hard work and academic prowess, typically framed as a student's merit. These themes also underlie some of the reasons that Linden students are uncomfortable talking about their financial backgrounds. For students at both ends of the economic spectrum, family financial status is tied to questions of who deserves to be a Linden student and why—who has true merit. Upper-income students worried that financial advantages would be interpreted as making the path to college easy, that they had paid their way in or that they were accepted because of family connections. Lower-income students worried that low income would be conflated with low intelligence or that they were admitted merely to bump up the college's statistics for diversity. Because of these worries, students from a wide range of backgrounds were invested in keeping a low financial profile.

Describing a fear that seemed to resonate for many students from less-advantaged backgrounds, Meredith, whose somewhat reserved nature belied her friendliness, reflected one afternoon during an interview: "I think a lot of people think I'm a scholarship kid—I'm only here because the college needs me to be here, not because I need to be here. So the college wants more diversity, and so that's why I got in, not because I'm smart." Being smart, of course, is the coin of the realm. It's what provides Linden students with their identities and worth as students, and it underlies the equality that Linden promotes as existing between students: we are all here with the same abilities, regardless of background. To be admitted for some other reason thus undercuts a student's membership, her legitimacy as a Lindie.

This same concern can also be heard in a discussion during a CAL meeting in which Genesis, the president during that year, began the meeting by bringing up a news editorial she had read about how affirmative action should be based on class not race. She tells the group assembled that the article prompted her to think about what affirmative action based on class could mean for her, as a working-class African American student: "I was thinking when I read it, okay, okay, I'm a student of color, so I benefit from affirmative action. But then once you are on campus, you want to know that you were admitted for your merit, not for some statistics, so that the college can represent how diverse it is." She sees this as a problem: "You don't want to feel like you are somewhere to add to the school's diversity statistics. It's a question of why am I here. You want to be here because of your intellect, not to diversify. You get a sense that you're here because we want to include you, not because you're equal." In other words, like Meredith, Genesis worried that her inclusion as a Linden student might be due to her ability to "diversify" campus rather than due to her "intellect," a "ticket" (to use bell hooks's term) extended to her rather than a symbol of earned admission based on merit. Victoria, who was just months away from graduating during our interviews, shared similar fears.

VICTORIA: Even though I get to come to Linden and stuff, people will always look at it as—if people know I have financial aid, people always kind of look at it as well, you were given this, you were given this opportunity. Which I was, and I'm grateful for it. . . . But it's not something that, if we're talking about privilege, it's one of those things where someone gave me this privilege to get to come here. It wasn't something, you know, [trails off]

LIZ: As in you didn't earn it, you mean?

VICTORIA: Yeah, which is, kind of takes something away from it. . . . Because I did work really hard to get here.

Thus Victoria sees financial aid, something she was "given" as part of the "opportunity" to come to Linden, as undermining and belying her legitimacy: if she was "given" the opportunity to come to Linden, does that mean she did not earn it? In some cases, this uncomfortable feeling seemed to last indefinitely: several years after graduation, sentiments like this still were being expressed during my final round of interviews with respondents.

Interestingly, upper-income students were reported to share similar fears. Low- and middle-income respondents described their impressions that their more affluent friends felt shy about revealing their own financial backgrounds. Alice, for example, reflected that "I guess each class has things attached to it. If you're upper class or wealthy, people may assume that you're snotty or you think you're better, so I feel people wouldn't want to admit that." She concluded, "Nobody wants to admit to anything, or confess anything, about their class."

Alice's impression was borne out through my observations on campus and other students' recollections of cross-income interactions.[8] As we saw with low socioeconomic status students, this reluctance seemed to stem from a deeply rooted concern about the nature of who may claim moral standing as "deserving" a Linden education. Meredith described a workshop she attended during her college orientation in which students had been asked to group themselves by income. As she told me, there were handfuls of students in each of the middle groups, with smaller numbers at both ends. She and one other student were in the lowest-income group, and one girl stood by herself in the highest-income group:

> And then there was one girl whose parents made over three hundred thousand dollars, and she looked incredibly guilty when she stood up. She stood up and kept her head down, and she seems the most ashamed out of everyone because everyone was staring at her and was, like, "Oh my God, your parents make that much money?" You could just hear the room, everyone's jaws dropped. We were all like, "What!" So I think it was even more [uncomfortable] for her. I mean it made people in the middle feel better because there was so many of them, but for people in the extremes, we were all just like, "What, what is this doing?" So now all of a sudden people have these judgments of us. Me and the other [low-income] girl we were like, "Oh, there's the poor kids," and the girl that's really wealthy, everyone's like, "Oh, she's just here on Daddy's paycheck." And some people automatically give these judgments. We didn't even know each others' names, and we're already judging because we know the class backgrounds of all the people.

Meredith describes how she observed this girl's body language, how embarrassed she looked, and Meredith's own perception of the room's reaction. In her description of the event, Meredith rhetorically places the "really wealthy" girl in with herself and the other "poor kid," describing the "judgments [people make] of *us*" (my emphasis), signifying that she empathizes with this more-affluent student as being subject to a similar kind of stigma.

Similarly, when I was walking around campus after lunch with Becca, a discussion of "legacy students" came up—students whose family members had attended Linden. I asked Becca if there were many such students around, and she replied that she was not aware of many. However, she stressed, these students might not be very open about their backgrounds: "It might be uncomfortable to share that kind of information, because it would imply that you got in easier that way, that you got in because of your family connections." I asked her whether she thought family wealth worked that way, whether it was something affluent students felt like they wanted to keep to themselves. "Maybe," Becca replied, "especially now that the college is open about taking a certain number of admissions need-aware [i.e., with attention to the student's ability to pay the full cost]. No one wants the implication that they don't deserve to be here, that they didn't get in on their own merits. It could be very awkward."

Upper-income students' defensiveness on this issue could also be seen elsewhere in exchanges on campus. For example, Linden students maintained an online bulletin board, a sort of internal Craigslist on which students could post about topics of interest to them either anonymously or publicly. It was mostly used for things such as seeking a ride or a used book, complaining about college policies or meals in the dining hall, and occasionally for social issues. Tensions around socioeconomic inequality and the meanings of difference sometimes came through in postings about financial aid and family money, engendering sometimes lengthy back-and-forth debates about the relationship between hard work, deservingness, and financial status. For example, a comment posted to the student online bulletin board about people being "spoiled" prompted the following responses:

Comment One: Just because someone is given money does not necessarily mean they are spoiled. My parents have money. We went on expensive vacations, had nice things, all that. It doesn't make me spoiled. My character wasn't affected by it. I'm not indulgent. I know how other people without money live.

Comment Two: Yeah, seriously. I had only worked once before I came to Linden, and that doesn't make me spoiled or lazy or lacking character or something.

Comment Three: Okay, since it offends you: You're not spoiled. I mean, I don't know you at all. You might sweat a lot and have a different outfit for every hour making the laundry super expensive. You might be allergic to everything besides filet mignon and caviar. Sounds rough. Hope you can use the resources at this school, get a fabulous job, and stop struggling.

The first poster clarifies that "just because" she has money does not mean she is "spoiled." In other words, she works hard and, by extension, deserves her place at Linden. These connections are even more clear in the following comment's word choices of "spoiled or lazy," while the implied accusation of the third comment is sarcastically direct about the putative nonconnection between money and hard work. Low- and high-income levels are therefore difficult and sensitive topics because they relate not only to one's home life or background experiences but also to students' qualifications to attend college as equals.

Moral Worries and Silent Inequalities

These interactions provide examples of what Mike Savage and his coauthors refer to as the "loaded moral signifier" of class, a quality that makes class a deeply personal and private issue.[9] While class itself is silent, moral meanings stemming from class positions are nonetheless a threat. Low socioeconomic status students did not want to open themselves up to questions about why they could not afford to join in certain activities—indeed, these kinds of questions seemed to be experienced more as questions about "what's wrong with you?" Moreover, in some cases, they did not want to expose themselves to having to manage friends' reactions, which were often along the lines of Michelle's recollection, "Ah, look you're poor!" This perception of morality and class shaped low socioeconomic status students' management efforts profoundly in the ways that they perceived the salience of class inequality and in terms of how to negotiate it within friendships.

Alice highlighted this issue in her discussion of why people didn't speak openly about class. She believed that low socioeconomic status students "don't want to be labeled as someone who's . . . from working class. They don't want to admit that they struggle. It's not—it's embarrassing, and there's a chain attached to having to struggle and not having enough money. So people don't want to bring that up. It makes them uncomfortable; it's just a really uncomfortable thing to talk about." In a later interview, Alice elaborated that people can sometimes talk about socioeconomic status in academic classes, perhaps in sociology or other courses where one can be confident that at least the listener will share the same concepts, making the latent burden of explaining why people might struggle a little less imposing. She thought that outside of class, however, with people who don't share the same formal institutionalized understanding about inequality, and especially people from different socioeconomic backgrounds, it's just "too awkward." In those circumstances, "you will have to explain everything, like a teacher. And that's too emotionally stressful to have to do all the time."

Meredith perceived similar potential problems in having to explain and anticipating others' negative beliefs about her. Her mother had long been a recipient of disability income because she was unable to work. This status is linked to assumptions about people who receive welfare and other forms of government support, in particular to their moral character:

> I know with me in particular, because my mom is disabled, we live off taxpayer money. We live off a government check, and so a lot of people find that really problematic because a lot of people think the government shouldn't support people like that—they're just lazy. A lot of people think people on disability don't actually need it; and there's actually a huge process you have to go through to get disability. . . . So it's a really hard process, so growing up we were on welfare for a little bit, and that's problematic itself because people think women are just pumping out children to get more welfare checks. A lot of times people just think if you're poor you're either abusing the system or you're lazy.

For Meredith, not having money comes from a family dependence on welfare that is specifically linked to "abusing the system or . . . laz[iness]." To stay out of this area of conversation and explanation, she avoids topics that will require her to impart any kind of information.

Brianna, also, spoke about this kind of questioning when we talked about how there sometimes seems to be a sense of shame attached to money. Nodding her head in agreement, she responded: "Right—when you don't have some. You know, there's something wrong, well, why don't you? As if it's just something you can go out and like collect in a bucket [laughs]."

Quinn shared this sentiment. She told me that "when class comes into discussion you invariably have to talk about yourself" in order to elaborate. Although Quinn says she doesn't feel uncomfortable with wealthy peers, she prefers to keep a tight conversational grip on the interaction so that she doesn't need to talk too much about her background:

> LIZ: So, do you ever feel hesitant to sort of talk about your own back-ground?
>
> QUINN: Oh yeah. I hate that shit. It invariably leads to pity or me feeling like I'm in these conversations that I just don't like having, ever.
>
> Liz: Right.
>
> Quinn: Ever. It's like it's never more clear in those instances that you are two people who are standing across from each other and are not the same. And no one wants to think of themselves as fundamentally different, you know?

This is exemplary of what many respondents described: managing the interaction so as to avoid difficult questions that led to further questions and details, what Genesis called "personal issues, private issues." Similarly, Alice told me, "People always ask questions like, 'Why can't you go out,' and usually I try to come up with excuses, like, 'Oh, I'm too busy.' But a lot of times it's that I just don't have the money, but I don't want to tell them I don't have the money because then they're going to be like, 'What do you mean you don't have the money?'" As we see in Alice, Meredith, Quinn, and other respondents' replies, the distinct, but typically un-named, moral semiotics of class that arises in direct conversation about inequality—or even discussions of topics that might make inequality more evident—compels students to avoid these conversations. Class is never simple to explain, and once you get started, respondents seemed to feel, you're going to have to tell the whole thing, exposing yourself and your family life to question, comparison, and possibly judgment. Your listeners may not be well equipped to understand such experiences, having little connection to them personally or perception that these issues might affect students on campus—economic hardships and other associated struggles were often represented as taking place with other people, off campus. Respondents often wished, therefore, to leave class inequalities below the surface in interactions, managing their conversations to make them of as little significance as possible.

Putting Inequality on the Backburner

In some cases, respondents described making these interactional efforts deeper than simple conversation management. Rather than trying to avoid talking about differences directly, they worked to avoid noticing them in the first place. As Aleisha put it, "sometimes I don't want to know about peoples' financial backgrounds because I don't want to align or put myself against them." When she is in the dining hall or the campus center or her residence hall she does not want to look around and imagine or assume that everyone else is affluent or to feel negatively about people because of that assumption. It is simply easier for her to grant a kind of anonymity to the people around her.

As these kinds of reflections indicate, knowing too much about friends' socioeconomic statuses often created interactional difficulties. It demonstrates the ways that willful ignorance is used as a tactic to sidestep the underlying semiotics of class morality. For example, Lynne described the contrast between too much focus on difference and being able to feel she "belong[s] here":

> You don't want to make them [affluent friends] feel like they need to apologize, you know? It's not their fault, but when it comes up, they feel it's their fault for some reason. I know it's not their fault, and I don't want to make it turn into a power issue. Like, okay, systemically, in society and the world, yeah, it's about power, it's about who has money. . . . But individually, I don't want to turn it into a power issue. I don't want it to be like [that] because you do want to feel like—as a normal living, breathing human being with emotions, I want to feel like I belong here or can relate to some of these people. I want to feel I can have friends here. That stuff gets in the way of me creating those healthy relationships. That's why I'd rather not talk about with my friends who is on financial aid and how much financial aid they're on.

In order to avoid making difference into "a power issue," and in order to avoid making other people feel guilty or uncomfortable, Lynne avoids topics like financial aid. While she sees that "systemically . . . in the world . . .

it's about power" and "who has money," she rejects those dynamics in her life at Linden. And, while she doesn't want her friends to feel discomfort, she also wants to ease her own social experiences, as well—to feel like she "belong[s] here or can relate to some of these people."

Similarly, Victoria described over coffee in the student center one sunny afternoon how she felt

> just so aware that I didn't want to be aware to a point where it was going to push me over. . . . It is not my job to analyze everyone else, and I don't want to be overanalyzing everyone else's actions towards me 24/7 and being like, "Was that a class thing? What is going on in this dialogue subliminally?" I think that was not what I wanted from this [experience], and a lot of times that happened anyways, but I didn't want to be conscious of it all the time.

By avoiding "overanalyzing" what other students might mean or not mean "subliminally," by pushing awareness of class and income differences to the back of her mind, Victoria is able to have more of the college experience that she wanted. This has not been without effort, as she noted when she reflected that she "personally didn't go to the CAL meetings" because "I saw the documentary that they showed last year, and after seeing it I was so upset that I—I thought it was wonderful, but it upset me so much to see it and be more aware of everything on campus that I couldn't go to their meetings because I thought it would really make me stressed out." Engaging with socioeconomic inequality, for example by attending CAL meetings, would have made Victoria too "stressed out." Although she is aware of differences—"a lot of times that happened anyways"—she prefers to let them lie dormant in her thinking in order not to focus too heavily on this aspect of her Linden life.

Magdalena reflected that "it adds an extra layer to any kind of even informal relationship you might have." That is, direct acknowledgement of inequality is undesirable because it creates an "extra layer" of stress or discomfort that must be dealt with. And, as Michelle stressed, people want to "make friends, not enemies."

Other respondents thought that pointing out class differences might be counterproductive because it might put people on the defensive. Anna explained her thoughts on this with what seemed like frustration that had built up over several years.

ANNA: It costs so much to go [to Linden]. The people here are gener-
       ally pretty well off. And I mean I think I am someone who is
       on financial aid or who is working-class background—it's more
       personal that you're here. It's more, it's not just a right that you're
       here, it's like a privilege: you fought to be here, and [you're] earn-
       ing your way. You're taking all these loans and whatever. And
       a lot of times you just feel other people don't understand where
       you're coming from. They don't understand how hard it is for
       you. These people, it's like they have life [handed to them] on a
       platter, and it's upsetting to everybody else because they don't. . . .
       You're jealous because they're rich and that they don't have to
       work for anything now.

LIZ: Right.

ANNA: And that they can complain about their BMW. . . . I am hoping
       my car makes it for, like, a couple months. . . . So I think that's
       the big difference, and so, it's just, I don't know—you look at
       people, and you think what a waste it is, they have all this money,
       and they don't even understand the gift they've been given.

LIZ: Right. And can you say that kind of thing to somebody? Can
       you say like, "I bust my ass to be here" or "I grew up with these
       circumstances"?

ANNA: No, because that's like pointing a finger at them. You can't point
       a finger at somebody else. And even if you did, they'd be like,
       "I worked hard in my life, and you don't understand what my life is
       going like." And they're, "Oh, give me a break." So there's no point.

For Anna, class differences seem clear in terms of resources and in terms
of attitude. Her more-affluent peers seemed to her not to appreciate their
opportunities, their cars, their free time, and the relative lack of stress involved in not having to take out loans. (Anna's thoughts on this may serve
as an illustration of what Aleisha says she is trying to avoid by not thinking
about class differences.) The moral differences between having "earned"
entry into college rather than having it handed to you "on a platter" and
not having "worked" are also clear, providing further evidence of the
kinds of judgments students at the wealthier end of the economic spectrum may hope to avoid. Anna nonetheless believes that "pointing a finger"
is the wrong approach, and she withholds her criticisms.

As Magdalena noted as she talked with me one afternoon in the student
center cafeteria, "sometimes [class is] an exhausting exercise that it can be

put on the back burner—other things take precedence." She explained that class differences and inequalities are so awkward and difficult to talk about that they distract from the "main goal" of college and other things that demand students' time and energy.

> Especially at school, we have so much other stuff on our plates. First of all, what's our main goal here: to get our education, our BAs, and leave. That's why we're technically here at Linden, fundamentally, so that's it. And then we have some other outside activities that we're involved in, and that becomes a stressful situation as well, and just adding one more stressful interaction is sometimes not needed.

In other words, students' shared experiences on campus, and their shared priorities of education and social interactions, are given "precedence" over the difficult work of sorting out inequality.

Managing Direct Conflicts around Class

There are times when inequality can't be left on the back burner, when it is simply unavoidable. In these cases, low socioeconomic status students often tried to negotiate the discrepancies between themselves and their friends in ways that would allow all parties to feel comfortable and preserve the friendship. This sometimes involved straining to make wildly different socioeconomic capacities interpretable as commensurate. Evelyn, for instance, described the challenges of figuring out how to negotiate shared social life with friends who have more money to spend. She described two interactions with her roommate, who was becoming a close friend despite the short length of time the two had been acquainted and their very different backgrounds. In each interaction, Evelyn needed to work out what felt like the right way to uphold her end of their friendship in the face of their financial differences:

> With my roommate, she's never been like, "Here, have a ton of money." But there was a situation where they bought this printer, this beautiful three hundred dollar printer, and it wasn't compatible with her computer. So I came back from work one day, and her mom was there, and the printer was—I don't remember where it was. She's like, "Oh, hey, do you want the

printer?" And I was like, "Well, what do you mean?" And her mom was like, "Yeah, I don't want to just throw the printer away, so I was thinking about putting it in the hallway with a free sign on it, but then I figured I'd ask you first if you wanted it." And I was like, "Well, I could pay you for some of it. I feel kind of bad just taking your three hundred dollar printer."

After some protestation, Evelyn was convinced to accept the printer. As she said, "Well, if you were just going to put it in the hall, then okay, I will take it," and her roommate went off to buy a new one. Evelyn continued by adding a story about her roommate buying her dinner one night when fish was being served in every dining hall—something Evelyn really disliked:

> So I was like, "Crap, do you think you could bring something back for me for dinner?" And I went to go grab money out of my purse, and she was like, "Oh, don't worry about it, don't worry about it." And I'm like, "No, really, here." And she's like, "No, no, no. My grandparents are paying for dinner. It's not a big deal. And even if I was paying for dinner, it's not a big deal." And then she just left and I was like, "Okay."

Here again, Evelyn felt reluctant to accept her roommate's offer to buy her something—even if someone is paying for her roommate's dinner. These two interactions illustrated for Evelyn not only the difference in her and her roommate's financial circumstances but how complicated it is to figure out what is the right way to interact in the face of that difference: Accept the offer even if it makes her feel uncomfortable? Turn it down and risk offending someone? And she noted that it's even further complicated by the fact that in these interactions, money is actually quite hidden:

> So it really is interesting because she never directly is outright with, "Here, have money!" But when we're doing something or the dinner thing, for me it's kind of like a battle. Part of me is like I wish I was at a point where I could just do this by myself and no big deal, and then part of me is like, "Well, if you're willing to, then okay." But then I think about the times when I have had a little bit of money and I go out to coffee with a friend and I'll be like, "No, I'll get your coffee." So maybe it's something similar like that, except we're just on different scales. For me coffee is what I can do. And for her, printers is what she can do.

Evelyn's reckoning of how to think about equitable exchange and the practice of "spotting" (paying for) someone was complicated by the fact that while she could afford coffee, her roommate could afford printers and dinners. Again, how can both parties enter social interactions equally on such terms?

In some cases, students' choices about how to manage these particular moments led to friendships being dissolved. As noted in the section on direct approaches to inequality, these kinds of forthright discussions were very fraught for low socioeconomic status students as well as for their more-affluent peers. Danielle had this experience. She had formed a close circle of friends, each of whom was wealthier than herself. At first, this seemed exemplary of what she'd hoped to find at a diverse liberal arts college campus, a group with different life experiences nonetheless united by shared interests. However, after Danielle confronted the group about issues around socioeconomic differences, the friendships became untenable:

> Last year, first semester, I had like a really close group of friends. All them had more money than I do, and I thought it was really cool that we were still able to be such good friends. But then things kind of came to a head at the end of the first semester, and really came down to not understanding each other and mostly not understanding me. One example they gave when they were telling me why they were upset with me, which is a really petty thing: they ordered food, and the person doing the math just divided evenly, and I said, "I can't pay that. I can only pay for what I ordered." She said, "You should just trust that everything is going to even out in the end; we're all friends." And I said, "You don't understand—I can't [because] my mom and I have financial issues." . . . And they don't understand that.

Her friends were not able to accept Danielle's need to pay strictly for her own portion and her inability to "just trust that everything is going to even out in the end." Danielle's choice to be open with her friends about this seems to have led directly to their shutting her out of the group.

Evelyn's experience ended up becoming somewhat similar. Despite working to understand her roommate's perspective, the vast differences in their socioeconomic positions made their friendship extremely difficult to maintain. Over the course of a year, they shifted from being very close friends to fighting often. While these fights were not always explicitly about class inequality, they seemed to often come back to their different beliefs about class. For instance, Evelyn told me about one such fight that ranged over a couple of evenings:

> We were bringing up a previous conversation about how lower-class people would be more thankful for money if they were to get it and have a differ-ent attitude to upper-class people who already have that kind of money. . . . I really had to hold my [tongue, because], she's like, "You're just bitter and angry because you don't come from a place of money, and you don't know if you'll ever get to that place." . . . So the subject got brought up again last night about class, and she was like, "We get along on everything except this whole class thing." So I was like, "So let's just not talk about it because I don't really feel like being pissed off."

Evelyn's account here recalls other respondents' efforts, and her own ear-lier attempts, to push class inequality to the margins in their social rela-tionships. In this case, however, it seemed to re-center itself, to re-emerge in new fights. By the end of their first year, they had decided to no longer room together and effectively ended their friendship. Notably, the qualities at the core of their ongoing argument were moral comparisons—greater or lesser levels of gratitude, hard work—and the pathway that Evelyn tried to take to keep the peace in avoiding discussion of class inequality, of what her friend called "the whole class thing."

Class inequality is a formative but often silenced aspect of shared life for low socioeconomic status students on campuses where the majority of stu-dents are more affluent than themselves. As we can see, students often seek actively to avoid talking about class inequality and, in some cases, even to avoid awareness of socioeconomic differences. These strategies are shaped both by the larger semiotics of class morality and, more specifically, by the way class morality is understood through the key lenses of merit and com-munity, each of which is crucial to Linden student identity.

Like the college, students struggle with concerns about inequality, with "how to be together but not the same," in the words of one Linden ad-ministrator. Students confront these concerns through their social inter-actions and relationships with more-affluent classmates. Instead of being isolated in separate social worlds, low socioeconomic status students must continually negotiate and renegotiate the meanings and salience of class through their friendships. Friendships are a key venue, in other words, in which students must negotiate the implications of class inequality. We see that the ways that inequality is manifested, understood, and negotiated are shaped by the broader semiotics of class morality that positions only some students as legitimate community members. Here, semiotics takes on particular importance through lenses of community and merit, two areas of special meaning to students. Moral threats in both areas shape students' choices to leave inequality "on the backburner," silenced but nonetheless important.

Rather than a scenario in which low socioeconomic status students are acted upon, here we have a scenario in which low-income students are active in maintaining a process that may serve their situational needs but ultimately does not address long-term concerns around campus equity and inclusion. On the one hand, low-income students' tendency to suppress or silence their differences supports the development of friendships by allowing everyone to avoid uncomfortable discussions. On the other hand, the silence around inequality and frequent refusal to acknowledge it reduces chances for students to address problems or dissatisfactions openly. Given that low-income students are more likely than others to drop out, repeatedly transfer, or "stop out" (i.e., take time off from school),[10] it is important to understand what happens in the years between enrollment and graduation. Better insights about how low socioeconomic students manage interactions with peers and friends can add to a broader understanding of their successes and even, as Laura D. Pittman and Adeya Richmond indicate, suggest avenues for action by college administrators to support positive social interactions.[11]

One primary lesson here is that, despite the college's efforts to manage inequality through policy and program actions, students nonetheless must confront and manage inequality individually within their own friendships and personal lives. While the residential system often precludes students from "boasting" about their advantages (in the words of one respondent), it also brings with it particular cultural practices that subvert and make untouchable students' class statuses. Rather than a seamless comfort zone of classlessness, this subversion feels false to many low-socioeconomic respondents and leads to a hiding of status rather than an acceptance of difference. These data again make clear that organizational structure and culture are important for the ways that inequality can be navigated at the individual and interpersonal level. This latter point is especially important for understanding elite colleges. In the next chapter I shift to an examination of how an organized group of students attempts to tackle these sets of issues as part of their advocacy for low-income, working-class, and first-generation students at Linden.

4

Activism and Representation

Organizing Class

When I arrived at the Class Activists of Linden meeting one early fall evening, club leaders Violet and Heather were already there, commiserating. Heather had just told Violet the outcome of their application for club funding: CAL was awarded only $296 for their annual budget by the student-run board that distributes money to campus groups. This was many thousands lower than the requested $14,000—in fact, it was thousands less than the prior year's awarded budget of $4,000. Heather had found out first and already had had a little time to let it sink in; Violet had just found out and was taking the news very hard. Standing, she sank her head into her hands. "I can't believe it," she groaned. She seemed to tear up a little and sank her head down farther, like a person who is trying to avoid hyperventilating. Heather gave her a quick hug and rubbed her back a little, telling her, "Don't stress too much. We will appeal." Violet looked back up and responded heatedly: "It's no holds barred! I want to put up banners! It's so insulting! It's so fucked up! I can't believe this!" She paused for a breath and sighed, "I'm sorry [that I'm so emotional], it just feels so personal."

The Class Activists of Linden presented an interesting and rare window into questions about how to manage class inequality. CAL is one of the few student-run campus groups in the United States dedicated to this specific topic, namely advocacy and education about class inequality on campus. How can a student group like CAL negotiate silences around class? Do semiotics of class morality shape possibilities for activism and advocacy around class inequality? Many of CAL's goals revolved around increasing talk about and direct recognition of class inequality as such. This pushes them to make difficult choices about how to represent or frame class inequality. On the one hand, creating evocative narratives of class using personal stories provides credibility and motivates listeners. On the other hand, framing class in personal ways is risky because it creates vulnerabilities—being part of a group doesn't mitigate social pressures about leaving class inequality unexpressed. The incident that opens this chapter expresses part of what is so challenging about efforts to provide advocacy and education on campus: the tension between presenting class as personal, which is how it feels, and presenting class as abstracted and political, which allows students to sidestep direct expressions of inequality.

In this chapter I examine CAL's collective efforts to engage in the group's explicit mission of class activism within the context of student- and institutional-level silences around class inequality. I argue that this work was made more complicated by the same semiotics of class morality that underlie peer interactions described in chapter 3 and is exacerbated by structural constraints in the ways that clubs are funded at Linden. Because there are so few similar clubs on other campuses, I begin by outlining a brief history of CAL. (An account of my time spent with this group can be found in the appendix, where I discuss my methods in detail.) I contextualize the potential importance of student clubs for low socioeconomic status students in the book's conclusion.

Background

Many nationwide campus clubs like the Class Activists of Linden, organized around so-called identity politics such as racialized, ethnic, or gendered identities, sprang from campus activist movements that agitated for many years for recognition. However, there have been few broad-scale social movements around class inequality or for low-income and working-class people, making for a different history for clubs like CAL. CAL itself was created in the early 2000s, though other groups with similar goals have existed at Linden on and off since the 1980s. Earlier iterations of the group were centered around activist approaches to welfare policy and other state-specific issues; in some cases, the group's mission of serving Linden students became subservient to broader political goals. For example, one earlier group took up local union organizing and subsequently shifted their mission entirely. The contemporary iteration of CAL at the time of my study was small, but its members worked hard to have a visible presence on campus. CAL had between four and seven students at most meetings. (Larger clubs had fifteen or more regular members.) In addition to its active participants, CAL maintained an e-mail list of over two hundred students, faculty members, administrators, and a few alumnae. CAL encouraged students from any background to join but was explicit about its goal of representing and advocating for low-income, working-class, and first-generation students.

During my time at Linden, CAL typically met once a week, with occasional extra meetings for planning special events. Meetings lasted about an hour and were run by the president or co-presidents. Topics included planning events, responding to new issues on campus, talking about members' feelings and thoughts, and broader discussions related to class and education. The meetings were often more instrumental than emotional, however, with the club functioning more as an advocacy organization than as a support group. As noted, I went to almost all CAL meetings for two years, spending many hours with the group. I interviewed all five of the CAL presidents and a number of regular and occasional members during the years I spent at Linden, as well as three earlier presidents who were by then alumnae. (I also sat in on meetings for an administration-founded effort to make class a more open topic on campus, which provides a counterpoint and secondary set of analyses at the close of this chapter.) During both years, CAL students struggled to develop effective ways of advocating for themselves and other socioeconomically disadvantaged students on campus. This entailed understanding what the most pressing issues facing low socioeconomic status students were, developing ideas for how to address them, and educating both peers and administrators about low socioeconomic status students at Linden. CAL's goals included both policy changes and what we might think of as cultural changes, shifting the way that Linden community members think and talk about socioeconomic inequality. And, of course, they needed to keep the club viable by recruiting new members each year and supporting the current members. Underlying these broad goals were more complex tasks of deciding what constitutes socioeconomic disadvantage in the Linden setting and how to represent those experiences to nonmembers.

Over the years, CAL has emphasized varying aspects of these missions. During some periods, CAL students were primarily interested in action and advocacy, while at other times the group functioned almost solely as a safe-space resource. It has also struggled with how to include students from varying backgrounds. Although the club described itself as being for low-income, working-class, and first-generation students, it also includes allies and students who see themselves as fitting into these categories in some way, even though the college did not recognized them as such. The inclusion of allies, in particular, has been difficult. As Heather told me, they got tired of having to explain everything to well-meaning but confused affluent students. These kinds of struggles over definitions and purpose bring us back to the focus of this chapter: CAL members' discussions about how to talk about class in their efforts to raise awareness of inequality on campus.

Representing Class

Each of CAL's primary goals required the group to push for greater attention to class inequality on campus, particularly the needs of low socioeconomic status students. Given their peers' reticence to talk about class directly—a reticence often shared by CAL members themselves—and the close emotional understanding of the campus community, CAL students had to think carefully about how to represent class inequality on campus.

Framing Class as Personal   These challenges can be examined through CAL's short-lived effort to create a documentary film about class inequality on campus, a project that was finally shelved after months of trying to pull together interviews. The project was intended to update an existing one-hour documentary made by past CAL students featuring individual club members telling their own stories.[1] Several years after the original film was made, at the time I was doing my field work, the documentary was still being shown. It had become one of the best tools for generating club interest, more effective even than holding "open table" information sessions during new-student week, making classroom announcements, or using online tools such as e-mail listservs or Facebook. During the second year I was at Linden, CAL showed the documentary twice, both times getting greater attendance than anticipated and generating discussion.

Based on the success of that documentary, the CAL students, spearheaded by co-presidents Amber and Genesis, decided to make a newer, updated version. CAL student members decided that the new film, in contrast to the earlier one, would include information about the campus more broadly, including how students thought about class and about as many people's backgrounds as possible—it would take the college's "pulse" on class. CAL members first decided to come up with a list of survey questions to measure a person's class. Working from a list of "icebreaker" questions from a workshop held by a class educator in earlier years, they selected the topics they thought would be most helpful. Of course, class isn't easily summarized, and the process was slow: as a group and over the course of several meetings CAL tried to work through the core experiences of living in a given class location. This process highlighted tensions between relying on personal stories and reticence to talk about personal issues, as well as the difficulty of finding markers to represent class positions.

The group first set out to develop ten questions. We began by reading the list of thirty-six questions from the earlier document aloud in the meeting, weeding out the ones people did not think were useful and combining those that could be combined. Along the way, the CAL students collectively gauged whether the statement seemed to really get at something that rang true in them. The test seemed to be whether students in the group did or did not do or experience the topic of the question, confirming whether or not it was a good measure of low-income or working-class life. I wrote down the questions because I volunteered to make the survey using an online survey tool, since I had experience with this. Some were easy to decide on: "Did your mother go to college?" got combined with "Did your father go to college?" Students also agreed on including a question about whether one had been supported in schooling through test prep classes, tutoring, or private lessons. After these few, things got more complicated as the participants compared their experiences of growing up with various levels of socioeconomic struggle.

As they discovered, students in the room who made up most of the core CAL group and ostensibly shared a low socioeconomic status had varied experiences, which made it difficult to evaluate whether these questions were reliable indicators. "What about summer camp, for example?" Genesis reported, "I went to summer camp; there was some free program." Another student agreed, "Yeah, that's probably not a good one." A question about home ownership is also less straightforward than it seemed. Meredith noted, "We owned our home, but it's a trailer." Questions about credit cards got some discussion because some people had debit cards that have Master-Card symbols on them and kind of function as credit cards. By contrast, Genesis said she's "kind of surprised," because she never had a bank account before she was eighteen. Other people chimed in to compare—they'd had them since sixteen. Meredith reported that she has a friend who got a credit card as soon as she turned eighteen (i.e., once you can do it without family cosigners) and that a lot of her friends who are poor have them and use them for financing and overspending. Finally, the issue of having to be aware of family bills while growing up could not be agreed on. Michelle said she wasn't sure that anyone knows that stuff, but Meredith responded, "Dude, I paid all my family's bills. I own my family," and added that she is now trying to help her older sister get out of a lot of debt.

In many cases, students didn't find the measures meaningful or came up with too many workarounds. For example, a question about whether anyone on TV looks or speaks like you got some discussion, specifically about whether people on TV who look or talk like you are represented in a positive light. One student says she doesn't really "get" this question. No one talks like her: she's unique and an individual, she says, grinning. Others seem to be ambivalent about the question. To me, it seemed like this question was clearly about whether people of color and low-income or working-class people are represented well on TV, but no one took it up. They pointed out that, like Paris Hilton, you can be white and wealthy and still be represented badly. A related question about clothes also gets some skepticism. Genesis took issue, saying, "If I am rocking something donated and looking fresh, that doesn't mean I have money. It's easy to get designer stuff on crazy sale." Meredith agrees, "I never buy stuff full price! Looking good doesn't mean you're upper class."

Other questions got different reactions because of geographic or urban/ rural differences. A question about museums, for example, didn't get much interest. Genesis chuckled that even if she had money she probably wouldn't go to a museum. Meredith chimed in that she grew up in the country and there aren't any museums around. Another question was about having a computer at home. Someone asks, "Does a computer at school count?" Genesis got one through a program at school and asks another student who grew up in the same city whether she did as well—no, comes the answer, but she agreed there are lots of nonprofits that provide opportunities to gain access to computers in such a large city.

By contrast, people seemed pretty enthusiastic about asking whether you pay your own cell phone bills. This seemed to fit in the same symbolic category as "using daddy's credit card," and people agreed that this is a sure sign of being middle class or wealthy. A question about getting a car before the age of eighteen that was not a hand-me-down also got agreement and strong reactions and led to an even more extreme comparison: Genesis mentioned that she knew someone at Linden who was given a yacht as a gift. People responded with incredulity: "What! No way! Can you imagine owning a yacht?" Working through these topics over the course of an hour, the group was eventually able to select ten questions to ask potential respondents.

That even within this highly self-selected group of students such an agreement was not readily reached is indicative of not only variety among students—a point often lost in sociological and other representations of class difference that flatten differences within groups—but also how slippery a topic class is, how difficult it is to capture adequately. More important, CAL's discussion of class markers highlights the way that students used their experiences as yardsticks for measuring class status. For CAL students, and presumably others, class is fundamentally personal because it is measured, illustrated, and understood in personal terms through story and experience. Extrapolating somewhat, their discussion suggests that responses to the resulting survey would immediately generate comparisons because students used their own experiences as sounding boards. We therefore see the ways that class quickly becomes experienced as relative and comparative.

Putting class inequality in personal terms was even more challenging as the group moved into the second phase of the process, looking for people to speak on camera about their own classed experiences. The goal was to have students from across the socioeconomic spectrum. However, CAL members found it difficult to get students from *any* socioeconomic background interested in appearing in a documentary about class. CAL students spread the word through other clubs, e-mails, and class announcements but got little response. In addition to potential problems arising from the topic itself, a related hurdle may have been that they opted to interview people at the weekly CAL meetings, a step that afforded little privacy and may have made people uncomfortable. As it turned out, the few students who volunteered all ended up backing out.

On the first proposed interview evening, two students stopped by to volunteer. The students, a pair of friends who were members of another activist group on campus, said they were interested in the documentary after hearing about it from a former CAL member. Both seemed to know almost nothing about the intended content or about CAL as a group. They had heard that a documentary related to "social justice issues" was being made. The two potential interviewees inquired about what CAL did on campus, the questions that they would be asked, and the overall process of making the documentary. They were interested in building a conversation about class, and they were handed copies of the ten or so interview questions that the group had developed. Genesis explained that "the questions are designed to give us a sense of your class background." Amber, the other co-president, quickly added that the potential interviewees would be talking about class and privilege at Linden more generally: "People you know's experiences," Amber said, shifting what Genesis had said onto somewhat more impersonal ground.

These explanations did not elicit an immediately enthusiastic reaction in either potential interviewee. One asked, "Did you want to interview us now, tonight?" as they looked over the list of question they would be asked. Both subsequently left without being interviewed. (One explained that she was late for another meeting, and the other wanted to think things over.) They'd get back in touch, both said, but neither followed up. In a separate instance, Genesis asked a friend to come in for an interview, a woman she knew shared a similar background to her own. This step followed the recommendations of earlier CAL members, who suggested interviewing group members and friends. This friend wanted to do the interview but did not want her face to be used because she was afraid of offending her middle- and upper-income friends. This effectively negated her participation.[2] Soon after this attempt, the semester ended and the idea of making a film was let go.

In large part, the difficulties the group faced stemmed from people's discomfort with attacking the issue head-on: asking people to talk about class, especially their own, while being filmed appeared to be a nonstarter. Notably, none of the CAL students themselves volunteered to be interviewed, possibly because they envisioned the project as more outward than inward facing. Their responses during our interview conversations also show how talking openly about their own class experiences made them feel vulnerable. This made the prospect of relying on their own or others' personal stories as a frame for action extremely challenging. Personal narratives make the issue around which one is trying to organize just that—personal. They may place the speaker as the object of study, action, or pity. CAL students themselves did not want to appear to be asking for too much, whether pity or some form of support, from their peers. Sharing their own stories made them vulnerable to the kinds of judgments discussed in chapter 3 about personal worth and legitimacy as students. As Genesis movingly described to me, leaning in and speaking more softly during this section of an interview:

> I feel maybe there's—I don't know, money, like, some kind of status [or] respect behind money, having it. You have that respect and status, so when you let someone know [that you don't have money], like you become vulnerable, like you don't have that same . . . respect. It's just uncomfortable. I don't know why it's uncomfortable. It's private matters, personal matters, because they want to know—in a way you're telling your life story. In a way everyone who has financial issues, there's some kind of story behind it. I know mine is just a whole story behind it. I'm not trying to tell you the story because in order for you to understand, I feel I have to tell you and that's like letting that person know way too much about you, you don't want them to know.

For Genesis, talking about money, financial need, or economic disadvantage was risky because it required giving information she did not want people to know about her. Her invocation of the implications of even beginning such a story seemed to be like a crack in the proverbial dam. This concern about personal exposure was already clear in individual students' responses discussed in chapter 3; being part of a political advocacy or support group clearly did not lessen these worries. Working within a semiotics that associated class positions with moral positions, CAL students and others felt hesitant to frame class through their personal stories.

There are, however, also risks to *not* providing some personal stories. Without this personal disclosure, a person may not be seen as an acceptable source of information or leadership: social movement scholarship indicates that the authenticity of "real life" experiences and drawing on powerful emotions are crucial for making authoritative presentations.[3] Indications of the way that authenticity might be important could be heard through my interviews in different ways. For example, Magdalena, who had thought a great deal about class issues on campus, told me that students at Linden seem to want to identify with the people for whom they want to advocate. However, as she also said, this "false" identification with issues that are not "one's own," through dress, through self-presentation, or through club membership and activism, affect students' credibility. In fact, Magdalena had never joined CAL because she thought that some of the student leaders in past years had fallen into this category. She explained that a former member of CAL whom she knew from her first year at Linden had taken up an interest in socioeconomic issues on campus. This student had told Magdalena about her affluent background before becoming involved with CAL. Magdalena found her subsequent advocacy galling, as she related to me:

> [I was] trying to push away my own class background, and then to see someone who was superprivileged, you know, that kind of [trails off]. . . . I was like, I don't buy it from you. I can't buy it from you because you have so much in life, and you don't know what it's like not to have anything and you don't know what it's like to want. . . . All these white bread people who have decided that these issues matter because they finally realized their privilege but they don't actually have anything to do with it. Like they can go and slum it, but at the end of the day they can always come back home to mommy and daddy.

The dissonance between being "superprivileged" and socioeconomic activism outraged Magdalena.

Apple, a middle-class student and briefly one of the co-presidents of CAL during my research, expressed her own "misgivings" about serving as a leader in similar terms. Apple's mother had completed a master's degree and her father, a college degree. However, due to her mother's health issues and her parents' estranged marriage, Apple's family was on unstable economic ground by the time she went to college. As she told me in an interview, she wasn't a first-generation student and she didn't identify as working class or low income, even though her family had recently come to fit those demographics. Apple explained to me that even though her family didn't have money right now, she had a lot of cultural capital. As a result, she felt that she didn't know how to support low-income, working-class, or first-generation students, and she worried about her role as co-president— could she be a legitimate leader?

Students like Apple and Magdalena thought that leadership should reflect personal experience and knowledge of the issue being advocated and that it should be reflective of the experiences of the people for whom one is speaking. One's personal story therefore becomes a source of authenticity and, accordingly, authority. This presents a complication for CAL students: although personal stories are important for credibility and for mobilizing change, CAL students neither wanted to share their own stories nor could they get others to share personal stories. However, framing class as political had its own challenges.

Framing Class Using Abstract Narratives   In order to avoid relying on personal stories, the CAL students might have sought more abstract means of framing the issues they were concerned about. Many student clubs on campus used similar framing—what I refer to as celebrating culture and social justice—to generate interest and communicate their goals. This might seem to make sense for CAL as well, especially in managing a difficult topic like class inequality. Tapping into an accepted shared narrative provides a template for the teller as well as for the listener.[4] By relying on already sanctioned terms (i.e., by virtue of having been already used and accepted in the public sphere), students can align their group with a broader cause, thus appealing to a wider audience of ostensibly like-minded peers. Moreover, students can recruit interest while avoiding offense or controversy. However, each genre of presentation has its own requirements and its own unique challenges. Indeed, although cultural celebration and social justice appear to be superficially apt narrative frameworks, each presented particular problems for CAL students.

CELEBRATING CULTURE   As at other colleges, Linden student clubs frequently made use of what I call a "cultural celebration" diversity narrative. Under this framework, students put forward their discourse through posters, online posts, and other materials celebrating "cultural" characteristics, including race, ethnicity, and nationality, to draw in new members, to encourage other students to attend their events, and to draw attention to their thematic concerns. Culture here is a colloquial usage—food or art, for example—rather than a formal sociological usage. For example, Linden Mujeres, a club devoted to Latina/Chicana cultures, held annual dance performances as well as small sales of homemade food several times a year. The Cambodian Students' Association invited students to learn about Cambodia by attending events that featured Cambodian foods and Cambodian music. As these examples suggest, the celebration model also had a strong educational component. By attending or participating in an event, or even just purchasing a treat from a bake sale, one can learn a little bit about another nation, ethnicity, or group of people. And, as my terminology suggests, the wording and textual presentations involved invite the participant to feel *celebratory* about their diverse campus and the group about whom they are learning, especially since events were frequently timed to coincide with national or campus-specific holidays. With its positive and educational connotations, the celebration frame was often relied on in student club publicity.

Cultural celebration is at best a complicated potential option for CAL students, however, when presenting their events or recruitment efforts. At an elite college, the presentation of nonelite class cultures, if such a thing could be agreed on as representative, carries a strong risk of becoming a parody. "White trash" and "ghetto" parties are already a college norm, albeit less common at Linden than at many other campuses. While these had not happened in recent years at Linden, they are widely publicized in newspapers and thus exist for students as examples of what happens elsewhere. CAL students were not the only ones with concerns here: I heard other students critique these kinds of approaches when taken by the college.[5] Moreover, class "culture" is a thorny subject. What would a celebration of low-income or working-class cultures include? I asked Amber whether she, as co-president of CAL, thought it would be good to celebrate class diversity and, if so, what that might look like. She responded:

> I found the website for the University of Wisconsin class group, and they had a Celebrating Class Day, or something like that. Yeah, they had, like, this food thing that they did. And [long pause] it's just such a hard thing....

> I feel like it, especially with like the hipster movement that's going on right
> now, where this fashion of basically they're kind of like reclaiming lower,
> poor people's aesthetics of wearing mullets and like acid-washed jeans.
> They're trying to reclaim that and make that hip. And I think it'd be a very
> dangerous thing to. . . . First of all, I don't know how we'd, you know, de-
> fine the sort of "What is this class culture?" because it manifests itself in so
> many different ways. And also, if we did, I feel like it could be really diffi-
> cult and really, really hard to not come across as lampooning in some way,
> or like making a joke.

Amber worried specifically that by placing low-income or working-class
cultures in view as such, she might be complicit in a kind of "othering," af-
firming that low-income and working-class students are not Linden students in some way: "There's just this assumption that they're just, they're
those people, like they're othered." She worried about this not only in the
context of CAL but more broadly on campus. For example, in her residence hall, someone had suggested having a "redneck party." Amber recalled, "I was like, 'Uh, I don't know if we can do that. . . .' It never followed
through or anything, but uh . . . [trails off]." Celebrating working-class
or low-income cultures might be understood in this offensive framework
or perhaps as legitimizing future similar ideas. Thinking about class culture celebrations raised similar questions about who can speak to and for
these experiences. If affluent and middle-class peers are invited to celebrate working-class or low-income "cultures," what would those students
be getting permission to talk about or to celebrate? Would they, through
that celebration, engage in denigrating stereotypes or simplistic reductions
of first-generation, working-class, and low-income lives as struggles to
"survive" (in Barbara Jensen's words)?[6]

Furthermore, for some students, being low-income is not something to
celebrate but rather a painful and difficult personal history, the details of
which they would prefer to keep private. For example, the opening speaker
at a conference that CAL organized on campus opened her remarks by
saying that she had grown up "poverty class" and that she never understood or identified with people who would say things like, "We didn't have
a lot of money but we were rich in love." "Being poor," she continued, "is
not romantic. It's not some form of simple living." She got some knowing
chuckles from the students in the audience, including Violet and Heather,
who sat near me. Being from a low-income background can be painful, and

as Genesis noted earlier, "it's private matters, personal matters."[7] In short, respondents' feelings of vulnerability to moral assessment—of themselves and of their home communities and families—made a celebration frame uncomfortable.

Open discussion of personal background also comes with complicated emotional and performance negotiations. Admitting one's lack or need openly might lead others to think that one envies, covets, or wants a helping hand or pity. Students already sometimes experienced this in direct interpersonal exchanges, as Lynne described in recalling a time when she had had to explain to friends that she needed to pay only her portion of a dinner check:

> I remember this one time I went out to dinner with two of my friends at Linden. Neither are on financial aid. You know, they're probably two of my closest friends, and we never talk about them not being on financial aid and me being on financial aid. But something came up during dinner about splitting a check or something like that and me saying, "Oh no, I can't get this because it's just too much money." Then for some reason my friend's like, "Listen Lynne, I know you don't have that much money but . . . She got angry for a second and blew up. It made me feel bad, like I was doing a thing where it was like, "Feel bad for me."

Lynne described how the emotional dynamics of that moment were so tense that she and her friend both began crying at the restaurant. Afterward, they never talked about it. Lynne's experience captures precisely the worry about asking for too much or asking to be pitied, in this case being understood as asking her friend to "feel bad for [her]" and let her off the hook of sharing the bill. "Too much" talking about relative deprivation can send unintended messages, invite unwelcome scrutiny or pity, or simply make one a conversational bore. Lynne's exchange and its anticlimactic fallout also highlight the way that class inequality can be so confounding or uncomfortable to discuss that even very close friends would never discuss a misunderstanding that caused tears.

In each of these ways, we see the complex moral meanings that adhere to class, meanings that would be challenging to fit into a "celebration" model. A semiotics that links class to being othered or having reduced legitimacy as a community member is incompatible with celebration, and the dearth of open conversations about class inequality meant that CAL students and others were ill-equipped to facilitate cross-class conversations within this frame. I never saw CAL use it during my time on campus or in archival records.[8]

SOCIAL JUSTICE   A second narrative motif often used by Linden students is the broad theme of social justice. This is especially used by students working on themes related to politically liberal issues such as the environment, hunger relief, urban poverty, and sweatshop labor. Clubs using these themes tend to underline the importance of their work on specific projects to rouse students to volunteer or sign petitions and to create discursive links to larger political themes.

Although class has obvious potential links to the social justice frame, this narrative also presents problems for CAL students. Demanding social justice posits a victim who deserves justice and on whose behalf one acts. For CAL students, this means they or their family members are positioned as victims, which would highlight their own socioeconomic disadvantage. Often, the social justice frame was deployed by students who didn't necessarily have firsthand experience of the injustice against which they were agitating. Indeed, the social justice frame was often presented as an "us" on campus who were helping and a "them" off campus who were being helped, which was problematic for CAL members and for other low socioeconomic status students, who were sometimes critical of this frame. For example, raising awareness about hunger might take the form of volunteering at a soup kitchen, implicitly framing the problem as something that takes place somewhere else and to other people. Students from low-income and working-class backgrounds told me that there was an underlying perception of Linden students as being middle class. For example, one respondent told me about overhearing another student say, "You know Linden—everyone is middle class here." Linden as a place and Linden students were thus perceived as exempt from having experienced hunger and poverty and other class-related injustices. Maya explained, "It's kind of hard to come back here [from home] and hear people write papers about like teenaged mothers or about people in the military or things like that" as though these are social problems to be dealt with or just so many statistics. She continued, "It's distant [to students here], and it's not distant for everybody. Like my friends [from home don't] ever come here, but it's more than like papers [for us]—or more than your thesis statement, you know. [But] it's kind of hard to get people [here] to see . . . talking about [these issues], it's not necessarily statistics." It rankles Maya to hear her peers positioning her friends and family as abstract subjects to be studied rather than real people. This positioning suggests again a sense of otherness, as though these circumstances are distant from the experiences of Linden students.

Such comparisons were troubling for others as well. Evelyn, who spent her childhood in a local small city that was on unstable economic footing, was annoyed by the dramatic-sounding characterization of her neighborhood as "inner city" by Linden peers who worried about how safe they might be if they ventured in to it. Amber also spoke about this tension between an abstracted other and the invisibility of Linden students who experience the same problems:

> I do think it's interesting that we're always [trails off]. There are all these events of like, you know, Human Rights Coffee House or like an auction to benefit Haiti. And I think these things are all really great, but at the same time—and I don't know if this is part of the upper-middle-class activist mentality—but [these are] obviously legitimate issues, and you know we all contribute to those kinds of issues through globalization and all that. But, I don't know, it just seems really [pause] contradictory to have these types of things and then to just ignore the injustice that's happening on your own campus that you actively participate in.

This concern was not only in the minds of students but seeped into a great deal of Linden's self-presentation and understanding. At a panel of mothers and their Linden daughters, two mothers spoke about ideals of social responsibility at Linden. One mother noted, "It should not be underestimated how much Linden promotes people thinking of going into helping professions and doing worthwhile work for those who are less fortunate." She spoke about how doing this kind of work "is a value" of Linden and how Linden students understand "we are lucky to be here, but we always understand that there is a responsibility that goes with that." The framing here is again around an abstract other, "doing this kind of work" with people who need your help (or charity), as opposed to acknowledging that Linden students themselves and their families and their communities are the very same "less fortunate" others. Again, the assumed position of comparison is looking out, if not down, at the "less fortunate."

By positioning themselves and other low socioeconomic status students as needing assistance, as being the "less fortunate" who are usually portrayed as outside the college gates, CAL students risked bolstering the semiotics of class morality. CAL students thus avoided drawing on social justice narratives to frame their activities. Although they sometimes partnered with other clubs working to sponsor events of mutual interest, such as a talk on the student loan industry, they did not overall consider themselves a "social justice" club. This was amply demonstrated one evening when a CAL member mentioned that a new social justice zine was looking for submissions. No one at the meeting expressed a willingness to contribute to it, and the announcement passed by silently without a single suggestion that CAL or a CAL member might write or otherwise add to its content.

As a way of disrupting silences, relying on an already accepted and positive narrative frame such as cultural celebration or social change would seem to be a clear choice. Both of these political frames were difficult for low socioeconomic status students to make use of, however, because of the moral issues associated with class. CAL therefore seemed to be stuck between personal and political representations of class. These complications were challenging in and of themselves as students tried to figure out how to communicate about class inequality. An additional hurdle also arose in the ways that certain narratives were more likely to garner institutional support, leaving CAL at a potential disadvantage in gaining funding.

Structural Constraints on Campus   At Linden (as at many liberal arts colleges) funds for student clubs are provided by the college and allocated by a board of student representatives on an annual basis. Clubs submit their proposed budgets to cover their events—for example, to offer pizza to students attending a film showing or the cost of a speaker or performer. Every Linden club applies through the same process for the same pot of funding, and each group receives a baseline grant when the club becomes formally recognized by the college. Budget proposals are due in the spring for the following fall, and funding decisions are made in early fall of each year. For new and small clubs, it is difficult to foresee what will take place in four to twelve months, since it isn't always clear how many club members will return in the coming year. The funding process is therefore considerably easier for well-established clubs with consistent membership, two qualities CAL lacked. There were additional challenges related to the structure of funding and club organization on campus that shaped how and what CAL students were able to do.

As organizers of both new and established clubs know, one way to increase the likelihood of receiving funding is to hold events that appeal to a broad range of students. Because the student club governing board—and presumably the college administration—wants to encourage as much participation across the student body as possible, and perhaps because they wish to build unity and collaboration, clubs are more likely to receive funding for events that are presented as inclusive. Events that appeal to a wider audience than just their own members or students like them (i.e., "only" Latina students attending Mujeres events) are seen as more inclusive. This principle influences the types of events that get funded, and clubs that offer more events of this nature presumably get the best funding and therefore have the best opportunity for growth. Moreover, funding is an iterative process: clubs must apply each year and show evidence of past successes. Having had more people at past events leads to better funding, which makes it possible to hold larger events, including more people, and so on in a cyclical fashion.[9] These events are important not only to the club members but also to other students because they contribute to public life on campus. Amber, in her role as co-president of CAL, told me:

> That's one of the things that, again, frustrates me about the institution of Linden, as it is embedded in this meritocratic higher-education system. Because we're doing the budget for next year, and we had a copy of last year's budget and we saw that they wanted to host [a] workshop or something talking about class issues in higher education, and [the students last year] asked for four hundred dollars or something for it. And the school wouldn't give—the [student funding board] wouldn't give them any money for it because they're like, "Oh, this is only focused for a small amount of students." But I mean there are so few opportunities to talk about these types of things on campus, and I think that [that] dimension of diversity, they really ignore.

The pressure to create events for everyone in order to secure funding encourages clubs to favor positive and externally focused events. It also discourages events or approaches that might be considered too radical. This does not restrict what happens within meetings, of course. If clubs sponsor events for themselves (e.g., a talk on how to ace a job interview by alumnae speakers who live close to campus, as Mujeres did) they are free to do so. And this does not stop clubs from organizing protests against college actions, as some other campus clubs did. However, the pressure to hold events that are for "everyone" constrained the kinds of work that CAL and perhaps other student clubs could plan and complete through the available funding structure.

Organization-Initiated Efforts

In at least one case during the years I was at Linden, there was a sustained effort by the college to promote campus-wide engagement with class issues.[10] There had been short-term efforts in recent years—a faculty reading club on social class issues, for example, and a recent survey on diversity that found that class was the least-talked-about issue in the college, as well as an orientation evening devoted to diversity conversations, where students could opt to attend sessions about class, gender/sexuality, and race. The college was also in the process of creating a new campus-wide administrative office to manage a broad range of diversity issues for students and employees, including faculty; in the meantime a "president's council" had been convened to study the issue. Working with a nonprofit organization called Cross-Class Equity (CCE), Linden joined a regional network of colleges seeking to broaden class-related discussions on their respective campuses. Staff and faculty were trained as interpersonal conflict resolution experts, and, as part of this effort, a series of discussion groups were organized by CCE, featuring faculty, students, staff, and administrators selected to be representative of the Linden community. CAL students' reactions to and participation in Linden's effort to engage issues of class directly are illustrative of the complicated interaction between the college and students around this issue.

Early in the process, CAL was contacted by a Linden administrator who wanted their student members to support the CCE partnership. The way in which CAL received the message about CCE made it appear that the college would be moving ahead with the initiative whether CAL supported it or not. CAL was even asked to consider putting in some funding for the project. Not surprisingly, this did not go over well with CAL members. Over the course of several meetings, CAL students talked about and reacted to the content of the communication they received from the administration as well as the roles they perceived that they were being asked to take. Regarding the content, they found the wording to be very problematic.

First, the proposal seemed to disregard students' efforts, and especially CAL as a club. Students noted, for example, that the initiative replicated some things CAL had already done. As Violet exclaimed, "Don't they know we already brought [feminist author] Rebecca Walker as a speaker!" Furthermore, CAL students were outraged that this external group seemed to be getting a great deal of funding—for example, to coordinate a "national summer institute"—while, as one student remarked, "CAL can't get student group funding." (The proposal came on the heels of CAL having lost a great deal of club funding from one year to the next, as described at the start of this chapter. This made the latter request particularly galling, though the administrators organizing the process would not have known about it because a student board rather than administrators decides club funding.)

CAL students also worried about the roles to be played by students and administrators and what that might mean for the shape, goals, and duration of the effort. Although they agreed that the administration should be more involved in class issues, CAL students worried that if the college took it on, commitment would be short lived. Students joked that there would be a workshop or two and then "the college will be like, 'Okay, done! We've dealt with class.'" Similarly, students were worried about the student leader roles because no details were included to indicate how these students would be chosen, and there was only a single mention of CAL. Ultimately, however, the student members of CAL decided that they had no alternative but to sign on and to try to affect this new effort through as much involvement as they could secure—a single formal seat at the table, provided through a work-study job in the office of the dean coordinating the program. CAL students therefore considered that their involvement was largely symbolic, which in turn greatly reduced their perception that the college was genuinely interested in their issues or ideas.

Getting students meaningfully involved in the CCE process was challenging for a number of reasons. The role accorded to students as community members and decision makers was unclear and not effectively managed in the view of CAL students. This was evident from the very start, since the first meeting of one key discussion group, organized to tackle issues in the residence hall system, had only two students. A sympathetic faculty member invited more to the second meeting, but even then the number of students was less than ten. The discussion group series was organized by administrators, who do not necessarily have personal connections to students and may therefore have limited knowledge of who would be interested and likely to attend. Although the administration attempted to operate through CAL, this ultimately proved ineffective because CAL as a body was not very enthusiastic and because of its small size.[11]

As the discussion group series moved forward, there was continued lack of clarity regarding what role the students would fill. For example, during the final spring semester meeting, the group was polled about whether to continue working over the summer. Students, who almost all live elsewhere during the summer, voted no. Other participants—faculty, staff, and administrators, who made up the majority—voted yes, and the yes votes carried the day. This suggested that students' roles were fairly unimportant: if the process could continue without their input, they must not be very central to it. This solidified the impression that several CAL members already held—that the process involved students in name only.

Cross-Class Equity's efforts on campus encompassed several universes colliding into one frame of "class equity" without much indication about how they might all be seen in a way that was meaningful to their various constituents. Although students were generally concerned with (if not solely then certainly materially) interactions with their peers and with college personnel, many of the nonstudent participants were interested in class dynamics operating in other interactional venues and constituencies. These included students and faculty being "snobby" (in the words of one facilitator) to blue-collar staff, generalized labor issues, conflicts in town-gown relations, and larger policy concerns about union organizing, wages, and benefits. The concept of class was spread across all these issues and permutations, making it so diffuse that immediate action steps were difficult to envision.

This element also brought complicated questions about students' own class statuses to the fore: CAL students might be working class or poor in their upbringing, but as students they were relatively advantaged and empowered. There seemed to be contradictory roles for low-income students as both the objects and makers of snobbish comments, and as both the beneficiaries and critics of an elitist system. Indeed, this was sometimes a source of internal conflict for CAL and other low socioeconomic status students as they struggled to get used to the idea of other people cleaning up and cooking for them. As Macy noted, "it is a total breakdown of what it means to talk about class" being at Linden. "I can talk about [class] here all the time, but there's someone cooking for me." Shifting the conversation beyond student-to-student relationships thus positioned low socioeconomic status students in contradictory roles, making such discussions even more difficult to navigate. What kinds of critiques could they make as members and beneficiaries of a class-exclusive institution?

Although there were some overlaps in the kinds of class conversations the Linden administration wanted to facilitate and the kinds of conversations CAL wanted to promote, the two entities did not seem to communicate well or work well together. CAL was not the first place the college turned to, inviting them (in CAL's perception) fairly late in the process to contribute to the formal institutional effort, which contributed to mistrust. Moreover, the kinds of class inequality being targeted and students' roles in the effort and their class positioning was murky. Similar moral questions emerged during these conversations, as we see in Macy's reflection about conflicts between worrying about class inequality while someone is "cooking for [you]." Thus, when CAL students' concerns about inequality were placed in larger contexts (albeit perhaps not as smoothly as they could have been), this also shifted salient moral questions in ways that left CAL students in a kind of status limbo. We thus see how the college as an administrative body had to determine how to effectively manage class inequality among students and across campus while involving those constituents meaningfully. And this was very challenging because of the same moral worries that shaped other dynamics for low-income, working-class, and first-generation students.

The Class Activists of Linden faced a complicated problem in its goals—namely, if students don't even talk about money with their friends, how can a club motivate awareness and activism around issues of socioeconomic inequality between Linden students? Violet's reaction at the start of this chapter illustrates an ongoing internal conflict between class as something personal and class inequality as the issue around which CAL students organized politically, between abstract political ideals and the deeply emotional bases of students' own experiences at Linden. On the one hand, CAL students mostly wanted to keep their stories private. Like other Lindies, they did not talk about class inequality in their social circles. On the other hand, CAL's primary goals included education and advocacy, which are best accomplished through the crafting of personal, connectable narratives. Such efforts require those stories, or at least the issues shaping them, to be shared widely. Evocative personal stories would also help CAL students in not only making stories about class more visible but in finding a coherent way to represent class inequality to peers who don't share their experiences. They also require students to open themselves to the same kinds of moral assessments that are typically avoided. And, as indicated in the interviews, many experiences that are associated with low socioeconomic status are related to privation and lack or are culturally stigmatized in elite settings. These identities risk being further devalued when they are shared and highlighted as lacking in comparison to the perceived typical upper-middle-class backgrounds of Linden students. Students also had to confront questions about who could legitimately speak about the problems that low socioeconomic students face, about who decides what, if anything, constitutes a shared class culture and who can represent that culture. Here again, we see worries about framing low socioeconomic status people or backgrounds as problematic within a context that seems to stigmatize these same cultural forms.

Much as in individual respondents' interviews, CAL students' interactions and reflections show the ways that the semiotics of class morality are active in shaping students' choices about managing class inequality. Strength in numbers does not seem to mitigate worries about class morality, being seen as less-than or lacking. Indeed, this system of meaning shaped the ways the students thought about activism around class and their own efforts at class representation in complex ways. Representing class as personal and exemplifying challenges through their own personal stories (and, for that matter, recruiting others to do the same) was often unsuccessful because of the silences around class inequality and the fear of moral exposure. At the same time, abstract rhetorical frames brought their own moral questions: Would CAL students seem to be positioning themselves as victims by utilizing a social justice frame or, alternately, as parodying some form of class culture by adopting a cultural celebration model?

The stakes here are not only about CAL's ability to raise Linden students' awareness of class inequality, although this is their primary goal. Studies consistently find what higher education administrators already know well—namely, that participation in extracurricular life supports students' social and academic integration and reduces the risk of adverse outcomes,[12] including a propensity to drop out. This makes participation especially important for vulnerable populations such as low socioeconomic status students, who are less likely to participate in the extracurricular life of the college and more likely to stop out or drop out.[13] Clubs that bring students together based around a particular and shared identity, such as sexuality or racial, ethnic, or national backgrounds, are often intended to provide support or a "safe space" to members. Very few such clubs exist for low socioeconomic status students, perhaps for the obvious reason that class remains an area in which Americans show little interest or understanding, and because low socioeconomic status students often feel their identities stigmatized on campuses that valorize middle-class and upper-class cultures.[14] Research on other under-represented groups at elite colleges indicates that these clubs can be crucial spaces for peer support, leadership development, and interactions with others who "get it." Above and beyond the benefits of campus engagement, participation in groups of like or homophilic others seems to be particularly important for vulnerable students.

Given that there are very few clubs geared toward discussion of students' class or income backgrounds, low socioeconomic status students may have few formal avenues of *emotional* support.[15] Class advocacy clubs can provide support that might otherwise be unavailable, since many colleges lack services specifically geared toward socioeconomically marginalized students other than financial aid. Low socioeconomic status students remain under-represented on elite college campuses like Linden.[16] These clubs may also provide low socioeconomic status students with one of the few avenues for making friendship ties with others from similar backgrounds; as Joan Ostrove and Susan Long have noted, this kind of peer support may be especially important at selective and highly selective campuses where the organizational context values elite cultural capital.[17] CAL's capacities for advocacy, activism, and perhaps even support, however, were unfortunately constrained by vulnerabilities stemming from a semiotics of class morality as well as structural factors.

5

Silence vs. Empowerment

Class Inequality in Formal Settings

During early fall of my second year at Linden, the Class Activists of Linden met with the assistant dean in charge of the residence halls. The topic was a sudden change in college policy on housing during vacation terms: CAL students had been surprised and frustrated to learn that the administration no longer intended to make staying in the residence halls free of charge during vacations, one of the budget cuts introduced during my field work. For several CAL students, staying on campus during breaks had been a salvation. Those who could not afford to go home, especially for shorter breaks, stayed on campus for free and ate as inexpensively as they could manage. The announcement was made in an e-mail sent to students only a couple of weeks before the first fall holiday, which, although just a few days long, would cost students forty dollars if they remained in the halls. Longer breaks would cost over one hundred dollars, charges that would not include food. The CAL students had begun collecting signatures to demand a reduction of these fees and had asked the dean of the residence halls to come in and discuss the policy in person.

Although we have examined the role that a semiotics of class moral-ity plays in college discourse, peer interactions, and efforts to organize around inequality, we have until now left aside interactions such as this one in which low socioeconomic status students manage class inequality in their interactions with the formal structure of the college, namely, the academic and other official venues, such as student support services. These settings are crucial to college life, providing what we might think of as the bread and butter of academic attainment. Respondents themselves sometimes highlighted these academic venues—classrooms, dean's offices, offices for academic and social services—as the spaces in which the pri-mary functions of the college take place, as possible safe spaces for difficult conversations, or as areas of frustration where college resources were not equally accessible to all. Interactions in these spaces attracted my attention during my field work, not only because they are linked to the core goals of college life, but also because they expose in new ways how class status is linked to concepts foregrounded as significant hallmarks of accomplish-ment at Linden, such as making use of one's resources.

There are also strong sociological reasons for examining these ven-ues. Scholars stress the ways that *habitus* and interactional approaches create inequality among students who nominally have the same oppor-tunities, even within the same school or classroom. Sociological exami-nations have mapped these dynamics especially clearly in the formative educational settings of elementary school classrooms. Annette Lareau's seminal findings and subsequent work by Jessica Calarco show clearly that low-income and working-class children and adults are less adept at utilizing forms of cultural capital that are particularly relevant in school settings, such as pushing for exceptions or asking for help.[1] These scholars also show that middle-class students are able to benefit from class-privileged interactional approaches, while working-class students either do not benefit or are actively disadvantaged by their lack of facil-ity with such approaches. In particular, Calarco's findings differentiate between middle-class parents' encouragement of their children to use "any means necessary" to succeed in school, including having excuse notes provided by parents when work was forgotten or not completed, and working-class parents' inculcation of a what Calarco calls a "no ex-cuses" approach to school work, in which students are not provided with excuses for work not completed.

One might wonder whether low socioeconomic status respondents at an elite college might not have adopted middle-class skills by the time they arrive at this late stage of education—indeed, one might hypothesize that this kind of cultural capital could be a prerequisite for accessing elite higher education. My data shows, however, that this is not always the case. Moreover, while examinations of students' interactions with authority figures primarily have to do with the classroom, college students often manage a broader range of interactions with faculty and administrators. These interactions are especially important to understand because colleges like Linden stress the availability of opportunities beyond the classroom as a crucial aspect of the college experience; study abroad, internships, campus leadership, and gaining financial support from the college all require students to navigate interactions with authorities. We must therefore broaden our analytical lens to understand how class dynamics may play out in these supplemental interactional venues. Here we can also look to Jenny M. Stuber's work on students' class-varied approaches to extracurricular opportunities, such as study abroad or internships, for additional insights.[2] Stuber shows that working-class students are less likely than middle-class or upper-class students to see such opportunities as valuable to their education or future careers as they deal with immediate concerns. These findings highlight the ways that class background shapes students' navigation of college structures and use of resources that are nominally available to all.

Lareau, Calarco, and Stuber also raise important questions about how students interpret the "hidden curriculum" of college as to what should be accomplished in order to attain white-collar employment on graduation.[3] Networking, framing extracurricular activities in work-applicable terms, and accruing leadership credentials through such seemingly social activities as Greek life or clubs are understood by middle-class or upper-class students as crucial activities in college—indeed, students often arrive with such abilities. Students from working-class backgrounds are less likely to have time, social connections, or cultural knowledge to recognize these imperatives, which tend to be framed as suggested or recommended but not required. This echoes the ways in which Calarco's elementary school respondents experienced what she calls "interpretive moments": while middle-class students recognized these as a chance to get extra help, working-class students were unsure of how to interact in such ambiguous contexts and hung back.[4] This points to the crucial question of the ways in which schools, while structured and orderly, still have elements of ambiguity. In these moments, class may play an unrecognized role in shaping students' experiences both in the classroom and in interactions with other formal college structures.

Rather than comparing levels of participation in activities or academic outcomes in the classroom, I examine here students' experiences of how class matters in the classroom and in the process of accessing campus resources. I focus especially on humanities and social science courses in which discussion is prioritized and on CAL's meetings with administrators; I selected these because I could not accompany individual students to one-on-one meetings about personal topics. I first examine the ways in which the classroom is both a space where class can be more openly discussed but also where worries about class morality are important in shaping how, exactly, those discussions take place. I then shift to looking at interactions outside the classroom to show how moral meaning making shapes students' and administrators' interpretations of how students utilize college resources for support.

Classrooms

The classroom looms large in sociological, policy, and individual thinking about college. As Magdalena succinctly told me, students' "main goal here [is] to get our education, our BAs, and leave." Accordingly, it is largely in the classroom that we expect students to attain skills such as critical thinking that will be used in later years. Adequate academic work is the baseline requirement for staying enrolled. According to a 2008 poll conducted by the college, a majority of enrolled students chose Linden for its academic reputation, intellectual rigor, and classroom facilities. Low socioeconomic status students, like others, worked hard to gain admission to this elite school and value the opportunity to attend a college that will provide them with both comprehensive academic training and a name-brand degree to signify that training.[5]

The classroom was, however, also a space of duality around class inequality and cross-class interaction. On the one hand, classrooms provided a space in which class could be named, analyzed, and discussed as a source of stratification. Students could learn about their social class location in an abstract scholarly sense, perhaps making the naming of class somewhat less intimate and uncomfortable. On the other hand, classrooms also exposed students to situations in which invidious distinctions could be made and class-linked moral worries provoked.

Naming and Analyzing Class Inequality as a Source of Empowerment

One of the most striking findings to emerge from my conversations with faculty members and students was a perception of students as empowered by academic discourse. Newly learned academic terms helped students name their experiences, and conceptualizing social structure through their course work influenced the ways students perceived their own circumstances. For example, one sociology faculty member recalled her students' occasional outbursts of emotion and sometimes tears when talking about Bourdieu's concepts of cultural capital, a set of ideas that clarified previously opaque experiences and put their college lives in a different context. She told me, "I can see that students begin to see their own lives through new lenses and now see the class dimension. They learn that there is a class hierarchy and where they are in it. They learn to see that power is relative, that their families have worth and value, that they're being judged according to certain parameters but those parameters are not the only way to look at things—to see the kinds of power at play." This faculty member also noted that "people literally have come up to me and thanked me for introducing them to these ideas."

Student respondents also recounted stories of empowerment, using terms such as "hierarchy," "structure," "oppression," and "cultural capital" in interviews as examples of new understandings. Amber related a conversation with her adviser that exemplified this: "There was a time a month and a half ago where the registrar didn't send the forms they were supposed to [to confirm health insurance coverage]. I wasn't sure what to do about that, and I was talking to my adviser about it. She said, 'Yeah, that's a perfect example of cultural and social capital. You just didn't know how to say the right thing to get them to do what they were supposed to.'" Amber's adviser reframed her experience as an example of cultural and social capital in action, linking Amber's immediate experience to systematic class inequalities. Amber in turn picked up this use and contextualized it as a larger set of lessons or strategies to be learned at college, as she suggested later in her interview, noting that you "have to . . . pick up on the rules . . . and catch on to how people play." Amber could thus both name and explain the frustrations she felt on campus as part of something larger than herself rather than as a personal problem. Moreover, she was beginning to be able to see how to use cultural capital to deal with problems that came up on campus.

Similarly, Lynne told me that she felt students might be especially attracted to courses that provided this kind of learning. She hypothesized that "a big reason people get into that field of study in [social sciences] classes is because they want to understand those experiences more and they want to understand themselves." I asked Lynne if she had already been aware of these differences before taking social sciences classes or if she had become aware of them as the result of her course work. Like Amber, Lynne pointed out the importance of having the right language to name and deal with issues she was aware of but unsure of how to manage:

> Yeah, I was aware of the differences. I just didn't know how to—I couldn't really make sense of them without that kind of language, and like I've been talking about, it's just been a constant buildup. Growing up in the same middle-class town my whole life, having specific events occur, like going on a free lunch system in high school, realizing I'm only one of a few who need to use this system. Carrying around that piece of paper with me was embarrassing; it was so awkward. A lot of it had to do with trying to reconcile why that was happening to me.

Classroom learning helped Lynne begin to "reconcile" what was happening in her own life, to understand it in a broader perspective than her own experience in her family, and consequently to minimize some of the hurtful emotional aspects of her childhood. She continued in a similar vein in a subsequent interview: "I feel like such a nerd right now, but the two theorists that changed my life are Bourdieu and Judith Butler. The performing gender thing and the cultural capital as separate from financial capital. I felt like, 'Why didn't anyone tell me this earlier?'" The phrase "changed my life" is a strong indicator of how important academic concepts have been to Lynne. Gender and sociological theories, the language and concepts, help Lynne to make sense of the circumstances in which she found herself and even helped her to manage her relationships with others.

Not all respondents thought that understanding concepts such as cultural capital increased their comfort level, even if it did provide an analytical framework. For example, Fiona, who was especially forthright and direct in her interviews, told me about the events she planned to attend or skip over the final weeks of her senior year. The spring semester included a number of college-sponsored gatherings—dance parties, a water-balloon fight, a Bloody Mary brunch, and others—to celebrate senior students, and Fiona laid out a schedule of only a small number of the possible events that she and her best friend had picked out:

> Yeah, we're going to those because it's free. We're planning to go to wine and cheese night, and there was actually an event at the alumnae building a few days ago before the classes ended, but I didn't go. It's just bullshit. I feel I have no cultural capital, and who's going to be there? Lindies. So I didn't go, but my friend went. She said it was fine—not a big deal, so whatever, I just wanted—I didn't want to go to a place and feel weird.

While Fiona understood well what cultural capital means, she thought it was something she both lacked and did not value. By comparison, she believed that other Linden students were more in possession of it. Because of this discrepancy, going to an event with them would make her "feel weird"—especially events with a theme that draw on images of upper-class lifestyles, like the Bloody Mary brunch.[6] Even here, however, we see the way that academic terms helped students to name problems they faced and to understand class inequality in systematic ways. These were notable counterpoints to narratives of silence around class inequality and were powerful specifically because they countered the semiotics of class morality that was otherwise in place: understanding class as a system reduced students' and families' perceived culpability or failure.

These kinds of experiences show us the ways that classrooms, especially in the social sciences and humanities, and academic learning more broadly, may be empowering for low socioeconomic status students. Indeed, classrooms have great potential as sites for the kinds of difficult conversations that might be engendered by class inequality beyond simply the mastery of academic concepts. Students sometimes talked about the classroom as a "safe place" (in Magdalena's words) to broach these difficult subjects or indeed the only place where issues of inequality along race and class lines were discussed. This is in part because professors serve as mediators or conversational managers. The chances that conflict will escalate or conversations become too emotional are low. Moreover, the chances of being directly called on to take responsibility for inequality are low, since classroom approaches are often abstract and scholarly rather than personal. As one faculty member told me, a central difference between the classroom and workshops or other venues in which these topics are broached is that workshops ask students to change and thus to admit that they have in some way been wrong.[7] All of these reasons likely contribute to the empowering experiences described in regard to academics. Respondents' descriptions, however, also provided examples in which class inequality may be named in the classroom but the resulting conversation still falls flat. These occurred when faculty or student attempts at tackling difficult subjects faltered in the face of prevailing moral worries.

Moral Semiotics in the Classroom: Silences, Comparisons, and Conflicts

Despite some respondents' empowerment through scholarship and faith in the classroom as a space in which to tackle difficult questions about inequality, classroom dynamics were nonetheless shaped by moral semiotics. Alice was one respondent who believed in the possibility of the classroom as a way to "open some platforms" for discussion of inequality. This was not easily accomplished, she reflected as we talked one afternoon. Alice thought that particular topics lent themselves well to discussions of class inequality "because we talk a lot about uncomfortable things [in my classes]. I don't have a lot of sociology classes, but they talk a lot about this, and so, I know students already have [inequality] in their minds [in those classes]. So I feel professors can really help open some platforms, so people at least, somewhere are comfortable with discussing it." But when I asked Alice what happened in her classes when such subjects as inequality are raised, she replied:

> People are really, they get really quiet, and I always look around and . . . people don't make eye contact, or they look like they want to say something but maybe they don't want to sound in a certain ways and just keep it to themselves. . . . And the professor ends up trying to rephrase the question

to avoid uncomfortable questions . . . but eventually people get, as some one person has a comment and then it kind of [drifts off]. We would start over [in the discussion]. It's really awkward.

Thus, although classes could open venues for conversation about issues that students were hesitant to discuss among themselves, these conversations were not necessarily the kinds of in-depth engagements that respondents believed could be transformative—or at least educational—and that they seemed to truly desire. As we see in Alice's case, attempts to bring up inequality in class did not always go smoothly.

One reason for this awkward silence in academic spaces, as indicated by Alice and other respondents, is that classrooms are not like Vegas: what happens in the classroom may not stay there. Comments made in the classroom from personal experience may have unintended consequences or life spans. Even without direct statements that draw such comparisons to the fore or make the speaker's background intentionally clear, sharing classroom spaces also facilitates interactions that foreground differences between students and exposes viewpoints offensive to socioeconomically disadvantaged students—interactions that were not always well handled by professors or peers.

A primary source of comparison centered on academic preparation. Genesis summarized this concisely when she reflected that "they're [i.e., more-affluent peers] better prepared." This sense of comparison was not only about high school training or academic skills. Rather, respondents were concerned about a broad range of perceived differences between themselves and their more-affluent classmates, including differences in available time to work on homework or study (that is, less need to work for pay) and comfort in seeking help, both of which constituted clear advantages in the classroom. Often these concerns were linked. For example, Meredith described the ways she felt some of her low-income peers suffer from being underprepared—a problem she only partially shared, she explained, because she had attended a well-funded suburban high school near her semirural Rhode Island hometown:

A lot of my friends went to inner-city schools, so they didn't have the background for Linden, and I know that a lot of people find that problematic and don't think that's true. But they're struggling with the amount of work we have to do and the quality of it, and I think Linden doesn't support that at all. They bring diversity into Linden, but then once it's here they're [i.e. the administration] like, "Okay, you're here." . . . So I honestly don't believe that someone with an inner-city school education and someone from a top elite private school [trails off]—they don't get the same education. They may have the same capabilities, but they haven't been taught how to use them, so it's really hard in a setting like this to expect everyone to produce the same quality of work.

Meredith went on to explain, however, that although she felt her high school had provided a fairly strong academic grounding in comparison to some of her friends' schools, she now struggled to learn how to ask for help and to talk to professors:

I know in my own personal experience I'm not used to having help, so it's a bit of a pride issue. I hate going to see my professors. I hate going to the Communication Center [for writing help]. I'm like, "I've done this before on my own, I can do it now." And I know it would really benefit me, but at the same time it's hard for me to do it unless I'm forced. If I'm forced to go to the Communication Center for a paper, if I'm forced to meet my professor, I'll do it. But, generally speaking, I won't because I've never done that. But I know people who have had tutors in high school, so they visit their professors weekly. . . . And it makes me really uncomfortable because I don't know how to interact with professors. I don't know how to act with people from the Communication Center. I hate people judging my work, so I'm just sitting there incredibly uncomfortable the entire time, and I don't know what Linden could do about that.

In comparison to peers who "had tutors . . . weekly," Meredith felt not only less well educated but also less comfortable seeking assistance. She disliked needing help, and she felt "uncomfortable" because she did not know how to approach her professors. On both counts, then, Meredith perceived a disadvantage.

Georgina echoed Meredith's perception, reflecting in a conversation the classroom approaches common to her middle-class and upper-class peers that she perceived helped them to net better grades:

Entitlement. That's the difference. That's what I think. . . . They [middle-class and upper-class students] come here with a sense of entitlement. And the entitlement consists of the professors are supposed to teach the way they want to teach and they're supposed to learn a specific way. They demand it, and I see it. People fuss and they argue about grades sometimes. Or like, "Could I get some extra credit? Well, how is my grade looking?" It's this whole thing. They question what the teacher is saying. They question how their grade is going, whether they want the grade to go up and how is it going to go up, because they believe already that it's going to go up.

For Georgina and her friend Dee, who also took part in this conversation, it is "entitlement" that enables classmates to question professors, to ask for extra credit, or to "fuss" about their grades with the understanding that this may improve their scores. This level of "demand" was simply not part of the classroom repertoire of Georgina, Dee, and other working-class and low-income students—even when they recognized the ways that it seems to advantage others to draw on such interactional approaches.

These examples provide a strong connection to Lareau's conceptualization of "concerted cultivation" reaching its potential in middle-class and upper-middle-class students.[8] They highlight the ways in which respondents were sometimes ill-equipped, despite their status as elite college students, to draw on college resources, to make requests or demands for accommodations, or to advocate for themselves. Maya recalled at length how at sea she felt during her first semester at Linden. Like Meredith, she did not feel comfortable getting assistance or even know how to go about seeking it:

MAYA: I had no idea what I was getting into [with my classes]. I didn't ask for help either. I didn't ask for help, and then I just . . . I mean I took my finals, but I know I didn't know anything. Like after I took my finals, "I have no idea what I'm doing, I just want to get out of here and leave." It was just [pauses], ugh, it was something else. And then, um, I went home.

LIZ: So the academic stuff [and] not knowing how to study—

MAYA: Yeah, like, compared to other people, like it just seemed—at Linden you can't tell who's a senior and [who's a] first year, so I figured everybody knew stuff. I didn't want to say anything because I felt like everyone else just got everything, and if they didn't, they didn't say anything, and if everyone else looks like they're getting it [trails off]. Yeah, it's like, "I don't care." It just took me a lot to ask for help, period. I didn't know how.

Although Maya knew that she was doing poorly in her classes, she was reluctant to ask for help because she didn't know how to do so. This was exacerbated by her perception that everyone else "knew stuff," which made her feel foolish or less-than for not "just [getting] everything."

A number of respondents were keenly aware of how this lack of knowing or lack of facility placed them at a disadvantage relative to their peers. Moreover, as we see in Maya's recollection, absent a greater context for peers' apparent achievements, they often struggled both to understand how to ask for help and to see asking for help as a strategic use of resources rather than a sign of failure or inability. These comparisons engendered complicated moral puzzles of how differences between those who have resources that support their academic achievements, including cultural capital, time, and money, and those who don't should be evaluated. How can these comparisons be fair? Alexandra, for example, was direct in her linkage of academic comparisons and class inequalities. A first-year student when we first met, Alexandra was the kind of dedicated student one imagines at an elite college. She always spoke enthusiastically about her courses, excited about the work she was doing in her labs and premed courses. She had nonetheless been nervous about how she might stack up against more affluent classmates: "I've noticed, one of the things when I came here from a public school, I've met a lot of girls like my roommate who went to [a private school] . . . and I'm like I never had that." When I asked Alexandra about whether she had worried about these potential class differences when she came to Linden, she returned to this same comparison: "I did. Because, especially, I come from a low-income family. I just figured, 'Oh my god, my roommate, how will it be?' My roommate now buys all these things, and I can't afford to. . . . We're in the same school, and we're going to do the same education, so when it comes to that [trails off]." By her senior year, Alexandra had become not only aware of but also critical of these differences. Just after her graduation, she reflected back on a phenomenon she had observed during her last year or two on campus:

> Several students kept posting like, "I will pay X amount and X amount of thousands of dollars if you're willing to, like, tutor me in this and that." And I'm like, "Whaaat?" I'm like, somebody has that much money that they're able to put an ad and say "I'm willing to pay several thousands of dollars for you to tutor me and help me with this class?" I'm all like, "Whoa, that's why

we have like tutoring sessions at Linden!" But I was just thinking, "Huh, I wonder how her time at Linden is?" I mean, not only is she probably able to take advantage of the free resources that Linden has, but she's also able to pay somebody and get help. And so then I was like thinking, "Well, how fair, how fair is the grade?"

While Alexandra had become comfortable navigating the tutoring and other resources available for free on campus, the idea that others could pay for even more support made her question the validity of grades that did not take these kinds of support into account.

Other respondents shared these kinds of concerns about the ways financial advantage shaped peers' relative abilities to pursue their educations and what that meant for a comparison between them as they were evaluated in the classroom. These distinctions could be drawn in broader ways than paying for tutoring, however. For example, Evelyn was frustrated by what she saw as wealthier peers' complaints about time management. While she worked long hours at an area restaurant, her peers could spend time getting their academic work done or relaxing:

> [Most days I] go to class in my uniform and hopefully try and find parking near the building that my class is in so that I can literally fly out of class, get in my car, and get to work on time . . . because class gets out at 2:30 and I have to be to work at 3. These students complain about, "Oh, I have to spend time in the library." I would *love* to just have my eight hours that I've got to work and use that to do my [academic] work, because I probably would not be so stressed out. . . . And I'd get a lot more work done, and I probably would understand it a lot more if I'm going over it more and for longer periods of time.

While Evelyn rushed from one place to the next, sometimes barely meeting her commitments, and worried about being able to find enough time to study, her peers who work fewer or no hours had the luxury of working "too long" at the library. Likewise, students who came to view the documentary about social class on campus made and screened by CAL shared the following after seeing it: "I get so angry at people who waste time or who have extra time—that's a privilege, and they don't see it. People who stay up all night partying or watching TV, then skip class to sleep in. It's so much easier for them—no work-study job, and they don't need to sweat because they can just work in daddy's company." Here again, not having to earn money allows many students to worry less than low socioeconomic status students—something especially galling when the "privilege" is wasted or unrecognized.

As we see here, the classroom was sometimes a place where cross-class comparisons prompted frustration. In some cases, this occurred more directly as students' class backgrounds shaped their moral assessments of people in other class positions—people assumed not to be in the room, since middle-class students tended to assume that everyone shared their backgrounds or was more affluent. (White middle and upper socioeconomic status students also sometimes made race-class conflations by presuming that students who were black or Latina came from the "inner city" or the "projects" while white and Asian American students were presumed to come from the suburbs. Unfortunately, professors sometimes made the same assumptions.) In these instances, the moral connotations of class positions were unavoidable and clearly stated. For example, a classmate of Victoria's characterized "white trash" as "if you live in a trailer and drink Bud Light." Victoria, who spent part of her childhood years in a mobile home, was aghast at the comment and equally angered by the fact that no one, including the professor, corrected the comment or responded. She concluded that "for [the student who made the comment], she probably maybe doesn't know anyone who lives in a trailer. And she probably certainly doesn't think that anyone who can afford to sit in a Linden classroom would live in a trailer. . . . So in her mind she probably thinks that everyone who's sitting in that classroom has a nice big house like she does." Victoria further perceived that she was the only person outraged by the speaker's words and very likely the only person in class who had ever lived in a mobile home. This comment fed into Victoria's existing beliefs about the typical background and social beliefs of most Linden students, and she responded by writing her final paper for the course on this kind of problematic statement.

Becca similarly described several instances in which class backgrounds were impossible to miss and too difficult to manage, despite the buffer of the classroom:

> I remember specifically an experience in a sociology course. I took Soc 101 my sophomore year second semester, and we were watching a movie and discussing teenage pregnancy specifically, but it also had to do with like

teenagers from lower-socioeconomic backgrounds living in bad neighbor-hoods, getting in trouble, how do you fix this, all this other stuff. At the be-ginning of this discussion before the movie [students] were spouting off, you know, all of the kind of left-wing [ideals].

After the documentary, however, her peers' responses were different from her own: "So we watched the movie and at the very end had the discus-sion again, and one of the people in the movie was getting into trouble for breaking the curfew, and so we're discussing it, [and] 75 percent of the people [in class] were saying, 'Well, that's [bad],' you know, and say-ing things like that." Her peers seemed to blame the young woman in the documentary for being out after hours. For Becca, this reaction exposed a discrepancy between their liberal self-presentation and their failure to comprehend the situation being portrayed in the documentary: "I was like, 'You're not listening at all, because the point of the movie was that she had to stay in, and she had to be home at a certain time, [but] it was an abusive home.' Where was she supposed to go? So she leaves and gets into trouble again. . . . It was just kind of like, 'You have no clue what you're saying. In theory you believe this, but in practice you're not understanding what this is saying.'"

Along the same lines, conversations about why low-income families might go to McDonalds instead of making healthier eating choices were frustrating:

> People were talking about how, you know, we shouldn't be in any way shape or form supporting those companies [like McDonalds]. I was like, "If you make below the minimum poverty line, and you can go to McDonalds and feed your three children for ten dollars a day, not everyone has the abil-ity to shop at Whole Foods or to get organics." Like it did not register. I re-member a very specific group of people saying, "They should try harder."

Here again, we see the distinctly moral positioning of low socioeconomic status people as making poor nutritional choices, having bad politics, and needing to generally "try harder." These expressions were profoundly frustrating to Becca and others, perhaps especially coming from peers who saw themselves as liberal.

How should respondents handle these kinds of circumstances? One way might be to chime in, making the speaker aware that someone who lived in a trailer, eats dinner at McDonalds, or experiences financial hardship is sitting right here, sharing the classroom. In other words, respondents might position themselves as educators, "giv[ing] that other perspective to students who don't come from [their] background," as Amber phrased it. While this might have been helpful to their affluent peers, socioeconomically marginalized students often felt that the burden of educating others through personal stories was simply too much. Violet, for example, noted:

> I think for as long as I've been here, as much time as I've been talking openly and explicitly about class and putting out information about it [through CAL], people are always shocked and surprised. It's always news to them. . . . I don't know how you'd pick it up in conversation, but [trails off]. Because class isn't talked about, especially if you have less privilege—personally I'm not offering my story all the time or really rarely ever. So like I think that's true for a lot of people across the board, I don't think there are a lot of opportunities for privileged people to hear [low socioeconomic status students'] stories and have consciousness raised about that.

While Violet speaks "openly and explicitly" about class as an abstract topic—elsewhere in the interview she spoke about "the distribution of wealth," for example—she specifically refrains from "offering [her own] story." She perceived this tendency of hers and others as a loss because it prevented "privileged people" from learning from these stories in meaningful ways. Interactions like the ones described above therefore sometimes go unanswered or unchallenged in ways that rely on a student's personal testimony of her own low-income, working-class, or first-generation identity.

Taking Violet's words into account, we might think about this silence as a form of cover for low socioeconomic status students. This perspective takes on additional strength when we compare it to classroom dynamics in which students of color are asked to speak about the experiences of their presumed community—often in ways that are conflated with class, such as when black students are asked about their experiences of "the inner-city" or "the projects" regardless of their socioeconomic background and where they actually grew up. Perhaps remaining silent is the more comfortable option. Following from Violet's discussion, however, we also see the ways in which class silence perpetuates the kinds of nameless moral fears that were discussed earlier. These comparisons are heavy with moral implications, featured in the classroom just as strongly as in other college spaces. The classroom therefore provided a specific, keen venue for moral comparisons.

As we see in these reflections, the practice of academic work, broadly, and classroom settings, specifically, are areas of class-boundary differentiation and reification, places where existing inequalities become further entrenched. Questions of class morality are therefore important for thinking about students' academic endeavors and classroom experiences. As we have seen, merit and achievement are the moral coins of the realm, crucial to legitimacy. Respondents described the ways that middle-class and upper-class peers, who were more comfortable seeking help, had stronger high school academic training, and had more money to potentially bring to bear, were seen as the norm, the pace car, with whom they were compared by faculty. Affluent peers, moreover, also often served as invidious sources of comparison in their own thinking, as low socioeconomic status students often had the impression others just "get it" and succeed, making their own struggles in the classroom a sign of personal (moral) failing rather than a signal to seek support.

Education vs. Life Experience

The comparisons just described take place in the classroom or with reference to shared academic endeavors, student to student. However, other sorts of comparisons were also invoked through academic learning: even as respondents pursued new sources of understanding, they sometimes perceived their gains as separating them from their home community as they compared both their daily lives and the ways they understood the world with family and friends from home. Violet, for example, valued her scholarly vocabulary, which allowed her to talk about power, gender, and class—issues that mattered to her personally. Her papers for classes were on hegemony and feminism, and she enjoyed talking about these topics on campus. She told me that at home, however, "it's not just avoiding conversations or talking to [my mom], it's feeling on a totally different place. We wouldn't even talk about the same things, much less try and talk about them in the same way." While Violet is talking about one set of topics, using one set of language, her mom is "dealing with how to get by, what jerky thing her boss said to her."

Rose similarly felt that the knowledge she'd gained at Linden helped her to understand more about the place she came from, but it also created some difficulties. She reflected on how her academic training made it difficult to talk with her parents about political issues:

> ROSE: Like it's really hard. I feel unless you're an academic and have
> taken sociology classes, it's really hard to understand welfare and
> things like teen pregnancy. Before I got here it was very easy for
> me to be racist or to be classist.
>
> LIZ: In what sense classist?
>
> ROSE: Just in like, why are so many—why do you have cable [TV when
> you're] on welfare; you don't have heat, but you have cable? It
> would piss me off, like, the lack of ambition . . . that's just one
> thing that drives me nuts, like not wanting more. . . . [Now] I re-
> mind myself of the sociology behind it and getting yourself settled,
> putting your money toward good things, good for your family but
> also morale. I guess that's where the cable comes in.

But, Rose continued, it's difficult to explain four years of new thinking to her parents, whose "life experience" leads them to very different beliefs than Rose's:

> You know, you can't—if they're all bashing the Latinas for not knowing
> English, it's like, a really fine line, and I haven't figured out how to go about
> it yet. It's hard because they're being racist. You want that activist [stance],
> like, "Hey, there's a certain way to see this." But, at the same time, be-
> cause you've had this college education, it's not your place, especially being
> younger [trails off]. It's kind of education versus life experience.

Thus new learning brought both empowerment and, sometimes, conflict with friends or family. Rose saw the ways she had learned to think sociologically about race and class stratification as conflicting with her parents' "life experience." Sharing her new insights as fact, privileging her scholarly learning to correct the views she now sees as incorrect, would be disrespectful, "not [her] place." Here, scholarly learning becomes a "double-edged sword" (in Violet's words), often serving to put respondents at odds with home communities and making maintaining those connections more difficult.

Gender as a Distraction

Respondents sometimes indicated that class as an issue could be overshad-owed by a shared, campus-wide academic dedication to gender and sexu-ality issues. Linden students seemed to be especially attentive to this one, largely shared, status—although Linden is a women's college, not all stu-dents identify as female—and issues of gendered oppression. Linden's founding and continued role in higher education is activist in the sense that it is intended to address one particular wrong, namely the lack of educa-tion for women. Moreover, the college stresses commonalities and shared disadvantages among women rather than differences between them.

The theme of gender empowerment is therefore often present in college discourse. For example, speaking on a panel about education, President Hartigan discussed the ways that Linden and other women's colleges have expanded women's access to education in very specific terms. She framed her comments in terms of "talking about equality of access and Linden's history" in terms of "women, who had few opportunities." She said that "at its founding, Linden did not start with exclusivity." She continued by noting that "injustice is built into systems; it is reflexive and steeped." She connected Linden's history and mission with providing access to women, countering "injustice . . . built into systems" that are "exclusive." Simi-lar narratives are stressed in Linden presentations about the reasons for single-sex education, the majors and careers chosen by Linden students and alumnae, and other exemplars.

By embracing the implication that one must claim what might other-wise be denied due to gender, Linden students may become particularly attuned to just one source of hierarchy. One faculty member reflected regretfully that Linden students get "caught up" in being empowered through sisterhood and womanhood, but she thought that a piece "falls away about examining other forms of privilege that one has," and a num-ber of respondents made similar observations. For example, Lynne told me that the core of Linden identity was entwined with thinking about gender: "Gender—obviously we're empowered women—but being a Lindie, more than anything else, is about being a woman. . . . Why do we talk about—as Lindies, we are always talking about gender and sexual-ity, and we're never talking about how those are impacted by race and class." Lynne, who strongly identifies as a feminist, began by noting that her fellow Lindies are typically economically privileged but liked to see themselves as aware enough to be "not a snob . . . modest." This awareness is undercut, however, by the focus on being a woman as a shared primary identity. Gender therefore seemed to act as blinders that prevented the recognition of other important sources of power in academic and extra-academic settings. Becca recalled how her seemingly progressive classmates did not seem to understand the ways that having few socioeconomic resources deeply constrained people's actions. But when the conversation turned to sex or gender, she noted, "they all get it." Similarly, when we spoke after her graduation, Michelle reflected that "class was also kind of invisible at Linden. . . . And not just, I mean not to belittle these things, but we'd talk about gender enough to like—we'd talk about, all we talk about is gender, that's the right way to say that. Gender and sexuality are *everything* at Linden." Although, as Michelle concluded, gender "is a thing that *should* be approached at a women's college," it still obscured other forms of difference. Thus, while this shared focus on gender was deeply meaningful for many students—as we saw in Lynne's comments about Judith Butler—it sometimes deflected important considerations of other forms of difference, notably class.

Faculty Interventions

Respondents sometimes hoped that faculty members could mediate difficult conversations. Some told me that the classroom was the only place where conversations about controversial or touchy topics were broached, class inequality being one example. Despite their evident positive intentions, however, faculty were sometimes stymied when they were met with silences around class inequality. What roles, then, did faculty members play on a campus like Linden in which students and faculty share relatively small classrooms and much higher levels of interaction than at most colleges?

Interestingly, although respondents described appreciating faculty members who shared their backgrounds and who reached out to them, sometimes with great emotion, they also reported being frustrated by faculty members' well-intentioned efforts to mediate classroom environments in ways that were intended to make them more open to low socioeconomic status students. Respondents described feeling annoyed when faculty members talked about how "most" Linden students are middle class or could afford to buy books, as part of making a point that not *all* Linden students share these privileges. At one CAL meeting, for example, students expressed annoyance that professors seemed to assume that everyone at Linden came from a privileged background. The students complained that the faculty said things like, "You all . . ." or "Most of you probably come from a middle-class background." Even though it's true that most people at Linden do—and even though low socioeconomic status students themselves hold this perception—the students resented being reminded of their otherness.

Faculty members' roles were therefore murky, not always effective, and sometimes defeated their intentions to reduce comparison making. This brings up the question of who was the intended audience, and it seems that faculty positioned middle-class students in that role. Ironically, this further marginalized low socioeconomic status students by making them a source of education for their peers. Like students, faculty members are not always able to manage class inequality adequately. In these circumstances, being in a classroom did not consistently provide a constructive space for bridging differences or speaking openly about class inequality. Faculty members sometimes would call on the next person or push conversation forward rather than engaging with comments made by classmates that enraged low socioeconomic students. Alternately, some faculty members would push students to discuss their beliefs or experiences but were unable to create a successful conversation about inequality.

Using Resources: Getting Help and Making Demands

The classroom is not the only place where students manage interactions with the formal structure of the college. As suggested in Georgina's and others' comments, the ability to use resources and advocate for oneself is often related to a middle-class or upper-class *habitus* and upbringing. Within the context of Linden, then, students' abilities to advocate for themselves, to take advantage of resources, is part of what makes a Linden student a Lindie, as we have seen. Failure to successfully navigate the administrative structure challenges students' identities as community members. How might a semiotics of class morality shape low socioeconomic status students' experiences in these venues?

To take up this question, I return to the CAL students' meeting with the dean of the residence halls described in the introduction to this chapter, in which the dean had come to meet with them to discuss a policy change. During this meeting, the dean attempted to establish herself and her office as relatable and trustworthy. She told the group "I usually go to bed around now" and mentioned her young son. She made efforts to find individual connections with students by asking about their work-study jobs and residence halls. She also pointed out the positive things the residence life and residence hall staff had done in past years, saying that they "would never" intentionally put a student in a bad situation. She addressed the new policy directly, apologizing for "the way the word was sent out, the announcement, and the timing of it." Finally, she asked for CAL's help in getting the word out more effectively about the housing fee and, crucially, to let people know that there might be help available for students who could not afford the new fees. As she stressed, her office would work with individual students to make sure that everyone had a place to stay who needed it. Throughout, she emphasized her good intentions and what seemed to be the key takeaway message during this meeting: students should contact her directly to make arrangements to work around the new policy.

While I was struck by her efforts to seem approachable, the CAL students heard her presentation very differently, as became apparent in the conversation they held after the dean left. Their reactions could be characterized collectively as distrust. For example, one student said she feels like Linden "appeases in the short term and then hopes that people graduate or forget over the summer so that the college can leave whatever controversial measure in place." Another noted that "it's not our responsibility to absorb their budget shortfall," implying that the college might be trying to pick up a little extra money through this fee. Students also used language that indicated a much greater trust in their personal peer networks rather than the official story, expressed through such phrases as "word is . . ." or "someone told me that . . . ."

This schism between a presentation that asks students to trust the college and students' perceptions of untrustworthiness highlights what I posit are two different ideas about the meanings of support, divergent understandings of how students make use of college structures that are deeply linked to the semiotics of class morality. On their side, administrators appeared to think that informing students of available resources and keeping their doors open to requests for help was sufficient support. As one administrator reflected in a meeting with other administrators, "Linden students feel very comfortable approaching people—administrators and faculty—when there's an issue." Consequently, administrators tended to use language and interactional approaches that assumed students would do just that. In the example above, the dean pointed out that her announcement e-mail had indicated that students concerned about the decision could "come in to speak with her," a direction she believed would allay fears and allow students who could not afford the forty dollar fee to seek assistance. She reassured listeners during her conversation with CAL that no student would be turned away or left with nowhere to live; they needed only to speak with her about their individual cases.

The dean's approach in this, exhorting students to ask for exceptions and personal attention, was not unique to this circumstance. Suggestions to individual students to stop in to see administrators were periodically offered in my presence as administrators told students to "come see me in my office" to ask for specific information, help, or exceptions. For example, during a public forum where students were encouraged to ask about various issues pertaining to campus life, one administrator told students: "If your hall isn't doing good diversity work, come see me or talk to your hall administration representative." Several other speakers closed their remarks by saying, "Come in and speak with me at my office hours or make an appointment to meet with me." This approach makes sense from a college organizational view. It saves the speaker from having to elucidate every possible situation and outcome in advance. It may also increase wiggle room by allowing exceptions to be made behind closed doors on a case-by-case basis.

Such an approach, however, presumes that students feel entitled to make requests. As we saw in the discussion of classroom dynamics, students were often both uncomfortable in seeking help and unsure of how to go about doing so, relying instead on a "no excuses" model of accomplishment. Perhaps even more fundamentally, however, the come-in-and-ask approach relies on students' being comfortable with vague talk and faith in the system as expressed in a presentation in which the rules are stated but an offer to make exceptions is also made. This approach conflicts with what findings have long indicated about working-class interactional priorities that favor "straightforwardness" or even "blunt honesty."[9] The official approaches are geared more toward middle-class and upper-class style preferences for abstract language.[10] It's easy to see how middle or upper socioeconomic status students, who have long learned not only to ask for exceptions but to be accustomed to rules being bent or broken on their behalf, would feel both more inclined and comfortable taking up this offer.[11] This individual-basis approach is the opposite of blunt talk, as it offers no guarantee of a positive outcome or even clear criteria for students to determine if they might qualify. Low socioeconomic status students therefore appeared to be wary of case-by-case decision making.

Asking for these kinds of exceptions also made the asker emotionally vulnerable: personal meetings might require students to share information they preferred not to share. The system of "come in and explain" means that students must go into detail about why they need extra support or are unable to pay for something that others can afford. Most CAL students, and presumably others, felt uncomfortable explaining exactly why they could not pay for room and board or other needs. They also felt that this information was already clearly communicated in their lengthy applications for financial aid and therefore should not need to be repeated. As one student exclaimed with frustration, "It's already on the FAFSA!" Here we might recall Alice's reflection in chapter 3 about why students may choose not to discuss their background with more affluent peers, when she said, "You will have to explain everything, like a teacher. And that's too emotionally stressful to have to do all the time." Despite the dean's efforts to be open and approachable, to my knowledge not a single CAL student, even after this face-to-face meeting, took her up on this offer. Instead, most worked out informal arrangements with friends. In other words, they sought out individual solutions that did not require them to ask for exceptions and give details about the reasons underlying their needs.

Students were sometimes proactive in questioning this ask-for-exceptions approach. In one exchange with the Career Center, Heather, the president of CAL that semester, asked about the types of opportunities available to alumnae, one of whom she was soon to become. She asked specifically about working with the career office after graduation—what kinds of services would be available? Bill Franklin, the director, described their system, whereby from zero to five years out "by and large" an alumna could work with the career officer and, after that, the Career Center contracted with a local consultant to do coaching. Had Heather not persisted beyond this response, the answer would have stayed answered as such.

Instead, Heather asked for a more detailed clarification: "So, is that without charge? And what does 'by and large' mean?" Franklin replied that in the first two years after graduation, consultations are free and after that there is a charge. "But it can be prorated—if you explain that you can't pay, it's no problem." Heather was skeptical of this and gave an example of a friend of hers who was charged and told that the fee was non-negotiable. Franklin said that the receptionist knows about the policy and that the alumna would have to explain her situation to the counselor. Franklin added that he had charged an alumna only once, and the person made six figures: "I didn't feel bad about charging her." Here, the initial explanation offered was that services are available "by and large" to alumnae, with no mention of charges. On following up, the fee was clarified, but, as seen in other scenarios, it was left to the discretion of the career officer and made the responsibility of the alumna to explain her exceptional need. Moreover, from the students' perspectives, the story of a peer who was denied clashed with the director's story of "only once" charging a fee.

Administrators' concerns for low socioeconomic status students and desire to provide support were evident in my conversations with them, and the offers of support reported here seemed genuine to me. However, the administrators' understanding of Linden students as a collective body that is comfortable with asking for exceptions or support shaped the ways in which support was offered. Here we see how students' class-related disadvantages were made invisible, hidden underneath a blanket under-standing of what it means to be a Linden student. Thus, some college support systems went underused by students, both because they exposed students to moral threats and because they rested on assumptions that students can comfortably advocate for themselves. Students from low-income and working-class backgrounds, however, often conceptualized making requests for extra help or exceptions to the rule as making them too vulnerable—particularly since there were no guarantees as to what might happen in response to such requests. A semiotics of class morality that links financial lack with a position of being a less-than-full community member makes it unlikely that students will choose to expose themselves beyond what has already been indicated on institutionalized forms, such as financial aid applications. Moreover, literature on the earlier years of schooling highlights the ways that students' *habitus* or world view may exclude learning about this kind of action. Students and administrators therefore often operated with different belief systems about the nature of help seeking, which diminished the likelihood of resources being fully used.

In the students' accounts in this chapter, we see how concerns about class morality manifest in two significant ways to shape the experiences of low socioeconomic status students in their formal interactions with the college. First, we see that although the classroom could at times be a positive place for conversations about class, it was also subject to the same silences around inequality and enforced by the same kinds of moral worries as other venues. Students and faculty often spoke of classrooms as safe spaces for talking about inequality and as a place of empowerment for students. However, classrooms were places where class-rooted comparisons took on special importance as the core of college life and meaning (as we saw with students' collective concerns about merit and legitimacy).

This duality arises, not only because of lower socioeconomic status students' perceptions of others' stronger academic preparation or cultural capital, but also because of the system of moral meanings attached to class status that makes openness around class threatening. Although faculty and administrators frequently acknowledge these issues, they are not always able to effectively mitigate the challenges that arise for their students. I therefore show that students' class backgrounds matter in ways beyond traditional understandings of access or preparation. While students did develop new forms of cultural capital and empowering academic knowledge—learning how to think critically about circumstances shaping their own lives, for example—this cultural capital was not always sufficient for them to make full use of college resources. This issue, in particular, continued to be important as respondents transitioned into their postcollege lives.

Second, students' and administrators' respective understandings about how students access support are informed by perceptions of how comfortable students are asking for exceptions. Administrators often seemed to rely on students' abilities not only to navigate the student-services network but also to speak up when extra help was required. This anticipation of requests for accommodation beyond the system in place seemed to be built into the formal structure of support, since administrators routinely advised students to seek out individual "customization" of college policies, to adapt Lareau's term.[12] Respondents, however, were uncomfortable asking for special help. Low socioeconomic status students described how they were unused to asking for help and unsure of how to do so—a finding that echoes work by Lareau and by Calarco. However, the reasons for not seeking extra support were not only rooted in a lack of understanding about how to navigate the college support system. Rather, respondents felt that their options were constrained by the same semiotics of class morality that prevails in other college venues: asking for help meant risking extended vulnerability. Students are asked to share information they feel is personal, possibly humiliating. Asking for extra help often touches a nerve for students already feeling sensitive about their roles or places at the college. A lack of firm answers and solid information from campus administrators creates doubts for students that their needs will be met. Students are told, "We will take care of you," but without a definitive statement (for example, rules or policies) it is impossible for a student to know what will actually happen, making it difficult to count on this kind of support. These effective declinations of support were presumably invisible to administrators, since one cannot easily track negative cases. Although faculty and administrators did want to support low socioeconomic status students, their efforts were undermined by the dynamics I describe.

6

After College

Class and Mobility

Several years after concluding the bulk of this research, I contacted as many of the original respondents as I could locate. What had happened, I wondered, as they moved through college and ultimately graduated? What were they doing now, and how did they reflect on the experiences we had spoken about during their time at Linden? In all, I spoke with nineteen out of the original twenty-six respondents, between one and five years after they had graduated. (This last round of interviews took place over several years, and respondents had a range of four cohort years among them.)[1] When I reached out to Violet by e-mail to ask about making a time for one last interview, she asked me to send her transcripts of our earlier conversations, which I did. In an e-mail, she wrote: "It's soooooo weird to read all those things I said that I don't remember *at all* . . . and yet I can so distinctly remember having other parts of that conversation almost word for word. . . . So many things feel like they have changed, but then reading over that interview reminds me that a lot of things are still pretty much the same." Violet's feeling that "so many things . . . have changed, but . . . a lot of things are still pretty much the same" speaks directly to questions about mobility: What *does* change for low socioeconomic status students by virtue of graduating from this elite college?

Mobility as an outcome of college completion is a central issue: one of the expectations of many scholars, administrators, and policy thinkers is that students from socioeconomically marginalized backgrounds who graduate from elite colleges will have strong opportunities to become upwardly mobile. That is, they will have access to white-collar, typically well-paid work that they would not have been able to obtain without a college degree. They will be able to benefit from the alumnae connections accrued through attending an elite college and become part of a network of white-collar workers and peers whose parents and personal networks are white collar. Attaining a degree from a four-year college is associated with wide-reaching outcomes such as home ownership, better health over time, ability to support family members and having a wider range of choices for one's children, neighborhood location, lower stress, and many other important long-term opportunities. Sociologists argue that there are a number of causes for these outcomes: while the learning we do in college is important, so are the friends we make (social capital), the prestige associated with a college degree (credentialism), the social "know-how" gained (cultural capital), all of which help connect alumni to white-collar jobs after college.[2]

However, we can also think about mobility in other, less tangible ways. As we have already seen, upward mobility—the movement from one class position to a more-advantaged one—does not simply mean having a better-paid job or more money in the bank. Rather, questions of status are implicated: What kind of esteem does our position accord, and how does it compare to others'? Issues of loyalty to family, maintaining the values of one's upbringing, and fundamental understandings of self-worth may all be connected to the kinds of class mobility shifts through which the students who became my respondents were moving. We might understand these questions as especially important given the kinds of narratives they shared about higher education, broadly, and Linden College, specifically. Allison Hurst has examined how this issue unfolds during college, asking how the experience of socioeconomic mobility shapes a sense of self and identity relative to one's home community and prospective future community. She has shown that the meanings of higher education, of what it means to have "academic success," are filtered through students' understandings of class—whether they embrace or reject the "hegemonic view that labor is less worthy" that is implied in many institutions of higher education.[3] She also shows how this touches students' lives in deep and profound ways, because assessments of class "worth" are relevant not only to the students but also to their families, home communities, and friends.

Perhaps because of these deeply personal issues associated with upward mobility, many white-collar professionals from working-class or low-income backgrounds describe what Alfred Lubrano calls "straddling" two class locations: having moved from one class location into another (though not all feel comfortable describing themselves now as middle class, despite having typical middle-class markers).[4] They often feel trapped between worlds, with one foot in each and totally at home in neither. Their recollections highlight the complicated questions of how mobility matters for relationships with old friends and family, as well as new social ties with contemporary (presumably middle-class) colleagues, friends, and partners.[5] How does one relate across what are now class differences, or within new similarities?

I found that, several years after graduating from Linden, respondents had reaped both benefits and hardships from their recent socioeconomic mobility. Although respondents had gained important hallmarks of middle-class status, such as white-collar professional occupations and incomes, they did not necessarily see themselves as middle class or feel comfortable with this shift in status. Although they had moved beyond the so-called ivory tower of college life, the implications of class morality remained important. Indeed, a semiotics of class morality is not limited to Linden or to college campuses; rather, such ideas permeate American life. However, moral worries specific to college and Linden seemed to remain, shaping respondents' experiences in three areas: sense of self, relationships with family and friends from home, and relationship to the college.

Sense of Self: Becoming and Being Middle Class

Several years after completing their degrees, respondents seemed well settled into young adult life in ways that capitalized on their college achievements. Most had begun or were about to begin graduate school; others had advanced in their careers. A few had bought or were about to buy homes, and a few had married. One had children. All seemed happy with their accomplishments. Genesis, for example, told me that after graduation she had returned to her home city to join a consulting firm for which she had interned one summer. When we spoke, she had worked there for two years. She was about to begin a master's degree in urban planning and joked that she might call me for advice when she had to begin teaching. Meredith was starting her second year with a nonprofit program providing short-term housing and food assistance to families in a small Southern city. She was about to move to New York to take a job in a similar field when we spoke, and like Genesis she had plans to stay in her field for the foreseeable future. Both jobs required four-year college degrees, had possibilities for further advancement, and had been obtained through the kinds of institutionalized pathways that Linden's college career office envisions for students—in these cases, internships or work fellowships.

Despite these accomplishments, questions about class status remained. Magdalena, for example, felt strongly that her class background continued to shape her life after college. When I spoke with her during spring of her senior year, she and a close friend were talking about moving to New York and trying to break into the clothing business with a pop-up store. Magdalena had worked in retail through college, and her friend had design experience. After graduating, however, Magdalena found herself called home to be closer to her parents and siblings and to help care for her grandparents. She made a life for herself not in New York but in her smaller hometown city where she managed the local franchise of a regional restaurant chain. She found the job through a hometown friend: they needed someone just when she was looking for work. Once she began, she discovered that she is extremely good at managing people. As she told me when we spoke, her job is fulfilling and she feels good about her role—in particular, about protecting the interests of the servers, bussers, and others who work for her from the pushy midlevel corporate managers who are her supervisors.

Despite her job satisfaction and enjoyment of her postcollege life, Magdalena was clear about differences between her pathway after college and those of her fellow graduates. When I asked her about whether she thought class still mattered, she was emphatic in her response:

> I remember learning about how you [pause], there is cultural capital, you know, where, because you are born into a specific class, you are afforded

a lot [more] opportunities than another person in another class. And I can honestly say that I still totally 100 percent agree with that. Because I mean, I come from a working-class background, [and] I don't think I have had as many opportunities after I graduated from college than other kids who I graduated from college with did.

For Magdalena, graduating from Linden and all of the benefits that accrued from her time there did not even out the differences between herself and her class-advantaged peers.

Given these kinds of remaining distinctions, questions about whether respondents had become middle class were complicated, both in terms of assessing class-status markers and in terms of class identities. Aleisha began working immediately after her graduation, taking a full-time position with an office where she had earlier interned. She was well paid—in fact, she noted that she paid off her student loans in under a year: "I saved and saved and saved, which wasn't that hard because I knew how to do it." This was made possible partially, she noted, because she was living in a new place, and she didn't know the area well or have many friends with whom to go out and spend money. But, more important, she wasn't accustomed to having or spending much money. She told me: "[The concept that] you have the income, you can afford to fly somewhere on vacation and stay in a hotel, that idea is still pretty foreign to me. . . . It's not what I'm used to; it doesn't feel right. So you know those habits of not spending are still a big part of how I operate. To me, I feel like I'm spending a lot of money, but when I look at my bank account, [I'm still saving a lot]." For Aleisha, this was symbolic of her class status, or more accurately her lack of certainty about how exactly that status might be adequately characterized. As she said earlier in the interview, "I feel like I'm still not fully a part of the echelon that my income grants me." Despite having a very prestigious job and an income that allowed her to pay off her loans within a year, she does not *feel* middle class or upper class.

This feeling of not having joined the social "echelon" indicated by her income or job went deeper than spending habits; for Aleisha and other respondents, the question of class status was in many ways framed along moral lines. Aleisha, for example, perceived that she and her new colleagues—people her own age with similar educational backgrounds and incomes—held different ideas about social and political issues. She related a story about a friend at work who wanted to open a new business in order to obtain a tax write-off. His plan to work the tax system to his advantage bothered Aleisha a great deal:

> Look, I know that I have a comfy wage, and I am not trying to support anyone except my big fat cat. But I grew up in Section 8 housing, on food stamps, the school lunches. I did programs like Upward Bound. I went to Head Start. I've had federal students loans that helped me pay for college. I have benefitted in so many ways from social programs. When I pay my taxes, yeah I bitch and moan, but it's mostly hollow because I've been on the receiving end of those programs. And so I don't—it's hard for me to pat you on the back when all you're looking to do, the sole purpose, seems to be so that you can not pay as much in taxes as you have. You know, it's hard for me to swallow. I realize that you are still obeying the letter of the law, the tax code, but it feels slimy.

Even though Aleisha now sees herself as making a "comfy wage" and told me later in the interview that she felt uncomfortable identifying with the Occupy Wall Street movement because of her keen awareness of how advantaged she is, her understanding of what is appropriate is shaped irrevocably by her childhood and teenage experiences rather than her contemporary class position. Although that background is perhaps invisible to those around her, she has not moved away from it in significant ways, such as her spending habits and her beliefs about public welfare. Significantly, Aleisha herself perceives that these distinctions between her own and her middle-class or upper-class colleagues' attitudes are rooted in her class background.

Alyssa was working through these same kinds of questions. After working for several years in a policy think-tank, she moved to Philadelphia to attend the University of Pennsylvania and begin a doctorate in communications. Being a student at an Ivy League university was challenging for the usual reasons, but also because of what it symbolized for Alyssa about herself:

> And then, I also have moments where people will ask me, "Oh, where do you go to school?" And this is something that I've been struggling with so much. And I'll always start off, instead of saying, "Penn, the [Annenberg] School of Communication," I always start off with "the School of Communication," and then I hesitate, and I cringe, but just a little, and I say, "at

Penn" [laughs]. And I'm like, Oooh [down-tone]. And I just feel so uncomfortable, and I don't know what it is. Sometimes, I mean, people, they're like really confused, because they're probably like, "Oooh, is she lying?" Or they're like, "Ooooooh" [awed sound], and I'm like, "No, no, no, no, no—those faces, stop it!" [laughs] Yeah, so that's something that's been like a little [pause] odd for me. I don't know when it'll get better.

The discrepancy Alyssa feels between her own sense of self and the image she has of a Penn student is large. She worries that people may think she is lying—how could she, Alyssa, be attending this university? At the same time, she worries that people will put her on some kind of pedestal at a remove from themselves. And she cannot reconcile this status as Ivy League student with her own sense of herself that makes her "hesitate [and] cringe" before admitting her specific graduate program, despite the accomplishment and hard work that it represents.

The contradictions Alyssa saw between being *herself* and being an Ivy League student became clearer when she described the fears she held about changing as she continued in an elite education system: "Because I don't want to—one thing I don't want to do is sound like that person, like, 'Oh, I go to this private university. I go to Penn. I go to school there' [braggy voice]. I don't ever want to be that person. I always want to be that person that's super humble [ends on a questioning tone]." Like Aleisha, Alyssa was concerned about the moral implications of becoming "that person" rather than remaining "super humble," despite her new status as a college graduate and Ivy League student. For respondents like Alyssa and Aleisha, the "echelons" that their hard work has netted are not fully comfortable places, not only because they include a different lifestyle but also because they challenge the moral connotations that attend to class-status positions. Staying humble or honest, or having other personal qualities, remained important to these respondents, but the practice of maintaining such an identity was made more complicated by their new surroundings.

Developing Relationships with New Peers

As implicated by Aleisha's narrative, the same moral comparisons that made locating respondents' individual class identities complicated were also evident in their discussions of relations with colleagues and new friends from affluent backgrounds (i.e., those with whom they now arguably shared a class position). These relationships were often still experienced as cross-class despite respondents' having nominally entered the middle class. And, although postcollege life was in this sense a continuation of the cross-class interactions they had experienced at Linden, some respondents reported that these interactions were hard to negotiate despite having moved upward. As Meredith noted, she "gets offended by so much stuff. People can't enjoy themselves around me, because I get offended, and I speak up." This creates problems, she feels, in interacting with those who grew up with greater financial advantages than she did. She continued: "I definitely felt [pressure to just get along on campus]. I feel it now—why can't I be okay with people pissing me off? I want to get along with people." Meredith reasons that she understands that people don't always know better. As she says, "people are ignorant; that's no fault of their own. That's part of why I do what I do, teaching people about class, because people are ignorant." Nonetheless, she perceives that others do not receive her attempts at education as helpful. Rather, her critical lens about class inequality and her unwillingness or lack of ability to just "make nice" are problematic for others.

Reflecting back on how people chose to hide their class backgrounds in college and after, Meredith concluded by noting that not only does she feel that her confrontation of classism is unwelcome but, indeed, even her self, in the form of her background, is unwelcome in her new life: "Class is so easy to hide, theoretically. Not as obvious as skin color or gender. You can hide it if you have the right tools. It's just awkward. I can feel the tension rising, whenever people find out I'm poor. All of a sudden it's like I opened a can of worms, like they can't joke around with me. They don't know how to react." Meredith's phrasing here implies a sense of expectation on the part of others. Class inequality is "awkward" and makes others uncomfortable, removes the social ease between ostensible peers. Meredith seems to become framed as the offender in these interactions: it would be easier for everyone else if she would refrain from making her class background clear. Moreover, her reflections suggest that the self-confidence and assurance that many respondents said they gained at Linden help them confront classism but not necessarily to feel better about it. That is, the process of cross-class interaction is difficult even with the benefit of solid discursive tools in one's pocket.

Alyssa was also frustrated by gaps between her own and her peers' experiences. Attending an Ivy League graduate program meant that Alyssa was surrounded by middle-class and affluent peers. She found that she was more aware of difference than she had been at Linden, perhaps because of the student support services at Linden that provided pockets of funding, and also because she was one of the only respondents whose social circle entirely comprised peers from class and race backgrounds similar to her own. When we spoke, Alyssa had just begun graduate school, and she recalled some experiences she had as she prepared to attend graduate school. Many of her co-workers were going through the same process, with many looking at the same kinds of professional programs. Alyssa recalled that she had not been able to afford the application fees for many programs and therefore needed to be very selective. Her peers, by contrast, were sending numerous applications and scheduling campus visits to multiple campuses. Alyssa was baffled as to how they could do it until she realized that those costs were largely paid by parents. This comparison became more emotionally tinged when a co-worker seemed to assume that Alyssa shared those same resources: "And their parents were paying for their schools, and I was just like, 'Man, I wish,' and I remember one time this girl that I was—actually, it *really* upset me when this time she actually said, 'Oh Alyssa, like, you wouldn't know what it's like paying rent because you live at home with your parents.'" This off-hand comment felt to Alyssa like a slur or an attack, since, although Alyssa lived at home, she was repaying student loans in amounts that very likely equaled the speaker's rent. Alyssa was incensed:

> So then I was, I was just like, "How dare you even say [that], you have no idea how much I struggle and how the little bit that I can I try to help my parents pay their bills. I remember I was totally capable at the time at my house. I mean it wasn't a lot, but it was just like 100 dollars less that my parents had to worry about for the month. You know? And just like trying to do what I could, and it's just so infuriating to me that everything you said, you don't know me at all. . . . I don't live that privileged lifestyle that you're thinking I live because I live at home with my parents and I don't pay rent."

Being assumed to share that privilege, being seen as a privileged person, offended Alyssa deeply. This not only was inaccurate but, more important, it seemed to impugn her sense of morality: rather than mooching off her parents she was contributing to her family and "struggling" to pay off her own debts.

These kinds of comparisons stuck with her as she moved through graduate school. She reflected that, although she liked her cohort, she found no one "like her" there. Her peers had attended good high schools and colleges, she said, and had parents who were white collar professionals. It seemed like "destiny" for them:

> For instance, certain people who did their undergrad at Penn or maybe their parents . . . came to Penn or their parents are professors or lawyers or doctors, and they went to really good schools and they went to private schools so they have sort of, they're sort of destined to [be enrolled here]. It's sort of the path you take. But that's not the path I have, so, it's—I could have easily been somewhere else, also. I could have easily, you know, been—I dunno, working at a really low-paying job. If certain things happened in my life, like if I went a different way, I could have easily been in that position.

Alyssa's time at Linden had helped her build academic skills and (as she told me later) become comfortable speaking with faculty members, which she understood as being important to her graduate school outcome. However, it did not seem to her to patch the differences between her peers' and her own socioeconomic background or somehow make them comparable in her eyes. As we saw in the discussion of respondents' senses of class location, the ways in which they were middle class on paper—job titles, college degrees, and income levels—did not lead them to feel kinship or understanding with others who had grown up in this class position. These feelings of discomfort with nominally similar peers, and of frustration with others' assumptions of middle-classness, are deeply reminiscent of their experiences at Linden, raising questions about what changes when one graduates.

Habitus and Class-Linked Skills

Respondents' uncertainty about their new class position seemed to have potential implications for their abilities to deploy the kinds of class-linked advantages that are associated with middle-class and upper-class *habitus*, such as requesting accommodation or networking. At least in some cases, respondents' narratives suggest that, although they have become familiar with middle-class cultural "tool kits,"[6] their world view continues to make these resources an uncomfortable option. The strongest example of this was Magdalena's clear description of class-linked skills that she still considered not within her grasp. Comparing her friends' postcollege job searches and her own experience finding work, she told me:

> You know, they have greater social networks that they can rely on because their parents . . . like how many people do I know that got a job, or got a position because their dad knew someone or their mom knew someone in this [field]. Like I knew someone who knew someone [to help me get a job], and that was great, and that was awesome, and I found I was really good at what I do, and I've actually been able to be very successful at it. But is it exactly 100 percent the way I wanted to go? No. I mean when I first came back I did a lot of applying to nonprofits in the area. . . . And it's all about who you know.

Magdalena's job did come through connections but not the kind of connections that get you the kind of job that Magdalena at first envisioned after college—and not the kind of connections that Linden career advisers, sociologists, and policy thinkers envision when talking about developing social capital networks. Magdalena could have opted to contact Linden alumnae as a supplement to her own local ties. This is something Linden emphasizes to students as a resource and one strong benefit of graduating from an elite college: one is an automatic member of a network. Despite being aware of this network, however, Magdalena did not feel comfortable calling on this network when the time came:

> I was very reticent about doing that because to me it just felt disingenuine, you know. I've never—I don't know these women from Adam, other than I get the Linden newsletter and the invitation to go to the Linden College Club events. I don't know who these people are [pause], and I'm just supposed to call them? I'm supposed to just like call them and be like, "Hey, I need help" or "Hey, I want a job in this. You don't know me from Adam. I don't know you from Adam, but apparently we're supposed to have a connection with one another because we went to the same college." That never made sense to me. But like I said, I'm scrappy and I know people [here], and I found something that I'm very good at, that I'm doing well at. However, do I think that if I had come from a different socioeconomic background, would I be on a different path right now? Absolutely.

What is crucial here is not only that Magdalena refers to the kinds of network connections, or social capital, that scholars have long argued constitute an important aspect of intergenerational class transmission, but also her reflection on her inclination to take advantage of her college connections—her *habitus*. While Linden College offers the alumnae network as a resource for job seeking and other opportunities, and Magdalena understood that this pathway existed, she felt uncomfortable capitalizing on this option. This suggests that graduates from low socioeconomic status backgrounds may not only wrestle with incongruities between their nonelite *habitus* and their newly elite cultural or social capital but also that they may not make as full use of these resources as their middle-class or upper-class cohort peers. Thus, the benefits of elite college graduation appear not to be evenly accessible.

We can relate these data to a respondent in Jenny M. Stuber's discussion of social class in college life, in which she compares middle-class and working-class students' approaches to extracurricular opportunities. Describing her thinking about activities such as networking and the practiced presentation of a professional self that seem to be expected skills of middle-class students, a working-class respondent told Stuber that "later on in life, I don't really see how being in all these clubs and stuff [will matter]. . . . I just hope that interviewers will be able to see that I'm someone who's grounded and understands the importance of being at work every day."[7] This reflects what may be a shared feeling about how one earns a position or other opportunity. While Linden encourages all alumnae to make use of its network, a form of institutionalized social capital, not all alumnae feel at ease with this option. Although Magdalena did not frame her response in these terms, her response may indicate a moral conflict between earning a position on one's own and her peers' abilities to call on parents or alumnae to provide a job.[8] Here again we see that college graduation did not necessarily lead to the assumption of middle-class or upper-class inclinations, or at least not within the first few years.

Changing Relationships to Home

The other side, so to speak, of respondents' mobility is formed by their relationships with family and friends from home. I asked each respondent about changes to these ties, ways in which their time at college or transition into adulthood might have changed those family and high school bonds. It is, of course, not uncommon to see relationships with high school friends or one's family change during college. People develop other interests and senses of identity or simply lose touch, and social ties are often frayed or severed. For low socioeconomic status students, however, these questions may have additional implications. For these students, going to college—especially a selective college like Linden—means entering a world with a different class ethos than the one in which they grew up, one associated with the classed rhetoric of "bettering oneself," as Diane Reay notes.[9] In most cases, they enter this world alone, because friends and family do not experience the same mobility trajectory. Indeed, as we saw in chapter 2, hometown friends and family are often framed as outsiders to Linden and to respondents' adult lives. Thus, one of the most important topics in these final interviews was respondents' ties to home. Here I discuss friendships and broader community ties, as well as relationships to parents.

Friends and Home Community

Most respondents noted that their high school or hometown friendships had already frayed during their college years for simple reasons of distance—this dynamic had frequently been mentioned in earlier interviews. After graduating from college, this trend of attenuated ties continued, sometimes in ways that respondents perceived as related to class mobility, other times not. For example, Genesis reflected: "It's too late now, I think. We're all so different. [It's] got to the point where we're all different people. One friend I've known since third grade or something. She doesn't live in the city, but we keep in touch and hang out when she's in the city." In narratives such as this one, the role that attending Linden played seems ambiguous. Most respondents indicated that their former friendships had changed and largely fallen away, but it was not clear whether this was because of time and distance or because of discrepant class positions. Several respondents, however, discussed changes in former friendships in ways that were clearly related to socioeconomic changes, though not always in ways we might expect. For example, several respondents maintained strong ties to hometown friends but reported discomfort, awkwardness, or pain in managing what had become differences when one graduated from an elite college while the other either did not go to college or did not attend a similar institution.

Maya, for instance, spoke movingly about her relationship with friends and family from home, who looked up to her. While she felt good about being a positive role model, she also felt uncomfortable with the distancing and othering that is inherent in being positioned as a role model.

> Sometimes when I go home it's like, you're kind of on this little platform [ends questioningly], like whether you want to be or not. And so what you say and how you act, people look at [you] more closely. . . . I feel like, you can't put your finger on it sometimes . . . but people tell me, and it kind of makes me uncomfortable, that I look up to you or I look up to you for what you are doing or I'm jealous, I wish I could be [where you live]. I wish I went to college or I stayed in college or went out of state.

Maya tried to encourage friends and family but also to remove any implication of status difference between them. She noted, "Maybe they don't have somebody or a parent or whoever telling them, community college is just as good as four-year colleges or your job at the store. Your full-time job promotion from part-time hours is just as good as whatever I'm doing in [my job]. Like I don't think that what I'm doing is more important than what you're doing, and I don't think they should see it that way either." In order to manage these interactions, Maya told me, "Sometimes I might downplay stuff that I'm doing a little bit." She described feeling like she has to remind people that she "falls off [her] bike all the time or gets lost" and other personal foibles, or she talks about the downside to her life in the big city and talks up her hometown.

Alyssa perceived similar challenges. When telling me about her graduate school enrollment, she noted that "when other people ask me where I go to school, I just have trouble saying 'I go to Penn' a little bit. Because so, so many assumptions come with that." When I asked her about those assumptions, what kinds of impressions did she think might people get of her, she elaborated on the ways she worried that she might be seen as too different from people in her home community:

> Like maybe, "Oh, she must be very, very smart," and I think I am smart, but I'm not a genius. And then those other people it's like, "Oh wow, how did she get there?" And that's just like sad because it's just [unclear] community,

where it's just like, you, you could be here too! And you can do this, but it's just unfortunate that things have happened in your life, where like you can't be where you are now. . . . I'm like, "No, actually, you could be here too, but certain things happened in your life where—I don't know—certain things happened that just didn't allow you to be here, but if you wanted to, if things were different for you, you could easily be here successful too. It's not because I'm a genius."

Alyssa's unease with feeling exceptional, at feeling fundamentally differ-ent from her home community, is palpable. She does not want to be seen as a "genius," someone so marked as different that they become unapproach-able. This discomfort in being picked out as special and therefore othered from her own community echoes Maya's recollection of her hometown pushing her simultaneously toward education and out of their commu-nity: to "make it" means leaving. Alyssa and Maya both spoke of trying to show people how they were not special, how "if things were different for you, you could easily be [successful here] too." Rather than seeing her at-tainment as affirmation of a specialness and individual hard work, or cele-brating this further step into middle-class or upper-class life, Alyssa seeks to minimize difference in order to confirm her home community member-ship and sameness.

For these and other reasons, hometown friendships sometimes become complicated. Some respondents described managing what have in some ways become cross-class interactions. Amber, for example, noted that she has kept up with a number of friends from high school but that their lives are very different. She told me that, in addition to being in touch with her best friend, she stays in touch with a group of friends from home now who are doing a wide variety of things in their early adulthood. Some went to college, some are still working in their high school jobs. Some went to technical school, some are working two jobs. Some are working for their parents. But, described Amber, "everybody's just really settling down . . . just like in a really different place in life than I am. . . . They're my friends, and I care about them, but I don't really know much about them on a deep level." Although she has been able to maintain these ties to home, her friends' and her own life have become so different that Amber no longer "knows much about them." This reflection speaks to large questions about the elasticity of social ties: What does friendship mean when you "don't know much about" the other person or feel that you meaningfully share their world. Amber used to be immersed in this world, but now she feels a distance.

As seems to be the case here, friends from home brought socioeconomic mobility into starker relief for a number of respondents. Comparisons between forms of work, choices about family, and tastes in food or leisure all served to differentiate and in some cases to make maintaining ties difficult for simple logistical reasons, as when one person has become a parent or works different hours. Not all respondents experienced these difficulties: Evelyn and Isabel, for example, both moved back to their home communities and reconnected with friends there, renewing their friendships as adults with friends from high school or the neighborhood. Maya and Amber also retained close ties with old friends, despite struggling to reconcile these friendships in the contexts of their own and their friends' adult lives. Ultimately, however, these friendship ties—whether maintained or severed—provide additional ways to think about the process of socioeconomic mobility and what may be both gains and losses. We see similar struggles in respondents' ties to parents.

Relationships with Parents

Comparisons with parents were heavily implicated in questions of socioeconomic mobility as respondents approached or moved past their parents' earning, purchasing power, and occupational statuses. Several had described struggles with parents during our interviews while they were at Linden.[10] These struggles continued as students graduated and became young adults. Although most respondents reported being emotionally close with their parent(s) and in some cases becoming closer after college, some nonetheless felt a change in their relationship that was shaped in some way by their college-graduate status. Money, careers, and even graduation brought new sources of tension. For example, Rose said that her relationship with her parents had already been "complicated" and was not getting easier as she moved into her twenties: "And it makes you feel so. . . . I remember when I first left Linden, and I immediately got a job, my first job, you know, to me I was making big bucks. I was making, I think, thirty thousand dollars, which in my world was like huge bucks. Even then, my parents—that was more than [my mom] had ever made in her life." She concluded by saying, "They had a job, not necessarily careers per se, and it was difficult" to bridge that gap and still relate to them in the same way.

Rose elaborated as she spoke about her recent enrollment in a graduate program that would help her continue to advance in her professional field: "I grew so much intellectually at Linden, and then with my job, professionally, it's really made my connection with my parents difficult." Although she noted that they are "still [her] parents," Rose told me that "they can't really relate to school. They can't relate to grad school, and they can't relate to my job. You know, I'm in management now. So when I talk and I complain about employees or grad school or something, it's just totally not on their radar; it's really hard for them to comprehend." Rose has moved to the other side, as it were, of the labor-management relationship that has shaped much of her parents' blue-collar working lives. Rose's workplace experiences and day-to-day frustrations are therefore even more remote and difficult for her parents to connect to. Rose's enrollment in graduate school has not made that connection easier as she moves further and further away from her parents' world, despite remaining emotionally attached.

Evelyn also experienced struggles with her parents as she moved through college. Although they had been supportive of her intention to go to college, once she was enrolled she found that her parents could not understand how much of her time course work required, which often competed with family expectations, since her parents lived only a short distance away. Although this tension was eventually resolved, it rankled Evelyn a bit to hear her parents bragging about her accomplishments a few years later after she completed her degree and made plans to continue her education:

> I think to them to them it's kind of like a trophy. Like I'm like this little trophy. They're always like, "Look, this is my daughter!" Like my dad was [pause] it drove me crazy when I was getting ready to graduate from Linden, but it was endearing at the same time. I was wanting to have little gatherings and celebrations, and he was saying, "I earned this too." Like, you know, "You're my daughter, and I've wanted this for you and da da da da da." And at the time, it was annoying, and [I felt], "You did not earn this, *I* earned this. I worked very hard for this. As a matter of fact, if it wasn't for you *not* supporting me, I would not have gone to Linden. And, so, and now I'm finishing Linden." But, you know, it is what it is.

Evelyn's parents had pushed her to enroll in a local community college rather than looking for a four-year college. This is what got her to

Linden—her first campus had a standing transfer relationship with Linden. Thus, as Evelyn points out, had her parents supported her four-year college goals initially, she might have begun at a four year college elsewhere. Now that she has completed her time at Linden and is looking into graduate work, they seem to lay claims to her achievements that seem unfair given their inconsistent support and sometimes added stresses. She resents being positioned as a kind of "trophy" when she has struggled for her achievements. However, Evelyn concluded this segment of the interview by noting how thrilled her parents are about her upcoming doctoral work, and she no longer minds their bragging that she will soon be "Doctor Evelyn" and will have her own office.

Genesis echoed Evelyn's frustrations of being seen as a kind of trophy or shared victory. In her case, long-time frustrations with her mother became exacerbated by her college graduation. Genesis described her relationship with her mother as being "like a mountain": it was a long, difficult climb to get to a good point, and now it has gone back downhill. As we talked about her relationship with her mother since Genesis graduated, her frustration was clear: "She doesn't say it to me, but she goes around bragging about me going to college, graduating, [that I] got a job. It's annoying to me 'cause [she] didn't do any of it! She talks as if she did so much, but I can't call her out on it. . . . [I feel like] 'You didn't ask how I paid for my books. You didn't even visit once, what are you talking about?'" Genesis's experience of college, the struggles she had there, were very much her own. Her mother had not been especially supportive during difficult times at Linden, despite being generally supportive of Genesis's college plans. Now that the hard work has been done, it is frustrating for her to be asked to share that experience as an accomplishment for them both.

Even when relationships are not as antagonistic as that of Genesis and her mother, postcollege lives sometimes introduced uncomfortable silences around respondents' new lifestyles, incomes, or financial capacities as compared to those of their parents. For example, Aleisha explained at length about her process of budgeting for a new car and how difficult this had been to talk about with her mother. Aleisha paid for the car with her savings, after carefully researching an affordable nonluxury model. Her mother also bought a brand-new car that year, her first ever. But when Aleisha mentioned her own purchase, her mother's response was, "Oh, Miss Moneybags." This was emblematic of Aleisha and her mother's broader relationship when money came up. As she told me, "I don't talk money with my mom because I am uncomfortable about it. And I know that if I am, then she must be. And I know that she is not comfortable talking about how much money she brings in. I can only guess [what she earns]." In a related instance, her mother included Aleisha on an e-mailed inquiry about a house. Aleisha saw the address and looked it up on Zillow. As with the car, the purchase of this modest house would have been a first for her mother, achieved after many years of saving and financial struggle. And with the purchase, her mother's mortgage would be two hundred dollars less than Aleisha's current big-city rent. Aleisha told me, "I looked at that [price] and went, 'Shit mom, I'll give you a down payment.'" She concluded, "It's weird for me to think that if I saved up for a year and a half, I could buy my mother a house with a check. This is why we don't talk about money." Aleisha's upward mobility brought the comparison between their two worlds so vastly out of range that communication about money was unmanageable.

These comparisons sometimes caused respondents discomfort not only with parents but also with themselves, bringing about introspective questions about who they had become. While Maya maintained strong relationships with her mother and father—and in many ways had become closer to each of them since graduating—she found that her perspective on their lives had changed in ways that were not comfortable for her:

> My parents' house is a mess. Like it's the house I grew up in, but it's so different from where I live now. And I don't know [pause], if I saved more money or didn't go out as much and saved that money, I could probably help them out a little or more than I am now, especially because houses are cheaper at home. It wouldn't take much. And that's something I'm really planning to do in the next few years. . . . That's become really important to me, even though it's the house I grew up in, getting them out of that house. . . . Every time I go home and I see the house and I see the condition of the bathroom and the condition of the kitchen and, to be honest, I see roaches, and I'm like, you know, it's not fair. And I think that's what changes the relationship with my parents.

Maya's words speak volumes about the conflict she feels in determining how much to support her family and how to balance that with a young adult social life: How does one balance family responsibilities with one's own goals? She also seemed uncertain and uncomfortable with her new-found assessment of her childhood home: what was once home now seems perhaps not good enough.

As we can see, respondents had questions about supporting or caring for their parents, particularly given their increased financial abilities. Despite being only a few years out of college, several reported increasing their caretaking of parents or other family members. Although these anecdotes were not always explained in terms of class, they are related to parents' economic status and respondents' desires to provide better lives for their family—a desire that was sometimes uncomfortable, since it was evidence of distance and change. Meredith told me: "Really, my family situation is so complicated. I don't think it has to do with being lower class." She explained that she had long had a strained relationship with her mother, who had initially not wanted her to go to college and then wanted her to stay home and commute to community college: "First year there was a lot of tension." But in recent years her mother has been sick, and Meredith has been trying to help care for her when she can, albeit from a distance. Describing her mother's health struggles, she noted, somewhat contradicting her earlier statement: "But that has a lot to do with class, because she gets bad [medical care]," because her income does not provide her with access to many medical resources and she does not have private health insurance.

Similarly, Amber's mother has faced medical issues in the last several years. Because Amber's parents are divorced and Amber is an only child, there are few other sources of support for her mother to rely on: "All of that was a huge stress for me. . . . Your life needs to go on. You can't keep worrying about your mom 'cause there's nothing you can do to control that. . . . Family life just like weighs on you so heavily and the responsibilities that you feel. I'm an only child, and neither one of my parents are super well-off." Although Amber has pursued employment and now graduate school out of her home state, the thought of her mother's illness and isolation sticks in the back of her mind as a stressor and responsibility.

Although respondents often did not see themselves as inhabiting new class positions—or at least not fully or comfortably—the changes in their lives relative to their friends, families, and home communities nonetheless changed their relationships. Very few respondents reported real breaking of ties, but many reported strains and struggles. Whether these arose because respondents were earning more than their parents, shared less in common with friends and family, or felt othered as the result of having "made it," questions of how to maintain relationships across new differences were profound. Barbara Jensen talks about some of these issues as "survivor guilt" at having been able to remove oneself from many of the things that make working-class and low-income positions difficult in daily life.[11] We can also see these as associated with moral worries, since respondents are likely to be accorded the kinds of legitimacy and esteem offered to (and by) middle-class and upper-class people, while friends and family who remain working class and low income are not.

In thinking about respondents' putative upward mobility—putative because not everyone believes that living a middle-class life is "better"[12]— graduating from college is seen as the entryway to the middle class. As noted, graduates of four-year colleges, and especially those who attended elite colleges, make gains across cultural, social, and human capital fields, drawing on each of these capacities to produce exactly the kinds of tangible life changes discussed here. This very large role for college is reflected in current political discourse and legitimated in the comparative earnings of college graduates versus high school graduates.

I began the book by examining the ways that low-income, first-generation, and working-class students are positioned and understand themselves within their college context. I want to conclude this chapter by examining how respondents themselves looked back on their college lives and on the college itself. In particular, based on those earlier interviews, did respondents see themselves as members of the Linden community after years of enrollment and alumnaeship?

Looking Back on Linden: "Blessings" and Challenges

Overall, respondents thought that they had benefitted from their time at Linden. Michelle and Maya, for example, both talked about how much they missed the intellectual conversations at Linden, which were not as easy to find after graduation. Alyssa talked about how she was more self-assured and felt more comfortable speaking with faculty than many of her graduate school cohort as a result of having gone to Linden. However, roughly a third of respondents spoke ambivalently about their time as students, as though still feeling the sting of "hidden injuries" experienced there.[13] These were not hardships that had been ameliorated by the passage of time or experiences looked back on as merely of the moment.

Genesis provided a strong example of this duality. She described Linden as "a blessing" and told me that she felt very lucky to have attended Linden: "Looking back, I'm really grateful." At the same time, she added:

> I mean I was grateful, but certain things I hated it for. But now, now that I think about it, who am I? If it hadn't been for Linden, maybe I would have gone [to some other college]. But there would have been no other way to go to private school if Linden hadn't given me as much financial aid and hadn't been as patient with me paying my tuition late. The financial aid office was rude and everything, but they helped me figure out the best financial aid package, helped me find a balance that worked out for me. Now I am "in" already—the name of Linden is all it takes. Looking back, I'd do it again.

Genesis said that she would "do it again" and clearly felt that her time at Linden benefitted her. But she also spoke about how hard her life at Linden had been: she had sometimes felt excluded and noted elsewhere in the interview that, even in retrospect, she thought Linden "was not meant for people like [her]"—she had sometimes "hated" being there.

Similarly, Rose took pains to emphasize in our interview that she had felt happy at college but in retrospect that she still felt uncomfortable: "I mean there were definitely times when I felt like a Lindie, but then there were also times when I felt not like a Lindie but like someone who was given a ticket to Linden." By "ticket," Rose meant she felt that rather than having earned her admission she had been "included" by the college for reasons not related to her intellectual capacities: she was selected to receive a special gift and thus marked indelibly as an outsider. This feeling had not lessened as she moved further into her postgraduate life as an alumna:

> I think I had, I would say, an elite experience. It's been an elite experience and an elite education, and I wouldn't say that it felt, looking back on it now, I don't think it felt like life. I don't feel that Linden ever became a part of me. I mean it was very important to me, and I value it tremendously. I'm very grateful for the education it gave me and the things I learned and the experiences that I had. . . . But it still felt like an experience, not like it was a part of me.

Respondents like Genesis and Rose highlight the ways these young women drew connections between class and belonging at college. They were not merely *different* at college—or rather their difference was not neutral. There were distinct negative undertones of exclusion, of feeling less-than. These findings remind us that class inequality and upward mobility are not only about access to advantages or opportunities but also concern larger and more deeply felt issues of stigmatization and belonging.

This was also evidenced in the ways they talked about their identities as alumnae. For example, Rose spoke at length about her involvement in an annual fund-raiser near her hometown. As a former recipient of a scholarship paid for through just such a sale, she felt somewhat obligated to attend:

> I remember getting that scholarship one year. So I always felt indebted. And I felt really guilty last year because I didn't go and volunteer at the fund raiser. I felt like I owed Linden, I owed the fund-raiser. And they actually did like this whole documentary on it. The [scholarship program] has been going on for thirty years or something ridiculous. But they were doing this little documentary thing on it for the archives. They called me [because] they really wanted to get me on camera to, you know, like an interview and get some little snippets of stuff. So, in some ways I kind of, it's kind of re-minding you that you're not a Lindie, and you were given this gift of a Lin-den education, but you're not, you didn't like pay for it yourself—or even just get *some* financial aid [but] pretty much just [a] free ride. And it's those types of experiences—that while I'm happy to help Linden out, they also make me feel more separated from Linden.

This perceived indebtedness seemed to separate her from Linden even in retrospect. Rose felt that, although she "loved" Linden, "it wasn't [her]." This distinction became clearer as she elaborated on how she sees herself interacting with Linden as an adult:

> And, you know, I don't know, going forward, I don't how involved I'll be with Linden, because when I can get involved in Linden—this is just kind of my own head space and my own mind frame—I always feel indebted. And I don't like that feeling. And it seems like I can't shake it. And I think, you know, when someone basically gives you, I don't know, probably like $170,000 worth of education, it's hard to not—and then they kind of exploit that—it's hard not to [feel indebted].

Rose's sense of indebtedness, something she "can't shake," speaks volumes about the ways in which she does not feel like a real Linden student, even several years after graduation—and even though Rose benefitted professionally and intellectually. Indeed, she took care to specify in our interview that she had loved many aspects of college at Linden. Rather than being entitled to that education like everyone else, Rose felt, however, that she was "given" rather than having earned her place. Even though she "loved it," her sense that she owes the college and may even be "exploited" by virtue of that debt tell us that moral questions of who belongs at Linden have not faded over the years.

Maya also perceived a complicated relationship between the college and students, particularly students from low socioeconomic status or racialized minority backgrounds (both of which describe Maya personally). Perhaps more than any other respondent, Maya seemed to embody Linden—confident, ambitious, accomplished in her career as a researcher for a lobbyist for green energy, and involved in her local Linden club leadership—she was even thinking about pursuing a greater role in the national alumnae association. She felt strongly that she had gained as a Linden student and felt comfortable building on those gains. However, when I asked her about the kinds of issues Rose and other respondents mentioned, it was clear that she understood these personal gains to exist within a broader and more dynamic relationship: "I don't want to sound like Linden is like my everything, benefactor, protector. I feel like they do a lot of that already on their own [laughs]. I mean, [it's] a strong word, but I think it's kind of true [laughs]—like, they use us. They use us totally in marketing; they use us in funding drives to pull at people's heartstrings." For Maya, being "use[d] in their stuff all the time" as a figurehead for low socioeconomic status students or for minority enrollment or as a person who helps drive up the "numbers game" that she understands as being important to both Linden and students was part of an equal exchange. She admitted: "Yeah, like, they use us, and I see that, and I recognize it, and I'm like, 'Okay, like I'm using you too [laughs]. I'm using your name; I'm using your networks; I'm using your resources.' That's why I really don't feel guilty, because I'm like, no, they use me in their stuff all the time, and it's not to say I have negative connotation of Linden, it's just realistic." In contrast with Rose, Maya feels that her relationship with the college is an exchange: she uses their name and resources, while they use her as an example of diversity in their materials. The nuances of this exchange relationship are immediately clear in Maya's framing of "they" rather than "us" or "we"—in other words, despite her extensive alumnae volunteer work and leadership, she does not frame the college as a community of which she is a part. Rather, it is a community with which she has a relationship.

Like Maya, a number of respondents were clear-eyed about the class and status benefits of going to college in this elite space. Aleisha, for example, thought that she had been a realist when considering her college options.

> I like to think that I went to Linden with my eyes open. I got in to [my local state university, and] I got in to Linden College. The reason you go to Linden isn't because the journalism program is better, because it's probably not. It's because of the connections that you'll make and because of the alumnae network and the benefits of being a Linden alum, instead of a [local] alum. . . . I mean Linden was also the only school that I could really afford, so it was kind of like well, it's got this great thing going for it, and it's got this great scholarship, thank you.

Thus, for Aleisha, the status-related benefits of a Linden degree outweighed any concern she may have had in selecting an elite college for herself, as well as the memory of bumps and bruises experienced during her time there.

The tension between having accrued benefits as well as challenges, being part of a community while also "used" by that community, is summed up nicely by Amber. Reflecting her earlier student ambivalence about her role in the college, Amber told me, "I do think that I wouldn't be the person I am today if I hadn't been at Linden and experienced that opposition [and seen] what is wrong with our class structure. . . . I don't hold a grudge against Linden. . . . It is embedded in a larger structure." However, she also said that ultimately, "I just never feel like I will completely claim that as part of my identity." While Linden to a great extent made her "the person [she is] today," and while she understands the challenges she faced there within a larger structure, it is something she remains in some sense outside of and apart from.

Although most of the former Lindies I contacted had experienced upward socioeconomic mobility, their experiences direct our attention to real complications and the jagged, rather than smooth, nature of this arc. Although we tend to conceptualize a person's life as a complete whole, these respondents' experiences imply rather a fractured, contingent, or still-shifting class sense, one in which the moral pains and "hidden injuries" of class are still at least sometimes in play. We therefore have a picture of uneven mobility—at least in this early adulthood stage. Respondents had obtained middle-class and white-collar jobs but not necessarily a transformation into the middle class in the sense of having become comfortable there or having gained the kinds of cultural capital and social fluency necessary to effectively maneuver in the ways that a person from the middle class might. In other words, their *habitus* has not necessarily changed. This observation raises interesting questions about upward mobility and what changes happen in the process: Can we separate respondents' *habitus* shifts and senses of self from their occupational, educational, and income statuses?

Several years after graduating, respondents seemed to be both adjusting to middle-class life and struggling to figure out how to locate themselves within this class position. While respondents no longer thought of themselves as inhabiting low-income or working-class positions in the same way they had before college, they clearly also did not see themselves in the same social space inhabited by the middle-class people around them. They framed differences between themselves and family, friends, and the college in ways that indicated the continued role of class morality. In particular, we see that, despite a sometimes emphatic appreciation of the benefits of having attended Linden, a perceived lack of belonging remains. Respondents saw themselves as different from peers who superficially share their class position and as not fully members of the college that provided a pathway into middle-class or upper-class membership. These remaining discrepancies—both between respondents and their home communities and between respondents and their potential new class communities—give insights into the ways that mobility is not merely a question of changing categories.

The evocative phrase of bell hooks—"the price of the ticket"—seems especially relevant here. She writes that "there was no place in academe for folks from working-class backgrounds who did not wish to leave the past behind. . . . Poor students would be welcome at the best institutions of higher learning only if they were willing to surrender memory, to forget the past, and claim the assimilated present as the only worthwhile and meaningful reality."[14] As respondents reflect on their college and postgraduation lives, what was the price of their upward mobility, if any? These final interviews with respondents showcase their many accomplishments: they have graduated from a top liberal arts college, obtained employment and in many cases admission to graduate programs, and overall they describe being happy with their lives. Put into more theoretical terms, they have reaped many of the arguable benefits of elite college education by obtaining white-collar occupational status and incomes and the institutionalized cultural capital of a college degree.

Close attention to their discussion of job-search processes and senses of self, however, shows the ways in which this mobility is uneven. While their *habitus*, or world view, has almost certainly changed as they have moved further into adulthood and completed college, it remains unchanged in ways that are noticeable to respondents themselves and that constrain their abilities to obtain some aspects of socioeconomic mobility. This partial mobility allows us to distinguish between facets of class advantage and to ask about what kinds of mobility may or may not be desirable to young adults from working-class and low-income backgrounds. Here we can also think about the questions asked by Sennett and Cobb in their discussion of the "hidden injuries" acquired through class mobility as one moves into a middle-class world that does not value one's background or, indeed, any working-class or low-income experiences and orientations. To what extent are these recent graduates experiencing their own hidden injuries, and how can they navigate socioeconomic mobility without needing to excise or repudiate their class background? Can one obtain the economic benefits of middle-class life without necessarily taking on the *habitus* or attitudes of a middle-class person?[15] These questions were still unanswered at the time of my last interviews with respondents.

Accordingly, respondents described deep and complex feelings of discomfort with becoming middle class. Some, like Aleisha, were still adjusting to having extra funds, while others, like Rose, were adjusting to the ways their salaries, which seemed generous in the abstract, did not afford them what they imagined middle-class life to include. Many found differences between themselves and friends whose class backgrounds were more affluent than their own; in some cases these differences took on new importance after college. Significantly, these misgivings and differences from friends were framed, subtly or more overtly, in moral terms.

Respondents' accomplishment of middle-class status, however incomplete, had implications not only for respondents' senses of self but also for their relationships. Respondents found themselves having rifts with college friends as they moved out of a shared social world. They continued to manage rifts with friends from home and family. Graduation and postcollege life also opened up new venues for comparison as respondents found new ways in which family support and resources were significant differentiators. Despite sharing with their college cohort this institutionalized status marker, family background remained important both materially and symbolically. These data fit well with Elizabeth A. Armstrong and Laura Hamilton's examination of college women from discrepant class backgrounds.[16] They observed that upper-middle-class graduates were able to move smoothly into well-paid jobs through family connections and social networks developed in college, despite or because of having prioritized social life over academic learning. Graduates who did not have such well-placed connections were penalized if they engaged in the same social-first behavior, because they were unable to translate social time into work gains. Like Armstrong and Hamilton's, my findings showcase the ways that even among graduates of the same institution, family socioeconomic status continues to be significant.[17]

Respondents' postcollege lives highlight important questions for future research and current understandings of upward mobility. First, respondents' descriptions of their jobs and postgraduate lives more broadly direct our attention to the benefits of elite colleges such as Linden and how these translate into the students' postcollege lives. The expectations placed on college—by students, families, and other stakeholders such as scholars and policymakers—to provide students with a crucial rung on the mobility ladder are great. Although we know statistically that college graduates earn more money over a lifetime than nongraduates, these data also present implications that not all benefits are as transferrable as the credential itself. The use of cultural capital and maintaining connections to affluent peers and friends may not be fully solidified gains, especially if they conflict with graduates' existing *habitus* or disposition. This complicates the view of simply providing access to elite benefits or spaces, reminding us that—as Lareau argues—forms of capital must be applied to be effective.[18]

Finally, looking at the gains from college, we see that students' scholarly knowledge about class and their increased levels of self-confidence do not necessarily reduce the pains of class inequality. This is especially notable as the young adults reporting these feelings are now members of the middle class, if not upper middle class. A deeper understanding of how upward mobility takes place and the emotions of this process is needed for both sociologists and college administrators—especially where these findings may help us understand how students and young adults do and do not benefit from the opportunities provided to them.

Conclusion

My purpose in this book is to contribute to two conversations: one about low socioeconomic status students at elite colleges specifically and another about cross-class interactions more broadly. What I hope readers will take away from the narratives included here is that these cross-class interactions and negotiations are difficult to manage because of the moral meaning making that accompanies them. Although we are not always explicitly aware of the semiotics within which we operate, Andrew Sayer and others have shown persuasively that class terms are deeply infused with moral assessments.[1] Most Americans consider themselves middle class,[2] a term that seems to be colloquially more synonymous with "regular" than with sociological measures of income, occupational status, or education level. The adjective "hardworking" is often part of this self-definition, if not explicitly then by implication—as in, a regular hardworking American. Those who are for one reason or another not understood as "hardworking" lose out on the moral benefits of this positioning. Class is thus profoundly associated with moral accountings of worth and claims to legitimate membership in shared society. This web of interlinked meanings is pervasive in American culture, belying our national disinterest in class.

In this sense, then, Linden College is like many American venues in the ways that class is both spoken of and not spoken of: although we can fit class into a broad-stroke rhetoric of diversity or opportunity, we often lack a meaningful language to speak about inequality on an individual level. Though not discussed explicitly and often intentionally avoided, class positions are nonetheless tied to membership on campus through a semiotics of class morality that positions middle-class and upper-class lifestyles as normative. These class meanings are understood through the vocabulary of community and merit woven into the college's self-presentations and students' own management of class inequality.

Sociologists of education have made continuing strides in understanding the mechanisms of class advantage and disadvantage in college broadly and in elite colleges specifically. Aries, Mullen, and Stuber have discussed the pathways leading low socioeconomic status students to college and the differences that are significant for them in benefitting from their college educations.[3] Along with Stuber, Hurst and Armstrong and Hamilton have discussed how students from low socioeconomic status backgrounds navigate campus life.[4] Karabel, Soares, Stevens, Stampnitzky, and Wilkinson have examined the ways that elite (and other) colleges' administrative structures contribute to various aspects of these students' experiences, whether by defining new admissions or aid criteria or by creating new sources of merit that students must meet.[5] However, the moral connotations of class and the ways these shape students' interactions, along with how this occurs on both student-to-student and college-to-student levels, has often been left implicit.

Although necessary, it is not sufficient to consider only the *mechanisms* of class distinction—that is, how people get sorted into class positions. Rather, when we think about class, it is crucial to assess how people draw comparisons between class positions and the saliency of class. Comparisons convey value: the value of a choice, the value of a lifestyle, the value of a person. This is key to understanding the *experience* of class and how class inequality emerges through interactions in particular spaces. Although privation is painful regardless of comparison, its indignity is exacerbated by the knowledge that we may be judged by others who do not share our experiences. Thus moral comparisons are crucial aspects of a classed experience, whether of advantage or disadvantage. Ultimately my findings show that the semiotics of class morality are pivotal at both the organizational level and the interactional level, both among students and between students and other actors.

One important issue implicit in my findings is how low socioeconomic status students are asked to change both by their colleges and often by sociologists as well. What do I mean by this? Analytically, we tend to home in on students' backgrounds as the source of class and, by extension and implication, class conflict. This has a clear logic, particularly because it allows us to consider interventions that may be important. For example, if we know that having social capital connections to affluent peers is helpful, we can think about how to institutionalize social capital. However, this is also problematic. Allison Hurst and Deborah Warnock invoke Bourdieu's formulation of "*les miraculés*," the "miraculous" survivors of working-class and low-income childhoods who go on to higher education.[6] They have pointed out that this framing positions a nonaffluent background as something to be overcome rather than a valuable life. This "miraculous" student is presumed to desire a transition not only into greater knowledge but also into middle-class or upper-class life: such students must change themselves in order to become legitimate.

Focusing on students' backgrounds as problematic also shifts our collective gaze away from the organization and the ways that it is classed. Instead of asking students to change, we might ask organizations to change—not only to improve support for students but also to change their own internal workings so that being a successful student and member of the college does not require students to repudiate their home communities or take on elite social practices. Bell hooks has referred to this as the "price of the ticket," noting that low-income and working-class students at elite colleges— "the best institutions of higher learning"—must accept middle-class and upper-class lives as the only "worthwhile and meaningful realit[ies]."[7] Sayer likewise has noted that "the poor are typically expected to attempt to strive to escape from their unfortunate position."[8] Thus, socioeconomically marginalized students are expected to learn not only critical thinking skills, anatomy charts, and famous sonnets but also elite ways of being, thinking, and doing: they are also expected to change their *habitus*. Moreover, as hooks and Hurst and Warnock emphasize, they are also pushed to acknowledge the moral rightness of middle-class and upper-class positions and to strive, gratefully, to be "better."

The importance of gaining dominant forms of cultural capital should not be understated, particularly for students who plan to seek employment in the kinds of white-collar worlds in which social relations with middle-class and upper-class peers will be important in meetings over golf games, dinners with clients, and so forth. Not everyone wants to maintain a working-class identity or lifestyle: part of the selling point—for socioeconomically marginalized students and for others—of elite colleges is the elite aspect itself. These colleges are by nature exclusive, designed to meet the needs of the very "best" students. And they carry real caché in the world beyond college.[9] My intent in raising these questions is not to denigrate efforts toward upward mobility or to paint challenging economic circumstances as a "romantic . . . form of simple living," in the words of the Linden speaker quoted in chapter 4. Rather, I question the moral discursive structure that positions people with less money, preferences for nondominant cultural forms, or fewer choices as unworthy. This is certainly also a problem outside the academy in contemporary American society: we can look at movies, news media, and political rhetoric for examples of this kind of meaning making. It behooves scholars and others interested in higher education, however, to understand how these semiotics of class morality shape the experiences of low-income, working-class, and first-generation students at the kinds of elite colleges that provide the financial support to make a four-year degree affordable.

Commentators inside and outside of college campuses sometimes conflate increased access with lowered standards, and this accusation is sometimes leveled when colleges change their policies to become more welcoming to socioeconomically marginalized students and others.[10] Merit, the concept around which the college's conception of "best" is supposed to be formed, need not be associated with social practices or lifestyle. It is possible to have an elite academic experience without requiring elite social or cultural experiences. Excellence in writing, thinking, and analysis has nothing to do with spending money or preferences in social pursuits.

How to Support Low Socioeconomic Status Students

What would this look like, then? How might elite colleges better support low-income, working-class, and first-generation students? Elite colleges like Linden spend vast amounts of money per year financially supporting low-income students and providing support services that are intended to bridge some of the gaps that exist between students educated in resource-rich and resource-poor school settings. Moreover, in my experience at Linden, college administrators and faculty were to a person concerned about low socioeconomic status students' well being on campus and were invested in seeing them be successful. Several efforts were begun around the time I was doing field work, such as the partnership with Cross-Class Equity described in chapter 4. Another example of this came just after I completed my field work, when Linden put in place a new program designed to support socioeconomically marginalized students, based at least in part on lobbying by CAL students. These changes are also taking place at other campuses, as well: news articles have many examples of first-generation student groups that are pushing elite universities such as Columbia, Brown, and the University of Chicago to make campus work for them.[11]

However, Linden and other institutions serve many masters and are pulled in many ways. Colleges and universities are regulated by and accountable to accreditation boards, federal and state requirements, peer institutions, and more immediate forces including trustees, parents, alumni, and—of course—students. All of these may have competing needs for funding, data, or policy approaches. Elite colleges are also often inherently conservative, holding fast to tradition—faculty members sometimes grumbled about having their innovative ideas squashed with the phrase "that's not the Linden way"—and like large ships change course only slowly. Although they may have the financial resources to support groundbreaking initiatives, they do not always have the necessary constellation of actors and push.

Colleges currently support low socioeconomic status students primarily through the provision of financial aid and other monetary programs. Although we know financial aid in the form of grant aid makes a difference in students' enrollment patterns,[12] financial support is not the only factor in students' choices of which college to attend or success on campus. As press coverage shows, low-income and working-class students frequently choose to attend less-prestigious colleges closer to home rather than more distant elite campuses that might be able to offer greater funding via private grant dollars.[13] And, as noted, students who attend these colleges have different outcomes than their middle- and upper-income cohort peers, including slower time to graduation and lower levels of college satisfaction after graduation, which suggests that financial aid is not the only form of support needed. In other words, there is a partial but fundamental mismatch between the tools colleges offer to deal with class issues and the actual issues that low socioeconomic status students experience. A student, of course, has to pay to get through college, and I certainly am not criticizing strong financial aid packages. Rather, I am concerned about the lack of resources designed to help students adjust to these particular class settings—the unspoken academic expectations and social practices common to middle and upper socioeconomic status spaces—and manage discomfort or anxiety. I suggest we think about this in three ways: changing the narrative, changing the support structure, and changing the numbers.

Changing the Narrative

In chapter 2, I showed the ways that college discourse on low socioeconomic status students incorporates a semiotics of class morality. In chapters 3, 4, and 5, I showed the ways students' choices for managing cross-class interactions and self-advocacy are shaped by that semiotic structure. We see that such discourses are important: they create roles, structure relationships, and provide identities. Changing the narrative of what a Linden student is will be important for changing experiences on campus. Campuses such as Linden need to include low-income and working-class voices, not as examples of mobility or diversity, but as student body members like all others. Opportunities for this shift come in the kinds of campus ceremonies in which I conducted my field work and also in interactions with faculty and administrators, who were prone to seeing Linden students as connected to white-collar job opportunities or advice, entitled in their abilities to ask for help, and "mostly" middle class. The normative presentation of middle-class and upper-class life before, during, and after Linden, needs to change.

Changing the Support Structure

Although student organizations that provide "safe space" on campus are sometimes criticized, I believe in their capacity to support students—with the caveat that they not be framed as the solution: we should not be seeking to provide oases of safe space but rather to make the campus safer as a whole. That being said, clubs like CAL and Mujeres play important roles on campuses like Linden's and are beginning to be much more widespread, particularly on elite campuses. Moreover, these clubs increasingly facilitate political activism for and by low socioeconomic status students, carving out space for them to voice needs and demands.

These clubs could be better supported by the college administration. First, student organizations such as CAL and Mujeres that provide emotional support and advocacy should be funded outside of the existing student funding structure. The current funding process puts clubs that are profound sources of support in the same pool as recreational programming. Although friendships developed in any context can be important, these clubs exist for the sole purpose of supporting students who are minorities on campus and providing them an open space. And, as I showed in chapter 4, students running these clubs may feel obliged in their programming to offer events for "everyone" rather than the populations they intend to support.

Second, facilitators should be available for student groups centered on identity and belonging—or others—who wish to do work around class inequality. Although Linden has an assistant dean who coordinates multicultural programming, these programs are explicitly intended to support racialized and ethnic minority students on campus. It should go without saying that this is deeply important regardless of students' socioeconomic statuses. However, similar programming does not exist for those who work on issues of class inequality. CAL has asked for an adviser to do facilitation work, but so far it has been unsuccessful. Class inequality is difficult to talk about, even among a small group of students from nominally similar backgrounds. (As we have seen, students who may look similar when compared to a majority set of peers in fact have a broad range of experiences.) Nonpeer facilitators could help manage the emotionally fraught discussions. Moreover, programming around class inequality should not be limited to the brief orientation discussion of diversity and occasional student-organized offerings (leaving aside CAL's events). Class inequality is a significant enough issue to warrant sustained attention and learning opportunities on campus, rather than being framed as something that happens to other people somewhere else.

Changing the Numbers

Finally, Linden and other elite colleges are struggling to figure out how to enroll more low socioeconomic status students. Caroline M. Hoxby and

Christopher Avery have effectively charged elite colleges and universities to make better progress on this front.[14] Issues of enrollment and campus life are messily intertwined. A 2014 opinion piece in the *New York Times* describes the author's experience as a low socioeconomic status student attending a private college in the Northeast and her experience, as an adult, counseling students who share her socioeconomic background. She notes that students may not wish to attend a college that pushes them to "exchange [their] old world for a new world, one that doesn't seem to value where [they] came from."[15] In thinking about this observation, we might easily imagine that students might decline invitations to attend elite colleges—indeed, why would they want to spend four years in a place that tells them in subtle and not so subtle ways that they are not valued until they become middle class? Culture needs to change to attract more students, which in turn would arguably help change that culture. In particular, having greater numbers of students from low socioeconomic status backgrounds might shift the dynamic deplored by a student at Duke, quoted in a Forbes.com article, who asked, "Why is it not OK for me to talk about such an important part of my identity on Duke's campus? . . . Why has our culture made me feel afraid or ashamed or embarrassed that I felt like I couldn't tell my best friends 'Hey, I just can't afford to go out tonight?'"[16]

Above all, colleges like Linden need to de-center the relationship between class and selective higher education. Becoming well educated is important, particularly in an economy in which well-paid jobs are increasingly in the so-called knowledge economy. Political and news rhetoric reminds young adults daily about the importance of a college education. This education, the accomplishment of continued learning, need not involve denigrating those who don't participate—or come wrapped in moralistic comparisons. This shift can take place through changes in narrative, through helping students be more open about their backgrounds, through having more stories represented, and through simply being a less elite-classed place. To say that this will be a long-term project is an understatement, but it is deeply important.

In my critique of Linden's portrayal of low-income, working-class, and first-generation students as making up diversity, I echo scholars who have raised similar concerns about the discourse of race and ethnicity as constituting diversity. These scholars include, especially, Sara Ahmed, as well as Bryan McKinley Jones Brayboy, bell hooks, Susan V. Iverson, and Bonnie Urciuoli.[17] Colleges carve out and discursively put forward roles for different kinds of students for different kinds of audiences.[18] Students who provide diversity are positioned as important because of something extra they bring to the table, rather than intrinsically as students: in other words, no one argues that the "bread and butter" students, in Stevens's words, bring anything other than their own intrinsic value as individuals.[19] It is as if a special argument is needed for why so-called diverse students should now be included in this space that was previously closed to them, and that argument relies on a premise about what they bring to other students.

I have also questioned colleges' choices about forms of support for low socioeconomic status students (although not their good intentions), particularly given that Linden, like most campuses, provides support most clearly in financial terms. Financial support is crucial for low-income and working-class students, if not necessarily for first-generation students. Colleges face a complicated task in offering services for low socioeconomic status students that would include nonfinancial support. For example, offering academic or social support beyond those services available to all students might communicate that the college presumes low socioeconomic status students require such services, indicating lowered expectations for them. Indeed, my critique of the support offered to socioeconomically marginalized students and the ways these students are positioned as part of a larger panoply of college diversity is not aimed explicitly at Linden but rather at the prevalent treatment—both acknowledgment and lack of acknowledgment—of class in elite higher education generally. Other models of effective support systems do already exist. For example, Charles and her coauthors critique affirmative action programs for their potential to stigmatize students of color. The authors suggest that, rather than colleges' creating programs that frame targeted students as needing remedial support, college recruitment be framed around achievement, and that students be recruited according to broad criteria.[20]

Other Key Points

Although the primary subject of this book is the working of a semiotics of class morality and what that means for low socioeconomic status students, there are several other important implications that distinguish my findings from those of other scholars in this area.

Friendships

Low socioeconomic students are not necessarily isolated at elite colleges (though those stories are also important to voice and can be found elsewhere).[21] Much of the class inequality and socioeconomic mobility literature centers on exclusion and homogenous social patterning (homophily)—in other words, that we tend to be friends with people who are like us and that the benefits of ease, leisure, and wealth tend to accrue through systems that are closed to outsiders. Social capital, cultural capital, and even our national economic system reward those who have already accrued one or more of these forms of capital and make it harder to gain for those who have not.

In some ways, elite colleges function along the same lines, and sociologists of education have approached questions of class in higher education with a view toward these same issues of homophily and exclusion. Socioeconomically marginalized students do have disadvantages in these spaces because of their mismatched cultural or social capital or because their lack of economic capital doesn't allow the same kinds of activities as their peers can afford. Students who arrive with these forms of capital gain demonstrably more from their years at an elite college than students who do not.

In contrast to what we might expect based on these two broad principles, however, socioeconomically marginalized students do forge friendships with more affluent peers. As Stuber's research shows, the campus context can "push students in" or "pull them out" of campus extracurricular life.[22] I have shown that low socioeconomic status students are drawn into peer circles and community. However, as detailed in chapter 3, friendships and students' shared social lives are important venues in which class differences must be negotiated. On the positive side, cross-class relationships provide important benefits that sociologists and others argue are crucial for low socioeconomic status students, such as network connections, social know-how, or even personal tastes in food and leisure activities. These will help socioeconomically marginalized young adults transition into both middle-class and upper-class spaces, should they so choose, such as white-collar jobs or graduate-training programs. Friendships, whether with same- or cross-class peers, are associated with other inter-related benefits such as increased likelihood of completing college and feelings of belonging on campus.

On the more potentially more negative side, my data suggest that these friendships bring students into difficult-to-navigate interactional waters. As with race and gender, class microaggressions that are encompassed within friendships are more difficult to name and respond to than overt acts of discrimination or exclusion. Friendships make class comparisons more immediate, though they may be blunted or avoided, as we have seen. Moreover, the expression of alienation becomes more difficult because, rather than criticizing an institution or political system from a distance, one is criticizing one's friends. In addition to—or even instead of—class anger, we see constrained expression, emotional concern for the class other, and investment in a shared student identity.

This multiplicity of positive and negative outcomes associated with belonging is mirrored at the organizational level: low socioeconomic status students seeking belonging in elite institutions may have very mixed feelings about membership in an organization that excludes their families and hometown friends or that espouses values other than those of their families. Organizational language about shared identity and community does not encompass these conflicts.

Context

A second key point of this book is the way that colleges, through structure and discourse, significantly shape the ways that class is understood and provide the potential for cross-class relationships. The naming of some people as "diverse," for example, is dependent on the existing makeup of a population. Thus the students who make Linden College diverse are fairly similar in demographic respects—that is, those aspects that are measured as diversity—to their hometown friends, schoolmates, and families; they are diverse in the context of Linden. We therefore need to understand low socioeconomic status students not only in terms of their backgrounds and their natal class positions but also in terms of their relative class location within a setting that is itself classed. Context is a key part of the question.

The setting or context also sets expectations and norms; it sets the bar for what is considered normal and thus the bar for comparison. As other scholars have suggested, socioeconomically marginalized students experience different types of discomforts at different campuses. The experience of being isolated or alienated appears more likely at a small elite college than a large public university; thus we also see here that comparisons matter.[23] A focus on context also rightly prompts us to think further about what colleges can do to support low socioeconomic status students.

I have highlighted the language of Linden College as an organization and considered how formal discourses about students create particular roles—and perceived sources of difference—for students at the same time as the college welcomes and includes them. Low socioeconomic status students are simultaneously placed both inside and outside of the symbolic bounds of membership. There are also other ways that organizational structures matter for how class plays out, some of which I have touched on here (e.g., the residence hall system) and others I have not (e.g., the layout of the college, academic policies, or even campus signage). Although Linden is different in some of these particulars from many other elite colleges, there are nonetheless important lessons to be gained from looking at Linden. Sociologically, the data make clear that we need to pay attention to the dynamic between structure and experience, administration and students. Practically, the data suggest that colleges have an important role in mitigating discrepancies between students. Indeed, their actions are crucial and in many ways still lacking.

In thinking about context, it is valuable to examine the particularities of Linden's campus: How does an organization's structure and discursive presentation shape the interactions of its constituents? We should not, however, consign these findings to this single campus. These observations help us think about how students manage inequality that exists on all elite campuses and the ways that inequality management does not just happen. Rather, students adopt interactional strategies influenced by cultural and structural forces. This means that colleges as organizations, faculties, administrators, and staff have roles to play in structure, discourse, and other means of shaping the spaces in which interactions take place.

Moreover, these observations contribute to a broader and, I hope, growing examination of how individuals interact across social-class positions. Discussions of how class is managed within interactions remain too few.[24] As we move into an era of greater and greater class segregation, these insights will only become more important.

Final Thoughts

During my research, I periodically heard or came across stories about "this one student" who had a particularly dramatic backstory. Sometimes these took the form of a profile—for instance, the student who became homeless in ninth grade and nonetheless persevered to gain entry to Linden and then graduated as valedictorian. Other times a dean or faculty member recalled a personal conversation with an unnamed student. Occasionally, these stories came from respondents themselves. At first, I was frustrated by these narratives: few of my respondents had such dramatic stories, and I worried that a hidden pocket of students existed, a pocket I was not reaching. I eventually realized that these students, along with their peers on the upper end of the socioeconomic spectrum—the student whose parents bought her a yacht for her birthday, the student whose family owned a jet, or the student who spent five thousand dollars on her phone bill one month—were obscuring in some way more mundane differentiations and distinctions. Although these stories certainly illuminate the ways that class inequality may become apparent, I had to look at the more day-to-day experiences of both belonging and othering described by respondents in their friendships, campus activities, and feelings of community membership.

We tend to focus on extremes: the most visible or sensational students are used to frame the upper and lower class poles (akin to Barrie Thorne's "big man" theory of sociological bias).[25] When we single out these extremes we miss the rest of the students who are struggling to get through four-plus years of college while figuring out how to manage their academic and other work, find supportive friendships, and maintain relationships with loved ones at home. It is these more mundane student stories of day-to-day struggles that are the substance of this book and where we can gain important insights about the hidden management of class inequality.

To the best of my knowledge, all of the low socioeconomic status students I interviewed ultimately graduated from Linden. Like Becca, Maya, Fiona, and Violet, they may have done so despite delays and interruptions, or they may have moved more smoothly through their college years, yet each one achieved the college degree she sought. Each has now moved forward into the postcollege world with a degree from an elite college and has received the social and cultural capital stemming from that particular piece of paper. When we focus only on this single end point, however, we lose the complex processes along the way and thus crucial insights about class, inequality, and college life. Socioeconomically marginalized students attending Linden and other elite colleges experience a host of contradictions: great friendships but also hidden injuries; empowerment but also loss; belonging but also alienation. Respondents expressed both deeply positive and deeply negative feelings, along with attendant internal conflict. The complexity is no less for the college as an organization or for its individual faculty members and administrators as they seek to welcome students from a vast range of backgrounds. There will be increasing numbers of students like Violet who are able to attend Linden College and other elite campuses. While the deep complexities of managing class difference are unlikely to dissipate completely, I hope that opening discussion of the semiotics of class morality can further this work.

Appendix: Methods

It is customary for researchers to provide readers with a sense of the process by which they conducted their work and thereby reached their conclusions. In this appendix, I address issues of informant recruitment and sampling, the collective demographics of my respondents, and the process of gathering qualitative data.

The data gathered for this project are entirely qualitative, comprising a mix of interviews, participant observation, and media analyses. I gathered the data over the course of two years spent living in Connerston, the small town surrounding Linden College. (Both town and college are pseudonyms, as are all names and identifying information.) Each day, I walked to campus in the morning and stayed till evening or later, depending on what came up. I usually spent the days interviewing students and then, later, interviewing faculty and administrators, as well as attending a mix of regularly scheduled venues in the form of student club meetings, periodic appointments at classes, college events, or with students, and simply hanging around in the student center, library, or a local café, observing.

I was lucky that much of my field work fit seamlessly with the activities of most of my respondents—namely, sitting and writing—allowing me to fit easily into this field setting, though this was notably not the case for social settings. In what follows, I review in greater detail the students and other constituents who were interviewed, the process of data gathering, and some of the methodological issues that arose as I completed the research.

Respondents

The bulk of my interview respondents were undergraduate students (others are discussed below). I recruited this sample of participants with three limitations. I looked for students of "traditional age"—that is, between 18 and 24—who were also US citizens. Parent(s)' adjusted gross income levels were also used in establishing recruitment criteria and in categorizing respondents for analyses; this is described below. All (to the best of my knowledge and perception) identified as female. Sexuality was not an explicit component of the interviews but came up in discussions of students' personal lives, and I did not discern systematic differences between heterosexual and other respondents in relation to the topics presented here. Geographically, respondents were from a wide range of backgrounds, but as at many elite colleges, the East and West coasts were heavily over-represented, while the South was under-represented.

As discussed in the introduction, I recruited respondents with the assistance of the college administration, Class Activists of Linden (CAL), and a handful of faculty members. In addition to sending an invitation by e-mail to eligible students, the college also confirmed whether respondents' family income fell below $40,000, between $40,000 and $80,000, or above $80,000, allowing me to determine if they fit the economic parameters of the study selection and to add some nuance to the conceptualization of class. I considered students whose family's adjusted gross income fell below $40,000 as low income and those whose family income fell between $40,000 and $80,000 to be working-class. The income parameters were selected based on an approximation of the level (below $40,000 adjusted gross income) at which a student would be likely to receive a Pell Grant and then twice that figure as the upper limit. During first interviews with each respondent, I established whether anyone else in the student's family had graduated from college. The respondents included in the final sample, with two exceptions, are in the first generations of their families to complete a four-year college degree. (I discuss the exceptions below.) I therefore used a three-point measure of socioeconomic status, based on family income range, parents' education levels, and parents' occupations, the latter determined through interview data. Based on this information, I categorized respondents as either low income or working class.

Of the total 26 respondents within the study's selection parameters, 13 were from low-income families (below $40,000 adjusted gross income) and had parents who had not completed college (with the exception of two discussed below). Parents' occupational categories included jobs such as factory and clerical work, cashier, cleaner, and machinist. Seven were white, one was black, four were Latina, and one was multiracial. Of these, some had older siblings who had either enrolled in or completed higher education. In a very few cases, these students had grandparents or other extended family members such as aunts or uncles who had completed some college or a degree, or who were middle class. Others grew up with no close relatives who had attended college. I also include here data from two respondents who were in complicated financial circumstances that made categorization difficult. Lynne's father completed college and a master's degree before becoming disabled; her mother did not complete college. Lynne's family had helpful cultural capital, but she spent the majority of her school years receiving free lunch benefits, and she received a high level of financial aid at Linden. Similarly, Alexandra's father had completed graduate training in his Central American country of birth but was unable to use his credentials after coming to the United States. Her mother did not complete high school. Both held blue-collar jobs in the United States. For the purposes of the discussions in this book, I grouped them according to my best judgment but acknowledge here the complications associated with this aspect of analysis.

Thirteen respondents were from working-class families. These are students whose parents were first-generation college students but had incomes that were above $40,000 and below $80,000. In two cases, students' family earnings were at or above $80,000—Brianna and Anna's fathers both worked in unionized, skilled labor occupations that, in combination with their wives' earnings, placed the family's income above others in this pool of respondents. Parents in this category held jobs that included handyman, cleaning work, and factory work. Some had earned an associate's degree, and in a few cases, one parent had received a bachelor's degree later in adulthood. The students' race and ethnicity demographic variation was very similar, with six white, three black, one Hispanic, one Asian American, and two multiracial students.

I interviewed every student who responded to my call for respondents. Because of the broad initial recruitment criteria and the way the call for interviews was disseminated, I had respondents who were, according to their own accounts of family educational history and jobs, middle class or upper class. I also interviewed a small number of students who did not meet the study's specifications because they were older than the traditional age or because they were not US residents during the respondent's upbringing; their insights were nonetheless valuable. Because I wanted this book to be about low socioeconomic status students who share the demographic criteria described above, data from other respondents are largely not reported, with a few exceptions, as in the cases of recent alumnae from low socioeconomic status backgrounds (Macy), Apple (who identified as middle class but was briefly involved with CAL), and Heather (who participated in this study through her role as CAL president but not through extended personal interviews).

Analytical Categories

Like any method, my method for grouping students for analysis has its drawbacks. There is little consensus among sociologists about to how to define social class; income, occupation, and personal or parental education status are the most frequently used factors in a scaled definition. In life, these boundaries are imprecise: they shift over time, blur, and overlap. Colleges and education researchers are also increasingly likely to use "first generation" as a proxy for class. Linden administrators and faculty often prefer to use this term in public settings rather than talking about income or financial need. Moreover, the students in this study who are low income and working class hold this status in common. However, as Vincent Tinto writes, "the . . . problem of co-mingling of income with other attributes characterizes the growing body of research in first-generation college students. Though first-generation students are understandably more likely to be from low-income backgrounds, that is not always the case. More than a few are from middle-class backgrounds."[1] I therefore elected to use income as one primary measure because it is the most relevant organizationally: this is the measure used by colleges and universities, states, and the federal government that is the closest fit to class and provides organizational language to describe economic diversity. Parent education and occupation were additional factors, given that they strongly influence the lifestyle and *habitus* of students' childhoods. Although this almost binary categorization may not seem aligned with the qualitative data-gathering strategies of the research, grouping students according to roughly similar parameters as those used by Linden itself helped me to think about tensions around institutional categories and how these tensions are managed or overlooked by the college.

The Sample within Linden's Larger Student Body

Linden enrolls a larger number of low-income and working-class students than many other similar campuses, a point of pride for the college. Correspondingly, Linden awards a great deal of financial aid each year to a large number of students. For example, in a recent incoming class, roughly two-thirds of the class received need-based grant aid from Linden. At the time of this writing, Linden is primarily need blind but reserves the right to offer need-sensitive admissions to a small percentage of students from year to year—this means that the admissions office makes decisions on most candidates regardless of their ability to pay for college but may make some final decisions that take family income into account. It should also be noted that these figures can be misleading. Linden's high cost of attendance means that students from middle-income and even upper-middle-income families may be eligible for financial support from the federal government and the college, especially if the student has siblings in college at the same time. According to Linden's figures,[2] roughly half of the admitted students in 2008 surveyed came from families with annual incomes over $100,000. The college's financial aid figures include the full range of grants provided, from $1,000 to over $60,000, with an average of over $35,000. Thus, many aided students at Linden are not low income or working class.

My respondents included an over-representation of nonwhite students as compared to the campus overall. Although roughly 30 percent of Linden's students are African American / black / Caribbean, Latina / Hispanic, or Asian American—there are very few Native American students at Linden—half of my sample fit these categories. Despite this overrepresentation, in a sample of fewer than thirty students, there are too few students of any individual group other than white to be able to make meaningful analyses about race and ethnicity. This is a gap in the data that I hope will be remedied in future research. Religious background and sexual orientation varied but did not appear to figure strongly in narratives related to socioeconomic status.

Interviews with Students

I conducted a series of interviews with students over one to two years and then did follow-up interviews ranging between three and five years after students' campus interviews, depending on the timing (e.g., a respondent who graduated in 2009 and was contacted again in 2014 and a respondent who was last interviewed as a student in 2010 and contacted again in 2013). The typical number of interviews with each respondent was five; the range was three to eight. (Only one respondent was interviewed three times, and only one was interviewed eight times.) Virtually all respondents chose their own pseudonyms, and I changed personally identifying information (e.g., home state or region, parent occupations). In rare cases in which students' chosen pseudonyms were too close to their real names or in cases where students didn't select a pseudonym, I provided one. Interviews were between forty-five minutes and two hours long and averaged roughly an hour in length. All interviews were scheduled at times and locations of the students' choosing and typically took place at the student center but sometimes in dining halls, local cafés, or a student's residence hall room (interviews after graduation took place by phone or Skype). At various points during the writing of this book, I shared my writing with respondents and invited their feedback. I contacted all the respondents with whom I had conducted post-graduation interviews to offer chapters or, if they wished, the full manuscript. Copies were emailed to each respondent who requested them, which was the majority. Gratifyingly, no one expressed concerns or doubts about the findings or arguments, or my recounting of conversations and events.

TABLE 1. Respondent demographic and interview information

Pseudonym	Interviews	College year	SES[1]	Race/ethnicity	Job at time of fi interview
Alyssa	5	Sr.	LI[2]	Black / African American / Caribbean	Policy/advocacy; graduate school
Danielle	5	Jr., Sr.	LI	Biracial	
Alexandra	5	Fr.	LI	Hispanic/Latina	Graduate school
Michelle	5	So.	LI	Black / African American / Caribbean	Service industry and part-time teaching; upcoming graduate school enrollment
Fiona	5	Sr.	LI	Hispanic/Latina	
Meredith	5	Fr.	LI	White	Teaching; upcoming graduate school enrollment
Violet	3	Sr.	LI	White	Nonprofit administration
Aleisha	5	Sr.	LI	White	Business
Ramona	4	Sr.	LI	White	
Victoria	4	Sr.	LI	White	Nonprofit administration
Evelyn	5	So.	LI	White	Graduate school
Maya	4	Sr.	LI	Hispanic/Latina	Policy/advocacy; graduate school
Lynne	5	Jr., Sr.	LI	White	Nonprofit administration
Magdalena	5	Sr.	WC[3]	White	Management
Isabel	5	Jr., Sr.	WC	Hispanic/Latina	Nonprofit administration; upcoming graduate school enrollment
Genesis	8	So., Jr.	WC	Black / African American / Caribbean	Policy/advocacy; plans for graduate school
Brianna	4	Jr.	WC	White	
Anna	4	Sr.	WC	White	Graduate school
Amber	5	So.	WC	White	Teaching; upcoming graduate school enrollment
Quinn	4	Jr.	WC	Multiracial	
Georgina	5	Sr.	WC	Asian American	Law

(*Continued*)

TABLE 1. *Continued*

Pseudonym	Interviews	College year	SES[1]	Race/ethnicity	Job at time of final interview
Alice	5	Fr.	WC	Black /African American / Caribbean	Business
Allison	3	Sr.	WC	White	
Rose	6	Sr.	WC	Biracial	Nonprofit administration; graduate school
Becca	3	Sr.	WC	White	
Harmony	5	So., Jr.	WC	Black /African American / Caribbean	Nonprofit administration

[1] Socioeconomic status
[2] Low income
[3] Working class

Each respondent was informed that I, the interviewer, was an academic researcher; what the general goals of the project were; that I would seek to interview her several times over the course of a year or two; and that she was free to skip or decline to answer any question or to end the interview at any time with no questions asked. Respondents were also informed that interviews were anonymous and confidential. I e-mailed a consent document to each student that included all of the above information, as required by the institutional review boards that approved the study (those of Linden and of my home institution). I did not offer any remuneration or other inducements to participate. For the purposes of the respondents' anonymity and to avoid self-consciousness, I informed students that my book was about acclimation to college for students of different types of backgrounds, and I often emphasized—especially when being asked about who I was interviewing by nonrespondents or in a group of students—that I was interested in the experiences of students from all kinds of backgrounds. The consent document noted, however, that I was interested in student perceptions of social class on campus.

I interviewed twelve respondents in the first year and interviewed five of those the following year—others graduated or were studying away from campus. Fourteen were added in the second year, for a total of twenty-six students over the two years. The vast majority of respondents were recruited through e-mail contacts. Linden College forwarded an invitation e-mail from me to all students meeting my income criteria during the first month of the first year. CAL sent out additional e-mails that year and at the start of the second year. A few faculty members sent them to their classes. Other respondents came—very rarely—through word of mouth or snowball sampling. One of the biggest and earliest surprises to me was that respondents tended to indicate that they did not know other people's financial backgrounds and that their friends were generally of higher-income backgrounds. Thus, although I sometimes asked students if they knew anyone else who might be interested, only two interviews were generated that way. Finally, I occasionally asked students who had spoken out at public events or who were in CAL if they would be interested in participating. Several students did decide to participate as the result of my invitation.

I used an open-ended interview guide with a certain set of questions for each interview and followed up on students' responses to get greater detail or discuss relevant topics in more depth. In the first interviews I focused on the respondent's home life—questions included items such as Who is in your family? Where are they now? and What was your home and neighborhood like growing up?—and high school experiences, asking how she had decided to attend college and how she had chosen Linden. Subsequent interviews focused on Linden experiences both inside and outside the classroom, the respondent's relationship to friends and family at home, friendships and support systems on campus, daily life, and many other areas. I sometimes phrased questions the following way: "Other students have mentioned [topic X]; what do you think about that topic?" or "I was having a conversation with someone, and she told me [X]; has that ever happened to you?" or "I saw [X] in the *Lindeneer* [student newspaper] or on the campus website; what did you think about that issue?" I returned to questions over the course of several interviews or even within a single interview to approach the topic from a different angle or simply to double-check my understanding.

Student interviews were often made smoother because I attended a women's college for my own undergraduate years and thus had some similar experiences I could share with my Linden respondents. (There was, however, another side to this coin, which I discuss below.) As a fellow women's college alumna, I could ask informed social questions, questions that compared my own recollections with respondents' experiences and vice versa. For example, I was aware of the high importance Linden students place on their residence halls and so could begin conversations with a standard question—What hall do you live in?—that was an entrée into widely accepted conversational territory. Also, students were sometimes interested in my experiences, either during college or subsequently. Many seniors, not surprisingly, were concerned about their upcoming graduations and whether they might find jobs, attend graduate school, or do something else (such as join the Peace Corps or Teach for America) and asked about my first year out of college, how I figured out what graduate programs to apply for, and so forth. These were also relatively easy topics of conversation around which to establish rapport—especially when initiated by the student, which removed some of the loaded meanings that might have arisen were I, a somewhat older person, to bring up the topics.

Despite the ease of communication that this similarity sometimes helped me achieve, I also believe that it deprived me of a sense of strangeness or outsiderness in my respondents' eyes. I believe that many may have expected me to share a common body of knowledge, which led them to feel that less needed to be explained. I was very likely guilty of the same error and probably missed opportunities to ask for more information or clarification, because I saw certain things as "natural" despite my best efforts to look at each interaction or observation with fresh eyes. See below for further discussion of this issue.

Interviews with Others

I also conducted interviews and informal conversations with selected alumnae, faculty, and administrators. Most alumnae had been involved with the student organizations I shadowed, but some came from word of mouth or personal connections—that is, they were personally known to me or they were acquainted with another student or alumna in the sample. I selected faculty by asking administrators which faculty members tended to be knowledgeable about low-income concerns on campus and by snowball sampling. I spoke with ten faculty members whom students or administrators recommended as being supportive. I spoke with thirteen administrators who were immediately relevant (e.g., the dean for new students) as well as others who were recommended to me as knowledgeable by faculty or administrators. I interviewed administrators across several levels and across multiple areas of responsibility, primarily those involved in housing, student services, and academic or central administration. I did not interview service staff in blue-collar or support roles, and this is a gap in my data. I was fortunate, however, to gain some understanding of student-staff relationships through conversations with knowledgeable others and sitting in on discussions of those issues. As with student interviews, any personally identifying information from faculty, alumnae, or administrators has been changed, including, but not limited to, name, title, department or office of employment, role, and/or gender.

Participant-Observation Field Work

Since mine is a study that is in part based on ethnographic accounts, my methods for this study are in somewhat reverse order: acknowledging that socioeconomic status is a complicated and personal issue for many, and hesitant to make students uncomfortable by singling them out for such a private topic, I opted to begin by interviewing students and then building field work in part on those contacts. Other field work took place either in venues dedicated to students who identified publicly as being interested in this issue, primarily meetings of the Class Activists of Linden, or that were not directly related—that is, all-college events (as discussed below). I assigned pseudonyms to each office, club, and event, as well as changing identifying information when appropriate (e.g., Linden holiday traditions).

Student Clubs and Events

For all student events, I was either invited by the students coordinating the group or given permission to attend, and I identified myself as a researcher. The club where I spent the most time was the Class Activists at Linden. I attended weekly CAL meetings for two years as well as a conference held by them and periodic events such as speakers or film showings. This club had existed in different iterations in earlier years and then become dormant. It was resurrected by two women who are now alumnae with close ties to the women who were the presidents during my time at Linden. The group's purpose had originally been a combination of support and education. Students would come together to express frustrations about social life and microaggressions on campus during meetings and also to plan some events each year that would educate other students about social-class issues—namely, their own issues. However, as one of the presidents during my time at Linden put it, they got "sick of trying to educate" people with little evident outcome. They changed to an activist organization and put on events that put a spotlight on social-class issues on campus broadly, as well as lobbying for simple changes to better support low-income students. At the time I joined, the students from the prior year had requested funding for a book collection (denied), a bookshelf (denied), a staff person (denied); put together a guidebook to help students access funds available in different corners of the college as well as occasionally cheat the system; screened a documentary; and brought in speakers to run workshops on income and class inequality. It's important to note that the club expressed its membership and constituency as low-income, first-generation, working-class students and their allies.

Demographically, CAL meetings typically attracted a core of five to seven students, with a few additional members coming consistently to events. They also maintained a large e-mail list of a few hundred students and faculty who typically made up the audience of, for example, screenings of their documentary. During the first year of my field work, CAL students were almost only white and from rural or small town areas. At the end of that year, almost all of those students graduated or left the club and the new student members included more urban and nonwhite students, though not a majority. While some students were leaders or members of other groups, CAL students were not typically as connected to administrators as students in other groups (though a number of them did have close faculty ties).

For one semester, I also attended the weekly Hall Chairs Board meeting. Hall chairs are students elected to coordinate administrative logistics in the residence halls, preside over students elected to run hall subcommittees (such as a coordinator of social events for new students) and liaise with the college's formal administrative bodies, particularly with the offices that run residence halls. I attended these meetings weekly for the final semester of my field work. This group is made up of about twenty-five students, with one administrative coordinator. The group met to discuss policies and events relevant to all halls, plan events on campus, discuss problems that arose in individual halls or groups of halls, and provide moral support for students whose jobs were sometimes difficult. By the nature of the position, students on this board tended to have close ties with the administration and to be considered leaders by the administration, which gave them a comparatively large amount of access to Linden's administrators and formal organizational resources. Demographically, this group was primarily, but not exclusively, white. I did not seek to ascertain these students' socioeconomic backgrounds, though I knew a few through interviews or as friends of respondents.

Finally, one semester I attended many meetings and protests of an ad hoc student group formed to respond to proposed budget cuts. This group was also small, comprising about ten active members and a handful of occasional members as well as others who came to events when they were held. The group was formed to respond to perceived threats (including the rumored closing of a building used by student clubs and reduction of support programs) and because students did not believe that their voices were being sought or listened to enough by the administration. This group included students across all race/ethnic groups but was majority nonwhite, and most of them were considered student leaders on campus—that is, they were already involved with the college in some formal way through residence hall positions or through clubs with large memberships.

College-Sponsored Public Meetings, Forums, and Workshops

I attended a large and varied number of meetings, workshops, and forums held on campus. These ranged from public all-college meetings highlighting presentations by administrators about the budget cut process, smaller workshops on privilege, and even a dialogue on social class in the housing system. I also attended events in which presentations were made to students about being a Linden student, in which the identity of "Lindie" was expressed or inculcated. These included convocation at the start of the year, "Togs Day," when rising seniors attend a special ceremony with invited alumnae speakers, and orientation sessions for incoming students. For all events that were not public to the Linden community, I received permission from the relevant coordinating body (e.g., the administrator or faculty member speaking) to attend or was invited by a participant.

Because of the nature of these events, I rarely identified myself as a researcher. I identified no student or other community member by name or identifying characteristic in my field notes during these sessions, and field notes collected during these sessions emphasized the speakers rather than audience members.

Social Life

Whenever possible, I spent social time with respondents and other students. These were sometimes formal events coordinated by the halls, when I was invited by a student and announced myself as a researcher. In other cases, such as attending a party or an informal event (meals, watching sports on TV, etc.), I did not necessarily announce myself to students because I did not want to make my host or any other student uncomfortable, though students often knew my status through the person who invited me or as a result of the way I was introduced. When asked, I always indicated my role, and I did not take any notes at these events that identified students not enrolled in the study by name or identifying characteristic. My aim in observing social interactions was to gain a stronger sense of daily student life broadly and specifically to my respondents—in some cases, I simply asked respondents if I could tag along when they went to do something they enjoyed or spent a lot of time at—but also to understand the places and ways that social class might or might not arise in social life. This knowledge was reciprocally supplemented by interviews and informal conversations with respondents and other students. Examples of social situations include parties, residence hall gatherings to eat dinner or watch TV, club sleepovers, and hanging out on campus with students as they studied or ate or chatted with others or went to singing practice or their jobs. I explained to respondents that I was interested in learning about typical daily life on campus and about their lives in particular. Some respondents accepted my request, and others declined, in some cases because they felt their lives would be too "boring," an interesting set of responses (I return to this below).

Classes

I sat in on classes both on my own and with respondents. In all cases but one, I was identified by the student or faculty member or was given the opportunity to identify myself. By attending classes, I hoped both to gain a sense of academic life on campus and to observe interactions among students and between students and faculty. Respondents described classrooms in various ways, sometimes as the only place on campus where meaningful conversations around class occurred, sometimes as places where they first learned such terms as "cultural capital" that helped them understand themselves better, and sometimes as places where other students said offensive or thoughtless things. Because my interest was in discussion and interaction, I went almost solely to courses in the humanities and social sciences. I accompanied one respondent to a course in the hard sciences but did not seek out other courses in this area. In most cases, I went to a class only once or twice. However, I attended many meetings of one particular humanities course over a semester. In these meetings, I recorded general observations about how the class functioned rather than making person-specific notes. As above, I did not take notes that could identify any student by name or other characteristic.

Issues and Complications of Field Work

The single most complicated aspect of this research was gaining access to "the field." I put this term in quotes because, in reality, this single field on Linden's campus comprises many fields—namely, the social worlds of various respondents as well as administrative and academic spaces. Unlike the process followed by many ethnographers, I typically began by interviewing students and then built my field work from there; the student club meetings and college events I attended were exceptions to this arrangement.

I elected to do this for two reasons. The first was so that I could gain access to a wider variety of social worlds than I would be able to do if I had elected to stay in a single residence hall for the duration of the field work. This would have brought its own strengths, but it worried me because of the limited perspective and the differences of experience that students perceive to exist between residence halls at Linden. Second, I was concerned that students would not feel comfortable speaking with me about social class and income if that was the express purpose of the field work. This meant that recruiting students was complicated, since I could not e-mail or post (e.g., on posters or via Facebook) for a desired population of low-income, working-class, or first-generation students. I especially feared that students might feel exposed through associating with me if it was known that my study was centered on these issues.

I therefore generally interviewed students first, and in the second interview asked whether I could participate with them in selected daily life events, to be determined by the student herself, or eventually whether I could shadow her for a few hours or days. A number of respondents agreed to invite to me to particular events, for example the weekly coffee gathering in a residence hall, breakfast, a Mujeres meeting, or a rehearsal for a play. I spent the most concentrated time with Alexandra, Lynne, Michelle, and Amber, as well as a few students from middle-class backgrounds who helped me gain access to broader college social spaces. Georgina, Aleisha, Danielle, Violet, and Becca took me around their residence halls, to meals, and to other campus venues, as did several middle-class students. I also spent time with the CAL students, including Meredith, Amber, Genesis, Alice, and Michelle, and other respondents, including Anna, who attended the Hall Chairs Board meetings, and Maya, who organized other campus meetings that I attended.

Participant observation was challenging for several reasons, including two unanticipated complications. First, I was not sure how to explain to students why they were of interest to my study without potentially stigmatizing them. The nature of the relationship between researcher and subject is a controversial one, with its own set of power dynamics. I was concerned (as were several Linden administrators) about the possibility of making students who might already feel singled out or vulnerable feel even more othered in their own collegiate homes. Second, I was at a loss for how to explain to students the reason I wanted to follow them around, possibly day and night, without sounding very, very strange. This was exacerbated, I believe, by students' knowledge that I was familiar with Linden's campus and am myself a women's college alumna. Combined with my age—older than they were but not old enough to be their parent—I suspect that students thought there was nothing for me to learn about life at Linden, no special secrets they could fill me in on. I did not seem to need their help, perhaps, as informants. I finally settled on the term "shadow," which has a linguistic hint of documentary making or journalism and which seemed to need no further explanation. That said, I still sometimes faced confusion about what was expected from such a situation, as when a respondent I was shadowing brought me to the library and asked me to sit at one table while she worked at another. On our walk back to her residence hall afterward, she mused, "I should have asked you to sit with me, since I ended up chatting with some friends!" All in all, I spent field work time with thirteen of the twenty-six low socioeconomic status students in addition to our interviews.

Being Boring

One particular hurdle I encountered was the problem of respondents thinking that they were or that I might consider them to be "boring." More than once, a respondent explained that she was worried that I would get bored spending time with her, that I would think her college life was dull, or that I would be unimpressed with her activities, which included a lot of library study time, time hanging out in one's room studying, and time making small talk with friends. (I sometimes found that the library was the best place to run into people, especially during exams.) Perhaps respondents measured themselves according to a pop-culture ideal of college living that involved more partying or excitement of other sorts, or perhaps the thought that I, as an adult, had different, more sophisticated ideas of "fun" (see below). Regardless of the reason, this perception made it difficult to persuade students that time spent showing me around or sharing their daily activities was valuable.

Comfort and Discomfort in Social Situations

Although I read notes from other people's field work before beginning my own, I did not anticipate the feeling of being an outsider and the profound awkwardness I would sometimes encounter in my field work. This was especially the case when I attempted to gain access to students' social worlds. In some cases, this was simply the result of context, in particular within the close nature of residence halls. Many of the facets of daily life that were totally normal for students were uncomfortable for me, including the simplest of tasks:

> Alexandra and [her girlfriend] get ready for bed, and I do as well—I'm sleeping on a kind of long seat cushion on the floor of their residence hall room. I don't feel comfortable, once I have my pajamas on, going out into the hallway, since there are tons of girls there in party outfits, exchanging

outfit critiques, pre-gaming [drinking], playing music, gossiping, and getting clothes on in the hallway. It feels like too much contrast between social spaces. Last night was also the same, with them getting ready for parties, and I felt the same way and consequently didn't brush my teeth before going to sleep.

While walking to the bathroom down the hall in pajamas was a nonevent for the students hosting me, I could not bring myself to breach the social space of the hallway.

I found it especially difficult to explain to students why I would want to come to their parties or other events and even more difficult to explain my presence to other guests once I was there. I tried to be as simple and straightforward as possible in my explanations, although this did not necessarily help. For example, I was at a loss for how to answer one acquaintance of a respondent who had invited me to a party, who asked, "So, how's your study going?" and then whether I was studying the partiers "right now." I recorded after leaving a party:

> Earlier, someone asked how my project is going, which is uncomfortable for me, and I explained [to others in earshot] that I am no not at Linden, at Penn, in my fifth year, getting my doctorate, writing about college students, no not about drinking, but about acclimation and how people think about college. The girl who is asking me about this asks about what it's like to be at college all over again or something similar, and I say it's surprisingly similar to grad school, and she says it must be classier at grad school, and I say you'd be surprised. Someone asks, so are you researching us *right now*? (Do I lie and say no, or do I make everyone uncomfortable and say yes?) Amber, who invited me, also asked me later whether I was researching or just hanging out. I explain that they are not so different sometimes, and that part of what I want to write about is just what it's like to be a student.

These interactions speak directly to issues at the core of ethnographic methodology about how to explain oneself, who one is in relation to one's respondents, and what one is asking of one's so-called subjects. It also provides an interesting example of me, the researcher, feeling vulnerable and exposed rather than my respondents.

Further, although I typically tried to be honest in my self-presentation— that is, to dress as myself, to be up-front about my intentions in any given interaction, and not to feel that I was pretending—this was neither always a comfort to me or to respondents nor was it even clear how to do it. For example, I was often unsure about how to behave in social situations, even down to the simplest issues, according to this field note:

> I left the house around ten, planning to stop in town to get a six-pack of beer and then go up to a party to which I have been invited. I spent a fair amount of time worrying about whether I should or should not bring beer, but decided that since the student who invited me is a senior and I am bringing it technically for my own consumption, it would be weirder not to bring something to a party. I talk on the phone with several friends to discuss this decision and laugh about how odd this is. As with the last party I attended, I agonize over my outfit, changing several times, trying to look cool but not as though I am an older person trying hard to look cool. In particular, this evening I am conscious of my outfit because I have been scrutinizing students' outfits all week in an effort to figure out what one can surmise about socioeconomic status by looking at clothes. The respondent who invited me to her party is from a low-income family, and I worry that by wearing a new pair of high-heeled leather boots, I will stand out as flaunting my money. I put them on, then take them back off and exchange them for flats that don't go as well with the dress I'm wearing. Once I get to town, I learn that the local package store has already closed, so there will be no beer. Once I arrive at the party, I immediately regret not wearing the boots—people are wearing a broad range of outfits, from a couple of women looking like they raided a costume shop to dress up as 70's disco-goers, to others looking like they are channeling early Madonna, a solid handful wearing simple jeans and tees or plaids, a few wearing sophisticated-looking all-black stylish outfits, and some boys who don't look like they changed from whatever they were doing over the course of the day. I feel totally out of place and frumpy, and even more awkward than I already would have. The music is too loud to make conversation with anyone, and my few forays into the middle of the living room to dance are totally uncomfortable. My solution is to text my field note observations to myself, which at least lets me feel like less of a wallflower since no one knows I'm texting to myself.

In this situation, as in others, my choices seemed strained and of unclear benefit. Despite my best efforts to meet what I perceived as the expectations of students, I failed in some (bringing beer) for lack of local knowledge and others because I could not figure out how to engage with them (the style of dancing or chatting between students, how to socialize with others in this setting). However, it's also important to note that becoming "simply" an observer was not only often uncomfortable but also appeared to be ineffective. While I personally found it difficult and slightly creepy to be a silent watcher, preferring to join in social situations, this made my presence more comfortable for respondents as well. Thus, for example, when I asked Michelle if I could spend additional time hanging around with her and her friends, she agreed and specified that her friends felt at ease because I didn't "just sit there."

Beyond comfort, I worried about finding the appropriate line between ethical honesty, respect for respondents who were being asked to share very personal stories with me, and sharing information that would make me possibly more of a stranger, disinclining students to share their experiences with me. This stemmed most often from the difference in background between myself and many of my respondents—I grew up living mostly in houses with yards in mostly middle-class suburbs, went to well-funded public schools, and have highly-educated parents. A short field note excerpt is relevant here: "Thinking about last week's CAL meeting, when we stepped in and out of the circle. I was sort of uncomfortable that I was "outing" myself in the question where Heather asked, 'Did anyone grow up living in a house like the res-halls at Linden?' I stepped in; no one else did. Thinking about honesty, authenticity, and research ethics: How important is it to be honest about myself, and in what way?" As is clear from the notes recorded at the time, I wondered whether being truthful about my own background would be alienating to respondents or potential respondents, and to what extent this is balanced by an ethical and respectful need to be honest. During a separate incident at a CAL meeting one year later, I was singled out by a guest speaker as a person of middle-class background:

> We have sort of a slow start as people come in. [The speaker] makes sort of small talk conversation with Genesis, [another student], and me. She asks, "So what does this group do: Is this group on race and working class?" Genesis says, "CAL is working-class, first-generation, and low-income students." "So everyone in the group is from those backgrounds?" asks the guest speaker. Probably because I know one member's middle-class background, I said, "No, the group is for people who are interested in class issues

and students from that background who are interested in class issues." . . .
Later in the meeting, after all the stories, the speaker says she would like to
hear from the people who haven't spoken yet. One student says she's happy
listening, and I am getting ready to defer as well, but the speaker turns and
asks me directly, "You're middle class, right?" I say, "Yes." She asks that
I speak from that perspective, and I talk about how easy it is to not see these
issues at Linden if you're someone for whom the culture is not different
from home. If it's not your reality, it's easy not to see it. I find myself using
the "as a person of . . ." language, which I think is a default of nervousness.

Here again, I was unsure of how my responses might be perceived by students in the room, and in fact I still do not truly know to what extent people chose to censor their responses. Moreover, although I suspect that being
"called out" as a middle-class person in this context was the result of my in-
terjecting about the group's identity, these field notes also suggest that class
may be visible in ways one cannot fundamentally control. This possible
tension between disclosure and interviewer-respondent relationship was
an ongoing conversation with myself, and one that varied from respondent to respondent. Occasionally, respondents would also bring me back to
a more immediate set of concerns, as when one respondent became clearly
frustrated with my conversational chitchat before beginning the substance
of the interview. While I was trying to show respect for her personhood by
conversing rather than just getting to the interview questions, she was im-
patient to get going and get back to her preparation for a final exam.

Why Students Participated

I decided not to pay students for their interview participation, primarily
because I was concerned about transitioning between paid time for interviews and unpaid time as field work informants. It may be the case that
my sample of students would have been different had I offered funds; one
might expect that more low-income students might have participated. Because I was able to interview students at their convenience, I hope this effect was minimized. I also found, as other researchers have noted, that
student respondents seemed to appreciate the time and space to reflect on
issues of personal importance to them, and my conversations with students
often ranged across topics in ways directed by the respondent's interests.

The interview guide included many questions about their general college lives and experiences, giving students a venue to reflect on both positive and negative experiences. When asked, I offered advice, and sometimes shared my own memories from this time period. Linden students, like many of their peers at other colleges, were faced with a stream of decisions that felt weighty and consequential, and I believe that the opportunity to talk over their lives with a relatively disinterested outsider was beneficial; in one instance, I even received a thank-you note to this effect from a respondent at the close of our last interview. In addition to these reasons, student respondents described an urge to help me with my research both because I was a fellow women's college alumna or because they themselves had once had to do a study for a college course and remembered trying to gather respondents. Thus, in a significant way, the same bonds of community and responsibility to one another that I discuss in this book informed my respondents' participation.

NOTES

Introduction

1. Carnevale and Rose, "Socioeconomic Status."

2. Barrow and Rouse, "Does College Still Pay?"; for an updated estimate, see Pew Research Center, "The Rising Cost of *Not* Going to College."

3. Carnevale and Rose, "Socioeconomic Status," table 3.3.

4. Stuber, "Class, Culture, and Participation"; Martin, "Social Capital, Academic Achievement" and "Privilege of Ease"; Aronson "Breaking Barriers or Locked Out?" For a review, see Lee, "Elite Colleges and Socioeconomic Status."

5. Zweigenhaft, "Prep School and Public School Graduates"; Martin, "Privilege of Ease."

6. DiMaggio, "Sociological Perspectives," 25.

7. West and Fenstermaker, "Doing Difference"; see also Harris, "Social Constructionism and Social Inequality."

8. DiMaggio, "Sociological Perspectives," 16. See Leondar-Wright, *Missing Class*, for a detailed analysis of the ways activists from varied class backgrounds interact and Streib, *The Power of the Past*, for an analysis of cross-class couples.

9. Savage, Bagnall, and Longhurst, "Ordinary, Ambivalent, and Defensive."

10. See, e.g., Gorman, "Cross-Class Perceptions of Social Class."

11. Bettie, *Women Without Class*, 48.

12. hooks, *Where We Stand*.

13. See Jensen's discussion of class dynamics in daily life in *Reading Classes*.

14. Lareau, *Unequal Childhoods*.

15. Sayer "Class, Moral Worth, and Recognition"; and "What Are You Worth?"

16. I am leaving aside here important racialized meanings that are also implicit and relevant to the same moral questioning.

17. See, e.g., Sayer, *The Moral Significance of Class*; Sayer, "What are you Worth?"; Lamont, *Money, Morals, and Manners* and *The Dignity of Working Men*; Carruthers and Espeland, "Money, Meaning, and Morality"; see also Zelizer, *Social Meaning of Money*.

18. Ostrove, "Belonging and Wanting."

19. Hurst, *Burden of Academic Success*.

20. Urciuoli, "Excellence, Leadership, Skills, Diversity," 394. See also Urciuoli, "The Semiotic Production of the Good Student."

21. Mo Daviau, Anxious Waves blog, https://anxiouswaves.wordpress.com/2014/12/02/diverse-futures-the-myth-of-the-high-stakes-smithie/ (accessed December 18, 2014).

22. Ibid.

23. See also Hurst and Warnock's "*Les Miraculés*" on this precise point.

24. See, e.g., Sewell and Shah, "Social Class, Parental Encouragement"; Sewell, Haller, and Portes, "Educational and Early Occupational Attainment."

25. See, e.g., Jack, "Crisscrossing Boundaries," and Martin, "Privilege of Ease."

26. See Alon and Tienda, "Assessing the "Mismatch" Hypothesis."

27. Hoxby and Avery, "Missing 'One-offs'."

28. There is also a significant amount of research (such as Radford's *Top Student, Top School?*) geared toward understanding how a student's class background may limit him or her from gaining access to college in the first place; I leave these issues aside here.

29. Bourdieu and Passeron, *Cultural Reproduction and Social Reproduction*; see also Bourdieu, *Forms of Capital* and *The State Nobility*.

30. Stuber, "Pushed Out or Pulled In?"

31. Stuber "Class, Culture, and Participation," *Inside the College Gates*, and "Pushed Out or Pulled In?"

32. Aries and Seider, "Interactive Relationship."

33. See Aries and Seider, "Interactive Relationship"; Ostrove, "Belonging and Wanting"; Ostrove and Long, "Social Class and Belonging." See also Jack, "Crisscrossing Boundaries" for variation among low-income African American students' experiences based on high school pathways.

34. Stuber, *Inside the College Gates* and "Class, Culture, and Participation"; Armstrong and Hamilton, *Paying for the Party*; Hamilton and Armstrong, "Gendered Sexuality"; see also, Mullen, *Degrees of Inequality*.

35. E.g., Aries and Seider, "Interactive Relationship"; Stuber, "Talk of Class."

36. Armstrong and Hamilton, *Paying for the Party*.

37. Stuber, "Pushed Out or Pulled In?"

38. Stevens, *Creating a Class*.

39. Ahmed, "Doing Diversity Work" and *On Being Included*; Iverson, "Constructing Outsiders"; Brayboy, "The Implementation of Diversity in Predominantly White Universities." See also Urciuoli, "Excellence, Leadership, Skills, Diversity" and "Producing Multiculturalism."

40. Mullen, *Degrees of Inequality*. See also McDonough's earlier discussion of student and parent perceptions in *Choosing Colleges* and Perna's model of college choice, "Studying Access and College Choice."

41. Aries and Seider, in "The Interactive Relationship between Class Identity and the College Experience," are also attentive to the dynamics of large public versus small private colleges.

42. Khan, *Privilege*; Cookson and Persell, *Preparing for Power*; Demerath, *Producing Success*; Bettie, *Women without Class*.

43. Lamont and Molnar, "Study of Boundaries"; Lamont, Schmalzbauer, Waller, and Weber, "Cultural and Moral Boundaries."

44. See, e.g., Kusenbach, "Salvaging Decency"; Stuber, "Talk of Class"; Lehmann, "Becoming Middle Class."

45. For a thorough review, see Lamont and Molnar, "The Study of Boundaries."

46. Fiske, Moya, Russell, and Bearns, "Secret Handshake."

47. Stuber, "Talk of Class" and *Inside the College Gates*.

48. Hurst, *The Burden of Academic Success*.

49. Granfield, "Making It by Faking It"; Lehmann, "'I Just Didn't Feel Like I Fit In'" and "Habitus Transformation."

50. Reardon and Bischoff, "Income Inequality."

51. Ibid.

52. Carnevale and Rose, "Socioeconomic Status,"

53. For discussions of historic admissions to elite universities and the role of financial aid in elite college admissions, see Karabel, *The Chosen: The Hidden History of Admission and Exclusion at Harvard, Yale, and Princeton*, and Wilkinson, *Aiding Students, Buying Students: Financial Aid in America*, respectively. For a simple timeline of federal financial aid programs, see FinAid, "History of Student Financial Aid."

54. Wilkinson, *Aiding Students, Buying Students*.

55. Urciuoli, "Excellence, Leadership, Skills, Diversity."

56. Hout, "Social and Economic Returns."

57. I have changed or omitted details here and throughout the book—including traditional events, hallmark social customs, and the way the campus looks—to preserve the anonymity of the college and its students.

58. Moffatt uses the term "friend*li*ness" in *Coming of Age in New Jersey*, 43–44, as follows:

> giving regular abbreviated performances of the standard behaviors of real friendship— to look pleased and happy when you meet someone, to put on the all-American friendly smile, to acknowledge the person you are meeting by name . . . to make casual body contact, greet the person with one of the two or three conversational queries about the state of their "whole self" ("How are you?" "How's it goin'?" "What's new?")

59. As with all statistics cited in this book, I have approximated these figures to preserve the anonymity of the college and its students.

60. For work specifically regarding African American students on predominantly white campuses, see, e.g., Feagin, *Agony of Education*; Willie, *Acting Black*; and Winkle-Wagner, *Unchosen Me*. For examinations of Hispanic / Latino students' experiences, see, e.g., Perez and Ceja, eds., *Higher Education Access*. For a discussion of Asian American students' experiences, see, e.g., Museus, *Asian American Students in Higher Education* and Truong, McMickens, and Brown, "Intersections of Race and Class." For narratives by Native American college students, see Garrod and Larimore, eds., *First Person, First Peoples*. For discussions of multiple racialized experiences, see, e.g., Lee and LaDousa, eds., *College Students' Experiences of Power*, and Charles, Fischer, Mooney, and Massey, *Taming the River*.

61. As with many student clubs, the CAL leadership changed between years and in one case between semesters. During the first year, CAL had a single president for one semester, Heather, who was strongly supported by Violet, her vice-president. During the second year, Amber and Genesis shared the responsibilities of leadership after another co-president, Apple, stepped down.

62. See, e.g., news coverage in ABC, "Colleges Struggle to Connect"; PBS, "Top-Achieving Poor Students Go Unnoticed"; as well as the *New York Times*'s periodic coverage, and academic works by Carnevale and Rose, Stevens, Stuber, and Mullen cited in this book.

1. College Dreams, College Plans

1. Carnevale and Rose, "Socioeconomic Status, Race/Ethnicity, and Selective College Admissions."

2. Early work in this area includes Sewell and Shah, "Social Class, Parental Encouragement"; Sewell and Shah, "Socioeconomic Status, Intelligence, and the Attainment of Higher Education"; and Sewell, Haller, and Portes, "Educational and Early Occupational Attainment."

3. Lareau, *Home Advantage*.

4. Ashley Rondini, in "Healing the 'Hidden Injuries of Class'," has a different view on the subject of first-generation students and their parents.

5. Sennett and Cobb, *The Hidden Injuries of Class*.

6. St. John, Hu, and Fisher, *Breaking Through the Access Barrier*.

7. Hoxby and Avery, "Missing 'One-offs'."

8. Mullen, "Elite Destinations."

9. See Carnevale and Rose, "Socioeconomic Status." Although the National Bureau of Economic Research finds that college selectivity per se does not correlate with increased earnings over a lifetime (though college cost and spending per student do), this effect is indeed the case for low-income students: "The income gains from attending an elite college are highest for students from a disadvantaged background." NBER Twitter Digest, http://www.nber.org/digest/dec99/w7322.html (accessed December 19, 2014).

10. See, e.g., Pérez-Peña, "Efforts to Recruit Poor Students"; Thomason, "In 'New York Times' Ranking"; and Dreier and Carnevale, "Making Top Colleges Less Aristocratic" for a few recent examples.

11. Carnevale and Rose, "Socioeconomic Status."

12. See also Stuber's "Pushed Out or Pulled In?" on elite liberal arts colleges as structural models that pull students in to the extracurricular life of the college more than larger campuses do.

13. Carnevale and Rose, "Socioeconomic Status."

14. See, e.g., Dews and Law, *This Fine Place*.

15. Torres "'Culture Shock'." See also, Jack, "Crisscrossing Boundaries."

2. "Scholarship Girls"

1. Stevens, *Creating a Class*.

2. Iverson, "Constructing Outsiders," 154.

3. Goffman, *Presentation of Self*.

4. Iverson, "Constructing Outsiders," explores similar questions in her analysis of university diversity statements and the creation of racialized and gendered student categories.

5. Rebecca Nathan uses this same formulation to examine somewhat different questions in *My Freshman Year*. In chapter 3, "Community and Diversity," she discusses the way that dormitory life at "AnyU" is intended to be structured around the creation of community (e.g., through organized activities and meetings) but that in many ways the group fails to cohere, particularly in terms of race and ethnicity.

6. See, e.g., Ahmed, *On Being Included*, and Hacking, "Between Michel Foucault and Erving Goffman." See also scholars working in the black feminist tradition, who develop important discussions of insider/outsider positions in the academy. For a review, see Collins, "Learning from the Outsider Within."

7. See, e.g., Lareau, *Home Advantage*; Kohn, *Class and Conformity*.

8. See also Allison Hurst's critique of rhetoric around higher education in *The Burden of Academic Success*.

9. This is part of a larger issue about what it means to become part of this particular community and the possible ramifications among family and hometown friends. I take up some of

these conflicts in Lee and Kramer "Out with the Old, In with the New?" There is also a substantial memoir literature on this topic, particularly of academics, e.g., Dews and Law, *This Fine Place*; and Ryan and Sackrey, *Strangers in Paradise*. For another view on this struggle, see Hurst's discussion of "double agents," students seeking to maintain footing in both college and home worlds, in *The Burden of Academic Success*.

10. See, e.g., Becky Supiano and Andrea Fuller, "Elite Colleges Fail," and David Leonhardt, "How Elite Colleges Still Aren't Diverse."

11. Sauder and Espeland, "Discipline of Rankings" Sauder and Lancaster, "Do Rankings Matter?"

12. It was remarkably difficult to find statistics for this figure. Linden administrators first alerted me to this issue, but searches in academic and policy literature did not turn up a definitive statistic. I found references to 2% and 3% but without attribution to the source.

13. Ahmed, "Doing Diversity Work," 750.

14. Adair, "US Working Class/Poverty Divides." For an excellent discussion of this issue in terms of race and identity, see Sara Ahmed's work, particularly the article cited above and *On Being Included*.

15. See also Iverson's analysis of this issue, "Constructing Outsiders," esp. 164. The following argument runs parallel to Iverson's detailed analysis of college diversity statements.

16. For an excellent discussion of the question of student gratitude, see Hurst and Warnock, "*Les Miraculés.*"

17. Winston, "Subsidies, Hierarchy, and Peers"; see also Ehrenburg, *Tuition Rising*.

18. See here Hurst and Warnock, "*Les Miraculés.*"

19. See Ahmed, *On Being Included* and "Doing Diversity Work"; and Iverson, "Constructing Outsiders." See also Brayboy, "The Implementation of Diversity." Black feminist accountings of being simultaneously insider and outsider are also foundational here. See, e.g., Collins, "Learning from the Outsider Within."

20. Cf. Hacking's *Social Construction of What?* on becoming a refugee.

21. Interestingly, in the Linden archives I located the "Linden College Student Council, State of the College Report" on campus diversity, written earlier in the decade by students for the college administration. It included criticism of the college's failure to understand "the dynamic of being a low-income student while trying to live as an average college student" and perceived lack of data on low-income students' progress and accomplishments across each year of enrollment, which the CAL students of that iteration believed would "further encourage students" who feel unsure about their own abilities to succeed as well as demonstrate "the value of socioeconomic diversity on campus" to more affluent students.

22. This comparison becomes even clearer when we turn to statistics for faculty members and staff. Although the college can easily cite detailed statistics for employees at all levels by gender, race, and ethnicity, no such statistics exist for a faculty member's socioeconomic background. Indeed, it would seem strange and out of place to imagine tracking this kind of data for faculty members and staff. A similar gap exists for alumnae.

23. Administrators sometimes used the term "access" to refer to class or socioeconomic status. Access to college has become increasingly a topic of public and policy conversation, especially as costs of attendance rise. This is sometimes mentioned in public forums, especially in relation to budget cuts, and here linked to diversity, though interestingly, sometimes as a counterpoint. This may be seen in the following comments by Linden's president in a public conversation about the meaning of diversity. She noted that "the word *diversity* may be too narrow a framing—it's too easy to see as only demographics. We need to think about access and inclusion." Similarly, the dean of enrollment emphasized to students concerned about the college's potential budget cuts that "the one thing that was held totally safe, in fact the only budget that was increased last year was the financial aid budget. This is because of the college's commitment to access." An alternate organizational (and student) view of diversity concerns something closer to individuality. In this

schema, diversity means differences of opinions and experiences, though still generally attributed to race/ethnicity, among other factors. For example, the adviser for first-year and transfer students warned students in her session at orientation: "You all have different backgrounds, beliefs, and opinions." This pronouncement came under the auspices of diversity. Similarly, during a later event for new students about the Linden community, another speaker discusses the "diversity" of the class (according to my field notes):

> She runs through the list of differences—race, ethnicity, class or economic background, political and religious beliefs, sexual identity, etc. "We will not always agree with each other. Don't say someone is silencing you if they disagree with you. Diversity is challenging. Don't be afraid to discuss difficult issues. . . . Diversity is at base demographic differences, but don't make assumptions or stereotypes that people will have had certain experiences or hold certain opinions."

24. Ahmed, "Doing Diversity."

3. "Are you my friend, or are you classist?"

1. Vaquera and Kao, "Do You Like Me"; Haynie, South, and Bose, "The Company You Keep."

2. Reardon and Bischoff, "Income Inequality."

3. See the broader literature on the importance of friendships to college success, e.g., Nathan, *My Freshman Year* and Kaufman, "Middle-Class Social Reproduction."

4. See Nathan's discussion in *My Freshman Year* of college friendships, which provides an interesting look at how these relationships tend to be shaped by college structures; see as well, Moffatt's 1989 examination in *Coming of Age in New Jersey*.

5. Interestingly, two seniors at the table also talked about their discomfort bringing up their study abroad experiences in Europe because talking about "when I was living in France" made them feel "pretentious." They talked over strategies to counteract possible negative impressions. Low-income and working-class students sometimes pointed out that dinner-table discussions of spring break or summer travel plans were quick indicators of students' financial situations.

6. Although students sometimes wielded difference to make others feel uncomfortable, others revealed different goals. Meredith described how she encouraged her roommate, whom she believed to have a similar economic background to her own, to be more open about her background by coming to CAL meetings or events or simply by discussing it with Meredith herself, with little success. Students also sometimes joked to one another about status differences, as in the example of Daniela and Mari that opened the chapter.

7. See, e.g., Moffatt's *Coming of Age in New Jersey* and Nathan's *My Freshman Year*.

8. Although I did not interview many upper socioeconomic status students, low and middle socioeconomic status students provided me with their understandings of friends' social experiences. I supplemented these understandings with my own perceptions from participant-observation field work.

9. Savage, Bagnall, and Longhurst, "Ordinary, Ambivalent, and Defensive," 889.

10. Goldrick-Rab, "Following Their Every Move."

11. Pittman and Richmond, "University Belonging."

4. Activism and Representation

1. The presidents of CAL several years earlier had used video cameras from the college and gotten a friend enrolled in a video-making class to help them. They interviewed one another and then branched out to interview friends and acquaintances willing to speak about their own experiences. The documentary touched on the kinds of personal dilemmas or problems the students

encountered at Linden, their feelings, and their frustrations. The documentary was made, in part, the former presidents noted, to establish a visual record of their presence on campus—so that if there were someday fewer low socioeconomic status students, or CAL disbanded, the college would not be able to cover over their having existed.

2. Beyond the complications of bringing these documents into being, these presentations raise additional questions that weave through CAL's various iterations and members over the years, a conflict between a mission to educate about class and missions to more pointedly support low-income and other students or to take a more confrontational "activist" stance. Early in the iteration active during my research, the mission was seen as education, as Heather recalled to me. They had gotten tired of taking on responsibility for educating other students, which required them to meet those students where they were at, accept their sometimes ill-informed views, and patiently work to shift their outlooks. Heather, Violet, Macy, and other early members therefore became more activist in their stances. During my years there, however, the membership seemed to swing back in the direction of education as they shied away from a confrontational stance. This tension between education and activism shone through CAL meetings as new members sorted through their own feelings.

3. Moon, "Discourse, Interaction, and Testimony."

4. Ibid.

5. The "celebration" approach does not always sit well with other students who might be called diverse, even though student clubs often made use of this frame. For example, at a post hoc discussion of Plenary Day (founded as a day of reflection by the first African American dean and celebrated each spring) students, faculty, and administrators discussed what had gone well and what might be improved. During the public comments segment, an African American student rose to say that "this should be a day to educate yourself. [The dean]'s focus was on education. These days shouldn't be about stereotypical cultural stuff about art and food and dance—don't tell us what we should be!" The "cultural stuff" presented by the college—in this case, poetry readings, a dance performance, and thematic meals in the dining hall in addition to academic lectures, struck some students as not only "stereotypical"—that is, simply parroting what one expects to see—but also as sidestepping the real issues by taking a "celebrate culture" stance.

6. Jensen, "Across the Great Divide." There are important issues of trust implicated here—trust in a listener's ability to hear and understand rather than judge or devalue. For a discussion of trust across class groups, see Fiske, Moya, Russell, and Bearns, "Secret Handshake"; for a more specific discussion of distrust by working-class adults for middle-class others, see Gorman, "Cross-Class Perceptions."

7. This seemed not to fade over time for at least some respondents: in the final stages of writing this book, I sent Violet's interviews and a sample chapter to her for review. A year or so later, we connected again by e-mail, and she told me that she had never gotten through either document because they were too painful to read.

8. For a similar point, see Lubienski, "Celebrating Diversity," 32.

9. This also had implications for networking between clubs, as I learned at an alumnae panel sponsored by Mujeres, among others. A former leader of the African American student group on campus in the 1990s strongly encouraged students to network in immediately practical ways: to attend one another's events, to participate in the leadership of other groups—in other words to become enmeshed. This strengthens the position of each club on campus and also increases the number of students "served" through events, increasing the likelihood of funding. For CAL, a group that was not consistent on campus and poorly networked with other groups, this may have been an additional disadvantage.

10. It is conceivable that there were others that escaped my observation, but because I was in touch with administrators, students, and faculty, I feel quite confident of this assessment. There were shorter-term efforts, such as one-time workshops or forums in which the subject was class

on campus. And faculty I talked to mentioned earlier efforts that were also limited term, such as a faculty reading group that focused one summer on student class issues and a couple of college task forces. In the latter cases, especially, the faculty and administrators who sat on those task forces, whom I spoke with, thought that there had been little if any substantial change as a result.

11. This also connects to an issue that representatives of various student clubs frequently brought up—namely, that it is both difficult to get students not already involved to become involved and that it is tiresome for clubs with small membership numbers to be the constant and only people working on a certain issue.

12. Tinto, "Research and Practice."

13. Kuh, Cruce, Shoup, Kinzie, and Gonyea, "Unmasking the Effects of Student Engagement"; Stuber, "Class, Culture, and Participation"; Martin, "Privilege of Ease."

14. Reay, "Finding or Losing Yourself?"; Brook and Michell, "Learners, Learning, Learned."

15. There are many clubs that work on class-related issues that do not focus on students, for example, labor actions, sweatshop or hunger awareness, and programs such as Habitat for Humanity that help low-income families build or repair their homes.

16. Carnevale and Rose, "Socioeconomic Status."

17. Ostrove and Long, "Social Class and Belonging."

5. Silence vs. Empowerment

1. See Lareau, *Home Advantage*, and Calarco, "Inconsistent Curriculum" and "I Need Help!"

2. Stuber, "Class, Culture, and Participation."

3. See Jean Anyon, "Social Class and the Hidden Curriculum of Work," for a seminal discussion of how students from varied class backgrounds are effectively oriented to stratified work positions in their respective school settings.

4. Calarco, "Inconsistent Curriculum," 186. See also her findings on help-seeking in "I Need Help!" which show the ways that working-class students are much less likely to secure teacher assistance than middle class peers, despite being given the same instructions. For a discussion of older students, see Megan Holland's discussion of student-counselor trust, "Trusting Each Other."

5. Sometimes this expectation produced disappointment, however, as Macy, an alumna, explained. In high school, she idealized college as a place of lofty discussions about things that mattered. When she arrived at Linden, she recalled, "I was really excited because it was the first time I was around a bunch of people who wanted to have real conversations about the kinds of things I was interested in" like race, class, gender, and sexuality. When she arrived at Linden, however, she found that there were few mentions at all of class, and she felt hesitant to share too much of her background because there didn't seem to be anyone else who shared it: "During one of those exercises where people step into and out of the circle, I was the only person in the circle for first generation, out of twenty or thirty people. It was terrifying, isolating, to be the only one. For almost everything else, there were at least a couple of people." Thus, even her own ability to engage with these issues was tamped down by her feeling of being "isolated" as one of very few low-income and first-generation students.

6. This knowledge is also a "double-edged sword" once transported beyond the college gates because it also serves to enhance feelings of distance from families and friends who do not share it. See Lee and Kramer, "Out with the Old"; see also Hughes, *Sociological Eye*, on this point.

7. Respondents had different perspectives about what gains could be made through direct college intervention. Parallel to Meredith's feelings about how Linden could not solve the problem of her discomfort in seeking help from faculty, a number of respondents believed that the college's efforts were bound to be ineffectual. Others thought the college had a duty to educate students about white-collar or middle-class social forms. More unusually, respondents actively resented the

college's efforts to advocate around socioeconomic inequality and other social issues that impact students on campus. For example, Magdalena shared a recollection from her first year of college. A woman in her residence hall was highly involved with CAL, according to my notes from a conversation with Magdalena, and "began promoting events to highlight differences, and [she] alienated the hall. . . . This person pushed and pushed and pushed the [diversity] issue, and it made [me] really uncomfortable and upset." In her junior year, Magdalena was elected to a position in the hall that gave her responsibility for these kinds of awareness-raising events. She decided to take a different, less-confrontational approach. However, as she recalled, "at a training workshop for new leaders, people were being alienated by the awareness agenda—and I pretty much got shut down [when expressing my suggestions]. Leaders at the workshop basically said, we are going to push your buttons and talk about difficult things." Magdalena disliked this approach especially because, as she said, "we have to live together and figure out some way to talk with each other and live together," which is made harder when differences are so heavily dwelt on.

8. Lareau, *Home Advantage*. See also Calarco's discussion in "Inconsistent Curriculum."

9. See Bernstein, *Class, Codes, and Control*; Lamont, *The Dignity of Working Men*, 36–38; Lamont, *Money, Morals, and Manners*; Leondar-Wright, *Missing Class*, 11; DiMaggio, "Sociological Perspectives," 20–23.

10. Leondar-Wright, *Missing Class*, 152–57.

11. This may also be linked to the findings in Stephens, Fryberg, Markus, Johnson, and Covarrubias's "Unseen Disadvantage," about students' values of independence or interdependence; as the authors note, American colleges and universities tend to focus on individual choices and "independent norms"—including, we might assume, the kinds of self-advocacy and entitlement discussed by respondents and scholars.

12. Lareau, *Home Advantage*.

6. After College

1. To the best of my knowledge, all respondents from the original interviews graduated. I was able to locate some respondents, who did not agree to be interviewed, via social media and could see that they listed graduation dates; others I last spoke with during their senior years were on track at that time to graduate. I could neither locate to speak with nor confirm graduation outcomes for Fiona, Ramona, or Quinn. Brianna did not respond to my request for interviews, and Becca responded affirmatively but did not follow up when I attempted to schedule an interview. Allison and Danielle and I were not able to find a time that worked for an interview.

2. For review discussions of college outcomes and socioeconomic status, see Hout, "Social and Economic Returns," and Lee, "Elite Colleges." For a discussion of cultural capital in college venues, see Wildhagen, "Capitalizing on Culture." For a discussion of credential theory, see Collins, *The Credential Society*.

3. Hurst, *Burden of Academic Success*, 5.

4. Lubrano, *Limbo*.

5. See Lee and Kramer, "Out with the Old"; Haney, "Factory to Faculty"; and Grimes and Morris, *Caught in the Middle*.

6. Swidler, "Culture in Action."

7. Stuber, "Class, Culture, and Participation."

8. It is possible that middle-class and even some upper-class graduates shared this hesitation. Magdalena's explicit linking of her feelings with her class position indicates that for her, at least, this is a class-related issue. Moreover, this difference links clearly to a substantial literature on the ways that working-class and middle-class people approach schooling. For example, it aligns with Calarco's ("The Inconsistent Curriculum") discussion of the "no excuses" approach to school used by working-class parents. Indeed, Magdalena seems to embody this approach. Similar links are

easily drawn to Lareau's (*Home Advantage*) findings and Stuber's ("Class, Culture, and Participation") observations. Moreover, the implications of this hesitation are larger for working-class respondents than for middle-class or upper-class graduates. While college connections are likely the only links to white-collar job networks for graduates whose family members and high school friends are working blue- or pink-collar workers, graduates from middle-class and upper-class families are likely to have personal ties to white-collar work worlds that make drawing on the broader alumnae network less crucial for such linkages.

9. Reay, "Finding or Losing Yourself?"

10. For more on this topic, see Lee and Kramer, "Out with the Old."

11. Jensen, "Across the Great Divide."

12. See, e.g., students interviewed by Lehmann in "I Just Didn't Feel Like I Fit In."

13. Sennett and Cobb, *Hidden Injuries of Class*.

14. hooks, *Where We Stand*, 36–37. See also Hurst and Warnock, "*Les Miraculés*."

15. For further discussion of this topic, see Hurst's *Burden of Academic Success*, and Hurst and Warnock's "*Les Miraculés*." See also work by Diane Reay, in particular, "Finding or Losing Yourself?"

16. Armstrong and Hamilton, *Paying for the Party*.

17. Ibid.

18. Lareau, *Home Advantage*.

Conclusion

1. Sayer, "Class, Moral Worth, and Recognition," and "What Are You Worth?"

2. Political gaffes are indicative here—during the 2012 campaign, both Obama and Romney talked about middle-class Americans earning up to $250,000 per year, a number so vastly beyond what actually constitutes the middle of the American earning spectrum as to be mind-boggling. The median income in the United States is approximately $50,000 per year.

3. Aries, *Race and Class Matters*; Mullen, *Degrees of Inequality*; Stuber, *Inside the College Gates*. See also Hamilton and Armstrong, "Gendered Sexuality in Young Adulthood"; and Aries and Seider, "Interactive Relationship."

4. Hurst, *Burden of Academic Success*; Armstrong and Hamilton, *Paying for the Party*. See also Hurst and Warnock, "*Les Miraculés*."

5. See Karabel, *Chosen*; Soares, *Power of Privilege*; Stevens, *Creating a Class*; Stampnitzky, "How Does 'Culture' Become 'Capital?'"; and Wilkinson, *Aiding Students, Buying Students*.

6. Hurst and Warnock, "*Les Miraculés*."

7. hooks, *Where We Stand*, 36–37.

8. Sayer, "What Are You Worth?"

9. See Carnevale and Rose, "Socioeconomic Status."

10. See Haveman and Smeeding, "Role of Higher Education." See also Leonhardt, "Top Colleges, Largely for the Elite."

11. As of 2015, these efforts are often found online, often on Facebook through the hashtag #classconfessions or through Facebook pages organized campus by campus with the same tag. For news coverage, see, e.g., Pappano, "First Generation Students Unite."

12. See, e.g., Hurwitz, "Impact of Institutional Grant Aid."

13. See, e.g., Supiano and Fuller, "Elite Colleges Fail to Gain More Students"; Leonhardt, "How Elite Colleges Still Aren't Diverse" and "Better Colleges Failing to Lure Talented Poor." See also Mullen, *Degrees of Inequality*.

14. Hoxby and Avery, "Missing 'One-offs.'"

15. Madden, "Why Poor Students Struggle."

16. McGrath, "The Challenges of Being Poor at America's Richest Colleges."

17. Ahmed, "Doing Diversity Work" and *On Being Included*; Brayboy, "The Implementation of Diversity"; hooks, *Class Matters*; Iverson, "Constructing Outsiders"; Urciuoli, "Excellence, Leadership, Skills, Diversity."

18. See Hacking, "Between Michel Foucault and Erving Goffman" for a discussion of how creation of discursive roles is important for shaping people's lives around those constructed categories.

19. Stevens, *Creating a Class*.

20. Charles, Fischer, Mooney, and Massey, *Taming the River*, chap. 8 and especially pp. 200–204.

21. See, e.g., Aries and Seider, "Interactive Relationship."

22. Stuber, "Pushed Out or Pulled In?"

23. Aries and Seider, "Interactive Relationship."

24. A recent exception is Fiske and Markus, *Facing Social Class*. It is notable, however, that in the chapter dedicated to sociological work, the author, Paul DiMaggio, outlines the possible contributions of three theoretical perspectives rather than focusing on empirical examinations.

25. In *Gender Play: Girls and Boys in School*, Barrie Thorne contends that earlier social scientists missed important findings because they focused on the popular or charismatic students on the playground, leaving out the marginal or peripheral students, yet generalized to "all" boys or "all" girls.

Appendix

1. Tinto, "Research and Practice of Student Retention," citing NCES 2005b, table 1, p. 7.

2. I have approximated college statistics to prevent them from being identifiable.

Bibliography

ABC. "Colleges Struggle to Connect with High-Achieving Poor Students." *ABC/Univision*. March 18, 2013. Accessed 9/10/15. http://abcnews.go.com/ABC_Univision/colleges-struggle-connect-high-achieving-poor-students/story?id=18758261.

Adair, Vivyan C. "US Working Class/Poverty Divides." *Sociology* 39, no. 5 (2005): 817–834.

Ahmed, Sara. "Doing Diversity Work in Higher Education in Australia." *Educational Philosophy and Theory* 38, no. 6 (2006): 745–68.

———. *On Being Included: Racism and Diversity in Institutional Life*. Durham: Duke University Press, 2012.

Alon, Sigal, and Marta Tienda. "Assessing the 'Mismatch' Hypothesis: Differences in College Graduation Rates by Institutional Selectivity." *Sociology of Education* 78, no. 4 (2005): 294–315.

Anyon, Jean. "Social Class and the Hidden Curriculum of Work." *Journal of Education* 162, no. 1 (1980): 67–92

Aries, Elizabeth. *Race and Class Matters at an Elite College*. Philadelphia: Temple University Press, 2008.

Aries, Elizabeth, and Maynard Seider. "The Interactive Relationship between Class Identity and the College Experience: The Case of Lower-Income Students." *Qualitative Sociology* 28 (2005): 419–43.

Armstrong, Elizabeth A., and Laura Hamilton. *Paying for the Party: How College Maintains Inequality*. Cambridge: Harvard University Press, 2013.

Aronson, Pamela. "Breaking Barriers or Locked Out? Class-Based Perceptions and Experiences of Postsecondary Education." *New Directions for Child and Adolescent Development* 119 (2008): 41–54.

Barrow, Lisa, and Cecilia Elena Rouse. "Does College Still Pay?" *Economists' Voice* 2, no. 4, article 3 (2005): 1–8.

Bernstein, Basil. *Class, Codes, and Control. Volume 1: Theoretical Studies Towards a Sociology of Language*. New York and London: Routledge, 1971.

Bettie, Julie. *Women without Class: Girls, Race, and Identity*. Berkeley: University of California Press, 2003.

Bourdieu, Pierre. "The Forms of Capital." In *Handbook of Theory and Research for the Sociology of Education*, edited by John C. Richardson, 241–258. New York: Greenwood, 1986.

———. *The State Nobility: Elite Schools in the Field of Power*. Trans. Lauretta C. Clough. Stanford: Stanford University Press, 1996.

Bourdieu, Pierre, and Jean-Claude Passeron. *Reproduction in Education, Society, and Culture*. 2nd ed. London: Sage Publications, 1977.

Brayboy, Bryan McKinley Jones. "The Implementation of Diversity in Predominantly White Colleges and Universities." *Journal of Black Studies* 34, no. 1 (2003): 72–86.

Brook, Heather, and Dee Michell. "Learners, Learning, Learned: Class, Higher Education, and Autobiographical Essays from Working-Class Academics." *Journal of Higher Education Policy and Management* 34, no. 6 (2012): 587–99.

Calarco, Jessica McCrory. "The Inconsistent Curriculum: Cultural Tool Kits and Student Interpretations of Ambiguous Expectations." *Social Psychology Quarterly* 77, no. 2 (2014): 185–209.

———. "'I need help!' Social Class and Children's Help-Seeking in Elementary School." *American Sociological Review* 76, no. 6 (2011): 862–82.

Carnevale, Anthony P., and Stephen J. Rose. "Socioeconomic Status, Race/Ethnicity, and Selective College Admissions." In *America's Untapped Resource: Low-Income Students in Higher Education*, edited by Richard D. Kahlenberg. New York: Century Foundation, 2004.

Carruthers, Bruce G., and Wendy Nelson Espeland. "Money, Meaning, and Morality." *American Behavioral Scientist* 41, no. 10 (1998): 1384–1408.

Charles, Camille Z., Mary J. Fischer, Margarita A. Mooney, and Douglas S. Massey. *Taming the River: Negotiating the Academic, Financial, and Social Currents in Selective Colleges and Universities*. Princeton: Princeton University Press, 2009.

Collins, Patricia Hill. "Learning from the Outsider Within: The Sociological Significance of Black Feminist Thought." *Social Problems* 33, no. 6 (1986): 14–32.

Collins, Randall. *The Credential Society: An Historical Sociology of Education and Stratification*. New York: Academic Press, 1979.

Cookson, Peter W., Jr, and Caroline Persell. *Preparing for Power: America's Elite Boarding Schools*. New York: Basic Books, 1985.

Demerath, Peter. *Producing Success: The Culture of Personal Advancement in an American High School*. Chicago: University of Chicago Press, 2009.

Dews, C. L. Barney, and Carolyn Leste Law. *This Fine Place So Far from Home*. Philadelphia: Temple University Press, 1995.

DiMaggio, Paul. "Sociological Perspectives on the Face-to-Face Enactment of Class Distinction." In *Facing Social Class: How Societal Rank Influences Interaction*, edited by Susan T. Fiske and Hazel Rose Markus, 15–38. New York: Russell Sage Foundation, 2012.

Dreier, Peter, and Richard D. Carnevale. "Making Top Colleges Less Aristocratic and More Meritocratic." *New York Times*. September 12, 2014. http://www.nytimes.com/2014/09/13/upshot/making-top-colleges-less-aristocratic-and-more-meritocratic.html.

Ehrenburg, Ronald. *Tuition Rising*. Cambridge: Harvard University Press, 2000.

Feagin, Joe R., Hernán Vera, and Nikitah Imani. *The Agony of Education: Black Students at White Colleges and Universities*. New York: Routledge, 1996.

Fiske, Susan T., and Hazel Rose Markus, eds. *Facing Social Class: How Societal Rank Influences Interaction*. New York: Russell Sage Foundation, 2012.

Fiske, Susan T., Miguel Moya, Ann Marie Russell, and Courtney Bearns. "The Secret Handshake: Trust in Cross-Class Interactions." In *Facing Social Class: How Societal Rank Influences Interaction*, edited by Susan T. Fiske and Hazel Rose Markus, 234–52. New York: Russell Sage Foundation, 2012.

FinAid. "History of Student Financial Aid." *FinAid!*, http://www.finaid.org/educators/history.phtml.

Garrod, Andrew, and Colleen Larimore, eds. *First Person, First Peoples: Native American College Graduates Tell Their Life Stories*. Ithaca: Cornell University Press, 1997.

Goldrick-Rab, Sara. "Following Their Every Move: An Investigation of Social-Class Differences in College Pathways." *Sociology of Education* 79 (2006): 61–79.

Goffman, Erving. *The Presentation of Self in Everyday Life*. New York: Anchor Books, 1959.

Gorman, Thomas J. "Cross-Class Perceptions of Social Class." *Sociological Spectrum* 20, no. 1 (2000): 93–120.

Granfield, Robert. "Making it by Faking it: Working-Class Students in an Elite Academic Environment." *Journal of Contemporary Ethnography* 20, no. 3 (1991): 331–51.

Grimes, Michael D., and Joan Marie Morris. *Caught in the Middle: Contradictions in the Lives of Sociologists from Working-Class Backgrounds*. Westport, CT: Praeger, 1997.

Hacking, Ian. "Between Michel Foucault and Erving Goffman: Between Discourse in the Abstract and Face-to-Face Interaction." *Economy and Society* 33, no. 3 (2004): 277–302.

———. *The Social Construction of What?* Cambridge: Harvard University Press, 1999.

Hamilton, Laura, and Elizabeth A. Armstrong. "Gendered Sexuality in Young Adulthood: Double Binds and Flawed Options." *Gender & Society* 23, no. 5 (2009): 589–616.

Haney, Timothy J. "Factory to Faculty: Socioeconomic Difference and the Educational Experiences of University Professors." *Canadian Review of Sociology/Revue canadienne de sociologie* 52, no. 2 (2015): 160–86.

Harris, Scott R. "Social Constructionism and Social Inequality: An Introduction to a Special Issue of JCE." *Journal of Contemporary Ethnography* 35, no. 3 (2006): 223–35.

Haveman, Robert, and Timothy Smeeding. "The Role of Higher Education in Social Mobility." *Future of Children* 16 (2006): 125–50.

Haynie, Dana L., Scott J. South, and Sunita Bose. "The Company You Keep: Adolescent Mobility and Peer Behavior." *Sociological Inquiry* 76, no. 3 (2006): 397–426.

Holland, Megan M. "Trusting Each Other: Student-Counselor Relationships in Diverse High Schools." *Sociology of Education* 88, no. 3 (2015): 244–62.

hooks, bell. *Where We Stand: Class Matters*. New York: Routledge, 2000.

Hout, Michael. "Social and Economic Returns to College Education in the United States." *Annual Review of Sociology* 38 (2012): 379–400.

Hoxby, Caroline M., and Christopher Avery. "The Missing 'One-offs': The Hidden Supply of High-Achieving, Low Income Students." NBER Working Paper no. 18586. National Bureau of Economic Research. Cambridge, MA. December 2012. http://www.nber.org/papers/w18586.

Hughes, Everett C. *The Sociological Eye: Selected Papers*. New Brunswick, NJ: Transaction, 1971.

Hurst, Allison L. *The Burden of Academic Success: Loyalists, Renegades, and Double Agents*. Lanham, MD: Lexington Books, 2010.

Hurst, Allison L., and Deborah M. Warnock. "*Les Miraculés*: The Magical Image of the Permanent Miracle—Constructed Narratives of Self and Mobility from Working-Class Students at an Elite College." In *College Students' Experiences of Power and Marginality: Sharing Spaces and Negotiating Differences*, edited by Elizabeth M. Lee and Chaise LaDousa, 102–17. New York: Routledge, 2015.

Hurwitz, Michael. "The Impact of Institutional Grant Aid on College Choice." *Educational Evaluation and Policy Analysis* 34 (2012): 344–63.

Iverson, Susan V. "Constructing Outsiders: The Discursive Framing of Access in University Diversity Policies." *The Review of Higher Education* 35, no. 2 (2012): 149–77.

Jack, Anthony Abraham. "Crisscrossing Boundaries: Variation in Experiences with Class Marginality among Lower-Income Black Undergraduates in an Elite College." In *College Students' Experiences of Power and Marginality: Sharing Spaces and Negotiating Differences*, edited by Elizabeth M. Lee and Chaise LaDousa, 83–101. New York: Routledge, 2015.

Jensen, Barbara. "Across the Great Divide: Crossing Classes and Clashing Cultures." In *What's Class Got to Do with It?*, edited by Michael Zweig, 168–84. Ithaca: Cornell University Press, 2004.

———. *Reading Classes: On Culture and Classism in America*. Ithaca: Cornell University Press, 2012.

Karabel, Jerome. *The Chosen: The Hidden History of Admission and Exclusion at Harvard, Yale, and Princeton*. New York: Houghton Mifflin, 2005.

Kaufman, Peter. "Middle-Class Social Reproduction: The Activation and Negotiation of Structural Advantages." *Sociological Forum* 20, no. 2 (2005): 245–70.

Khan, Shamus Rahman. *Privilege: The Making of an Adolescent Elite at St. Paul's School*. Princeton: Princeton University Press, 2011.

Kohn, Melvin. *Class and Conformity: A Study of Values*. Chicago: University of Chicago Press, 1969.

Kuh, George D., Ty M. Cruce, Rick Shoup, Jillian Kinzie, and Robert M. Gonyea. "Unmasking the Effects of Student Engagement on First-Year College Grades and Persistence." *Journal of Higher Education* 79, no. 5 (2008): 540–63.

Kusenbach, Margarethe. "Salvaging Decency: Mobile Home Residents' Strategies of Managing the Stigma of 'Trailer' Living." *Qualitative Sociology* 32 (2009): 399–428.

Lamont, Michèle. *Money, Morals, and Manners: The Culture of the French and the American Upper-Middle Class*. Chicago: University of Chicago Press, 1992.

——. *The Dignity of Working Men*. New York: Russell Sage Foundation, 2000.

Lamont, Michèle, and Virag Molnar. "The Study of Boundaries in the Social Sciences." *Annual Review of Sociology* 28 (2002): 167–95.

Lamont, Michèle, John Schmalzbauer, Maureen Waller, and Daniel Weber. "Cultural and Moral Boundaries in the United States: Structural Position, Geographic Location, and Lifestyle Explanations." *Poetics* 24, no. 1 (1996): 31–56.

Lareau, Annette. *Home Advantage: Social Class and Parental Intervention in Elementary Education*. Lanham, MD: Rowman & Littlefield, 2000.

——. *Unequal Childhoods: Class, Race, and Family Life*. Berkeley: University of California Press, 2011.

Lee, Elizabeth M. "Elite Colleges and Socioeconomic Status." *Sociology Compass* 7, no. 9 (2013): 786–98.

Lee, Elizabeth M., and Rory Kramer. "Out with the Old, In with the New? Habitus and Social Mobility at Selective Colleges." *Sociology of Education* 86, no. 1 (2013): 1–18.

Lee, Elizabeth M., and Chaise LaDousa, eds. *College Students' Experiences of Power and Marginality: Sharing Spaces and Negotiating Differences*. New York: Routledge, 2015.

Lehmann, Wolfgang. "Becoming Middle Class: How Working-Class University Students Draw and Transgress Moral Class Boundaries." *Sociology* 43, no. 4 (2009): 631–47.

——. "Habitus Transformation and Hidden Injuries: Successful Working-Class University Students." *Sociology of Education* 87, no. 1 (2014): 1–15.

——. "'I Just Didn't Feel Like I Fit In': The Role of Habitus in University Dropout Decisions." *Canadian Journal of Higher Education* 37, no. 2 (2007): 89–110.

Leondar-Wright, Betsy. *Missing Class: Strengthening Social Movement Groups by Seeing Class Cultures*. Ithaca: Cornell University Press, 2014.

Leonhardt, David. "Better Colleges Failing to Lure Talented Poor." *New York Times*, Education section. March 16, 2013. http://www.nytimes.com/2013/03/17/education/scholarly-poor-often-overlook-better-colleges.html.

——. "How Elite Colleges Still Aren't Diverse." *New York Times Economix* blog. March 29, 2011. http://economix.blogs.nytimes.com/ 2011/03/29/how-elite-colleges-still-arent-diverse.

——. "Top Colleges, Largely for the Elite." *New York Times*, Economic Scene. May 24, 2011. http://www.nytimes.com/2011/05/25/business/economy/25leonhardt.html.

Lubienski, Sarah Theule. "Celebrating Diversity and Denying Disparities: A Critical Assessment." *Educational Researcher* 32, no. 8 (2003): 30–38.

Lubrano, Alfred. *Limbo: Blue-Collar Roots, White-Collar Dreams*. New York: John Wiley & Sons, 2004.

Madden, Vicki. "Why Poor Students Struggle." *New York Times*, Sept. 22, 2014. http://www.nytimes.com/2014/09/22/opinion/why-poor-students-struggle.html.

Martin, Nathan D. "The Privilege of Ease: Social Class and Campus Life at Highly Selective, Private Universities." *Research in Higher Education* 53, no. 4 (2012): 426–52.

———. "Social Capital, Academic Achievement, and Postgraduation Plans at an Elite, Private University." *Sociological Perspectives* 52, no. 2 (2009): 185–210.

McDonough, Patricia M. *Choosing Colleges: How Social Class and Schools Structure Opportunity*. Albany, NY: SUNY Press, 1997.

McGrath, Maggie. "The Challenges of Being Poor at America's Richest Colleges." *Forbes*.

November 27, 2013. http://www.forbes.com/sites/maggiemcgrath/2013/11/27/the-challenge-of-being-poor-at-americas-richest-colleges/

Moffatt, Michael. *Coming of Age in New Jersey: College and American Culture*. New Brunswick, NJ: Rutgers University Press, 1989.

Moon, Dawne. "Discourse, Interaction, and Testimony: The Making of Selves in the US Protestant Dispute over Homosexuality." *Theory and Society* 34 (2005): 551–77.

Mullen, Ann. *Degrees of Inequality: Culture, Class, and Gender in American Higher Education*. Baltimore: Johns Hopkins University Press, 2010.

———. "Elite Destinations: Pathways to Attending an Elite University." *British Journal of Sociology* 30, no. 1 (2009): 15–27.

Museus, Samuel D. *Asian American Students in Higher Education*. New York: Routledge, 2014.

Nathan, Rebekah. *My Freshman Year: What a Professor Learned by Becoming a Student*. Ithaca: Cornell University Press, 2005.

Ostrove, Joan. "Belonging and Wanting: Meanings of Social Class Background for Women's Constructions of Their College Experiences." *Journal of Social Issues* 59, no. 4 (2003): 771–84.

Ostrove, Joan, and Susan Long. "Social Class and Belonging: Implications for College Adjustment." *Review of Higher Education* 30, no. 4 (2007): 363–89.

Pappano, Laura. "First Generation Students Unite." *New York Times*, April 8, 2015. http://www.nytimes.com/2015/04/12/education/edlife/first-generation-students-unite.html?_r=0.

PBS. "Top-Achieving Poor Students Go Unnoticed by Some Elite Universities." *PBS Newshour*. March 27, 2013. http://www.pbs.org/newshour/bb/education-jan-june 13-eliteschools_03-27/.

Perez, Patricia, and Miguel Ceja, eds. *Higher Education Access and Choice for Latino Students: Critical Findings and Theoretical Perspectives*. New York: Routledge, 2015.

Pérez-Peña, Richard. "Efforts to Recruit Poor Students Lag at Some Elite Colleges." *New York Times*. July 30, 2013. http://www.nytimes.com/2013/07/31/education/elite-colleges-differ-on-how-they-aid-poor.html

Perna, Laura W. "Studying College Access and Choice: A Proposed Conceptual Model." In *Higher Education: Handbook of Theory and Research* vol. 21 (2006): 99–157.

Pew Research Center. "The Rising Cost of *Not* Going to College." February 11, 2014. http://www.pewsocialtrends.org/2014/02/11/the-rising-cost-of-not-going-to-college/.

Pittman, L. D., and A. Richmond. "University Belonging, Friendship Quality, and Psychological Adjustment during the Transition to College." *Journal of Experimental Education* 76, no. 4 (2008): 343–62.

Radford, Alexandra Walton. *Top Student, Top School? How Social Class Shapes Where Valedictorians Go to College*. Chicago: University of Chicago Press, 2013.

Reardon, Sean F., and Kendra Bischoff. "Income Inequality and Income Segregation." *American Journal of Sociology* 116, no. 4 (2011): 1092–1153.

Reay, Diane. "Finding or Losing Yourself? Working-Class Relationships to Education." *Journal of Education Policy* 16, no. 4 (2001), 333–46.

Rondini, Ashley C. "Healing the Hidden Injuries of Class?: Redemption Narratives, Aspirational Proxies, and Parents of Low Income First Generation College Students." *Sociological Forum* 30, no. 1 (forthcoming).

Ryan, Jake, and Charles Sackrey. *Strangers in Paradise: Academics from the Working Class*. New York: University Press of America, 1996.

Sauder, Michael, and Wendy Espeland. "The Discipline of Rankings: Tight Coupling and Organizational Change." *American Sociological Review* 74, no. 1 (2009): 63–82.

Sauder, Michael, and Ryon Lancaster. "Do Rankings Matter? The Effects of *U.S. News & World Report* Rankings on the Admissions Process of Law Schools." *Law & Society Review* 40, no. 1 (2006): 105–34.

Savage, Mike, Gaynor Bagnall, and Brian Longhurst. "Ordinary, Ambivalent, and Defensive: Class Identities in the Northwest of England." *Sociology* 35, no. 4 (2001): 875–92.

Sayer, Andrew. "Class, Moral Worth, and Recognition." *Sociology* 39, no. 5 (2005): 947–63.

———. "What Are You Worth? Why Class Is an Embarrassing Subject." *Sociological Research Online* 7, no. 3 (2002).

Scalzi, John. "Being Poor." *Whatever* blog. September 3, 2005. http://whatever.scalzi.com/2005/09/03/being-poor/.

Sennett, Richard, and Jonathan Cobb. *The Hidden Injuries of Class*. New York: Knopf, 1972.

Sewell, William H., Archibald O. Haller, and Alejandro Portes. "The Educational and Early Occupational Attainment Process." *American Sociological Review* 34, no. 1 (1969): 82–92.

Sewell, William H., and Vimal P. Shah. "Social Class, Parental Encouragement, and Educational Aspirations." *American Journal of Sociology* (1968): 559–72.

———. "Socioeconomic Status, Intelligence, and the Attainment of Higher Education." *Sociology of Education* (1967): 1–23.

Soares, Joseph. *The Power of Privilege: Yale and America's Elite Colleges*. Stanford: Stanford University Press, 2007.

Stampnitzky, Lisa. "How Does 'Culture' Become 'Capital'? Cultural and Institutional Struggles over 'Character and Personality' at Harvard." *Sociological Perspectives* 49, no. 4 (2006): 461–81.

Stephens, Nicole M., Stephanie A. Fryberg, Hazel Rose Markus, Camille S. Johnson, and Rebecca Covarrubias. "Unseen Disadvantage: How American Universities' Focus on Independence Undermines the Academic Performance of First-Generation College Students." *Journal of Personality and Social Psychology* 102, no. 6 (2012): 1178–97.

Stevens, Mitchell. *Creating a Class: College Admissions and the Creation of Elites*. Cambridge: Harvard University Press, 2007.

St. John, Edward P., Shouping Hu, and Amy S. Fisher. *Breaking Through the Access Barrier: How Academic Capital Formation Can Improve Policy in Higher Education*. New York: Routledge, 2011.

Streib, Jessi. *The Power of the Past: Understanding Cross-Class Marriages*. Oxford: Oxford University Press, 2015.

Stuber, Jenny M. "Class, Culture, and Participation in the Collegiate Extra-Curriculum." *Sociological Forum* 24, no. 4 (2009): 877–900.

——. *Inside the College Gates: How Class and Culture Matter in Higher Education*. Lanham, MD: Lexington Books, 2011.

——. "Pushed Out or Pulled In? How Organizational Factors Shape the Extracurricular Experiences of First-Generation Students." In *College Students' Experiences of Power and Marginality: Sharing Spaces and Negotiating Differences*, edited by Elizabeth M. Lee and Chaise LaDousa, 118–35. New York: Routledge, 2015.

——. "Talk of Class: The Discursive Repertoires of White Working- and Upper-Middle-Class College Students." *Journal of Contemporary Ethnography* 35, no. 3 (2006): 285–318.

Supiano Beckie, and Andrea Fuller. "Elite Colleges Fail to Gain More Students on Pell Grants." *Chronicle of Higher Education*. March 27, 2011. http://chronicle.com/article/Pell-Grant-Recipients-Are/126892/.

Tinto, Vincent. "Research and Practice of Student Retention: What Next?" *Journal of College Student Retention* 8, no. 1 (2006–7): 1–19.

Thomason, Andy. "In 'New York Times' Ranking, Elite Colleges Are Judged on Economic Diversity." *Chronicle of Higher Education*. September 9, 2014. http://chronicle.com/blogs/ticker/in-new-york-times-ranking-elite-colleges-are-judged-on-economic-diversity/85615.

Thorne, Barrie. *Gender Play: Girls and Boys in School*. New Brunswick, NJ: Rutgers University Press, 1993.

Torres, Kimberley. "'Culture Shock': Black Students Account for Their Distinctiveness at an Elite College. *Ethnic and Racial Studies* 32, no. 5 (2009): 883–905.

Truong, Kimberly A., Tryan L. McMickens, and Ronald E. L. Brown. "At the Intersections of Race and Class: An Autoethnographic Study on the Experiences of a Southeast Asian American College Student." In *College Students' Experiences of Power and Marginality: Sharing Spaces and Negotiating Differences*, edited by Elizabeth M. Lee and Chaise LaDousa, 11–28. New York: Routledge, 2015.

Urciuoli, Bonnie. "Producing Multiculturalism in Higher Education: Who's Producing What for Whom?" *International Journal of Qualitative Studies in Education* 12, no. 3 (1999): 287–98.

——. "Excellence, Leadership, Skills, Diversity: Marketing Liberal Arts Education." *Language & Communication* 23, no. 3–4 (2003): 385–408.

——. "Introduction: The Promise and Practice of Service Learning and Engaged Scholarship." *Learning and Teaching* 6, no. 2 (2013): 1–10.

——. "The Semiotic Production of the Good Student: A Peircean Look at the Commodification of Liberal Arts Education." *Signs and Society* 2, no. 1 (2014): 56–83.

Vaquera, Elizabeth, and Grace Kao. "Do You Like Me as Much as I Like You? Friendship Reciprocity and its Effects on School Outcomes among Adolescents." *Social Science Research* 37, no. 1 (2008): 55–72.

West, Candace, and Sarah Fenstermaker. "Doing Difference." *Gender & Society* 9, no. 1 (1995): 8–37.

Wildhagen, Tina. "Capitalizing on Culture: How Cultural Capital Shapes Educational Experiences and Outcomes." *Sociology Compass* 4, no. 7 (2010): 519–31.

Wilkinson, Rupert. *Aiding Students, Buying Students: Financial Aid in America*. Nashville: Vanderbilt University Press, 2005.

Willie, Sarah Susannah. *Acting Black: College, Identity, and the Performance of Race*. New York: Routledge, 2003.

Winkle-Wagner, Rachelle. *The Unchosen Me: Race, Gender, and Identity among Black Women in College*. Baltimore: Johns Hopkins University Press, 2010.

Winston, Gordon C. "Subsidies, Hierarchy and Peers: The Awkward Economics of Higher Education." *The Journal of Economic Perspectives* (1999): 13–36.

Zelizer, Vivianna. *The Social Meaning of Money*. Princeton: Princeton University Press, 1997.

Zweigenhaft, Richard L. "Prep School and Public School Graduates of Harvard: A Longitudinal Study of the Accumulation of Social and Cultural Capital." *Journal of Higher Education* (1993): 211–25.

INDEX

residential campuses: community ties at, 101; cross-class interactions at, 20–21

resources, use of, 145–46, 152–56, 164–70, 181–82

respondents, 216–25; administrators, 224–25; concern about being "boring," 231; faculty, 29; selection parameters, 26–29; students, 30

Richmond, Adeva, 117

Rose, Stephen, 15

"safe space" on campus, 205

Savage, Mike, 108

Sayer, Andrew, 5–7, 200, 202

Scalzi, John, 5, 6

scholarly learning: compared to life experience, 160–61

scholarships: and gratitude, 79–81, 87–88; and indebtedness, 193–94; "scholarship girls," 18–19, 74. *See also* financial aid; grants

Seider, Maynard, 11

selective colleges. *See* elite colleges

self, sense of, 173–82

self-advocacy, 164–70, 205, 245n11

self-presentation: of elite colleges, 135; professional, 182; of students, 91

semiotics of class morality, 4, 6–9, 16–17, 117–18, 200–203, 205, 213; in classroom discussions, 151–60; and community membership, 87–89, 99–104, 117–18, 168–69; countered by social theories, 150; and direct conflicts around class, 114–17; and diversity roles, 84; and framing class inequality, 121, 128, 142–43; and friendships, 91, 117–18; and legitimacy, 104–8, 117–18, 133; and merit, 104–8, 117–18; and mobility, 173; and silences around class inequality, 110; and social justice, 136; and use of resources, 165–66

Sennett, Richard, 36, 197

Servicemen's Readjustment Act of 1944, 18

sexuality, 162–63

shame, 110

silences around class inequality, 17, 91, 141–42; in classroom discussions, 151–60, 163–64, 169; in cross-class friendships, 108–14, 118; and discourse on community, 99–104; faculty intervention in, 163–64; and framing class, 133–34; "passing" by middle-class students, 94; through avoidance, 111–14

sisterhood, 99–101, 162

snobbishness, 45, 53, 94, 140, 163

Soares, Joseph, 201

social capital, 10–11, 66, 72, 148, 172, 182; definition of, 3; lack of, 196, 209

social dynamics. *See* cross-class interactions

social interactions across class-status positions. *See* cross-class interactions

social justice frame, 134–36, 142

social life, 20–21; and participant-observation field work, 228, 231–35; and spending money, 114–17

social networks, 2, 146, 172, 180–82, 198, 246n8 (chap. 6)

social responsibility, 135

socioeconomic segregation, 15

sociological theories: as empowering, 148–51

Southern Connecticut State College, 12, 44

spending habits, 68–69, 94, 125, 175–76

"spoiled," affluent students as, 107–8

Stampnitzky, Lisa, 201

state colleges, 51

Stephens, Nicole M., 245n11

stereotypes, 132

Stevens, Mitchell, 12, 60, 201, 208

stigma, 1, 107, 142–43, 193, 208, 230

stopping out, 118, 143

Stuber, Jenny M., 11–12, 146, 182, 201, 209, 246n8 (chap. 6)

student clubs, 130, 136–38, 243n5, 243n9, 244n11, 244n15; field work in, 225–27; as field work site, 225–27; institutional support for, 205–6. *See also* class activism student club